FRANCE in 1940

BELGIUM

GERMANY

LUXEM-BOURG

Dunkirk
Calais
PAS DE CALAIS
Lille

SOMME RIVER

Compiègne

Reims

Verdun

MOSELLE

Épernay
Mesnil-
sur Oger
Sézanne-en-
Champagne
Ambonnay
Châlon-sur-
Marne

BAS-RHIN
Strasbourg

CHAMPAGNE

Riquewihr

saille. PARIS

OISE

D ZONE

Ammerschwir
Colmar

Auxerre,
Chablis

HAUT-
RHIN

St.Thibault

SWITZER-
LAND

Bourges

Dijon
Clos de Vougeot
Vosne-Romanée
Combanchien
Aloxe-Corton
Beaune
Volnay
Châlons-
sur-
Saône

HUGEL

REUSE
Aubusson

VICHY

Mâcon
Vinzelles

BEAUJOLAIS

Lyon

BURGUNDY

RHONE RIVER

Grenoble

NOCCUPIED
ZONE

DRÔME

ITALY

LANGUEDOC

GARD

Châteauneuf-
du-Pape

PROVENCE

ALPES
MARITIMES

Nice

THE
CHAMPAGNE
CAMPAIGN

Cannes

The Riviera,
(Côte d'Azur)

LAC
ouse

Carcassonne

AUDE

Marseilles

Toulon

RHONE VALLEY

OUSSILLON
PYRÉNÉES

MEDITERRANEAN SEA

CHAMPAGNE
RÉSERVÉ À
LA
WEHRMACHT

KEY — MAGINOT LINE / AREA
— DEMARCATION LINE

Wine and War

Wine and War

The French, the Nazis, and the
Battle for France's Greatest Treasure

———————

DON AND PETIE KLADSTRUP

with Dr J. Kim Munholland, Historical Consultant

Hodder & Stoughton

First published in Great Britain in 2001
by Hodder and Stoughton
A division of Hodder Headline

Endpaper map illustration by Laura Hartman Maestro

10 9 8 7 6 5 4 3 2 1

A CIP catalogue record for this title is available from the British Library

ISBN 0 340 76677 8

Typeset by Palimpsest Book Production Limited,
Polmont, Stirlingshire
Printed and bound in Great Britain by
Mackays of Chatham plc, Chatham, Kent

Hodder and Stoughton
A division of Hodder Headline
338 Euston Road
London NW1 3BH

For Regan and Kwan-li,
our daughters and inspiration.

CONTENTS

INTRODUCTION

The steel door would not budge.

French soldiers had used everything from lock picks to sledgehammers in an effort to open it. Nothing had worked. Now they decided to try explosives.

The blast shook the mountain peak, sending rocks and debris cascading to the valley below. When the smoke and dust had cleared, the soldiers discovered the door was slightly ajar, just enough for Bernard de Nonancourt, a twenty-three-year-old army sergeant from Champagne, to squeeze through. What he saw left him speechless.

In front of him was a treasure connoisseurs would die for: half a million bottles of the finest wines ever made, wines such as Château Lafite-Rothschild and Château Mouton-Rothschild, Château Latour, Château d'Yquem and Romanée-Conti, stacked in wooden cases or resting on racks that filled nearly every inch of the cave. In one corner were rare ports and cognacs, many from the nineteenth century.

One thing, however, jumped out at de Nonancourt: hundreds of cases of 1928 Salon champagne. Five years earlier, while working at another champagne house, he had watched in amazement as German soldiers arrived in the little village of Le Mesnil-sur-Oger and hauled away case after case from the cellars of Salon. Now before him was the very champagne he had seen being stolen.

The young sergeant was thrilled and incredulous.

What was also hard to believe was that all this precious wine – sitting in a cave near the top of a mountain – belonged to a man who could not have cared less about it. In fact, he did not even like wine.

That man was Adolf Hitler.

*   *   *

The opening of Hitler's *cave* that day is something Bernard de Nonancourt would never have imagined; before then, he had not even known the *cave* existed. On May 4, 1945, Sergeant de Nonancourt, a tank commander in General Philippe Leclerc's 2nd French Armored Division, was only thinking how good it felt to be alive. Just a few days before, de Nonancourt had heard the good news: the last German units in France had surrendered. His country, at long last, was completely free. Now the Allies were pushing into Germany, their planes dropping thousands of tons of bombs on German industries, airfields and shipyards. Although pockets of resistance remained, German troops were in full retreat and had begun surrendering in large numbers. Everyone knew the war would soon be over.

On that lovely spring day as bright sunlight glinted off newly leafed trees, de Nonancourt's army unit found itself tantalizingly close to its destination: the town of Berchtesgaden in the Bavarian Alps, the 'Valhalla for the Nazi gods, lords and masters' as historian Stephen Ambrose called it. Hitler had a home here, the Berghof, as well as a mountaintop stone retreat called the Adlershorst, or Eagle's Nest. Other Nazis, like Göring, Goebbels, Himmler and Bormann, also had houses here.

It was to Berchtesgaden that the leaders of Europe had come in the late 1930s to be humiliated by Hitler, leaders such as Schuschnigg of Austria and Chamberlain of Britain. It was also where the Nazis shipped much of their loot: gold, jewelry, paintings and other treasures which they had stolen from other occupied countries.

The centerpiece of this Valhalla was the Berghof, Hitler's abode, which, from all outward appearances, looked like a typical chalet nestled on the shoulder of a mountain. It was anything but. As one visitor said, 'Behind those pleasant white walls and the flowers growing in window boxes was a palatial fortress unnerving in its strange inner proportions and medieval grandeur and in its display of wealth and power.' The living room of the Berghof was sixty feet long and fifty feet wide, 'so large that people seemed to be lost in it.' Heavy wooden furniture, typical of the Alps, stood in front of a huge jade green fireplace. Gobelin tapestries and Italian paintings decorated the walls. In fact, there were so many paintings from so many different schools that 'the room resembled a picture gallery in an eccentric museum.'

What few saw or ever were permitted to visit was Eagle's Nest, a fortress situated several thousand feet higher. Hitler himself is said to have gone there only three times, complaining that it was too high, that the air was too thin and that it was hard for him to breathe. Nevertheless, Eagle's Nest was a masterpiece of engineering. Built over a three-year period and designed to withstand bombardments and artillery fire, Eagle's Nest could be reached only by an elevator that had been cut into the solid rock of the mountain.

Now, with his column paused at the base of the mountain, de Nonancourt stared toward the peak, lost in thought as he tried to imagine the horrors that had been masterminded from that bucolic setting. Suddenly, his thoughts were interrupted by a shout from his commanding officer.

'You, de Nonancourt, you're from Champagne, right?'

Before Bernard could reply, the officer went on, 'So you must know something about wine. Get down here right now and come with me.'

Bernard jumped from his tank and followed the officer to his jeep, where a small group of other soldiers had gathered. 'Up there,' said the officer, pointing toward Eagle's Nest at the top of the Obersalzburg mountain, 'is a cave, a wine cellar really. That's where Hitler put the wine he stole from France. We are going to get it back, and you are in charge, de Nonancourt.'

Bernard was stunned. He knew the Germans had hauled away millions of bottles of wine from his country; he had even seen some of it stolen from the village where he once worked, but a wine cellar on top of a mountain seemed incredible.

To be the one who would open it was almost overwhelming.

Bernard knew his assignment would not be easy. The 8,000-foot-high mountain was steep and some of its slopes had been planted with land mines. He wondered if the cave itself was booby-trapped.

As Bernard tried to picture how he would get up there and what he would find inside, a sense of exhilaration swept over him. Ever since 1940, when forces of the Third Reich swept into France and occupied the country, Bernard, like many other young Frenchmen, had hoped the war would last long enough for him to participate in the liberation and to be a part of history. This, he realized, was his chance, for Hitler's *cave* was much more than a wine cellar; it was a symbol of cruelty and greed, of Nazi Germany's hunger for wealth and riches.

How a young man from Champagne got to Berchtesgaden and became one of the few people ever to set eyes on the treasures Hitler had amassed for himself is one of the most fascinating stories of the war.

And one we heard almost by accident.

It began with a guessing game.

We were in the Loire Valley interviewing Vouvray's Gaston Huet for an article about plans by the government to dig a tunnel through the area for the TGV, France's high-speed train. Winemakers, including Huet, who was then mayor of Vouvray, were up in arms. The train, they warned, would destroy their vineyards and ruin their wines, which were stored in the surrounding limestone caves.

'There are hundreds of thousands of bottles in those caves,' said Huet, who was leading the protest. 'Noise and vibrations from the train could spell disaster.'

Suddenly, Huet excused himself and disappeared from the room. He returned with a bottle and three glasses. 'This is one of the reasons I am against the train,' he said, holding the unlabeled bottle out to us. It was streaked with cobwebs and covered with dust. Without saying another word, Huet pulled the cork and began to pour. The wine was brilliant gold in color. We looked at each other in anticipation, then at Huet. A faint smile had crossed his face.

'Go on, try it,' he said.

The first sip left no doubt in our minds that we were tasting something extraordinary. The wine was dazzling. It was lusciously sweet, yet so fresh and alive one might have thought it had been made yesterday, and we told him so.

'So what year do you think it is?' asked Huet.

We guessed 1976, a great year for Loire Valley wines, but Huet only shook his head and urged us to try again. 1969? Same reaction. 1959? Wrong again.

Huet, looking more amused by the minute, was clearly enjoying himself. We decided to give it one more shot. 'How about 1953?' We tried to make it sound more like a statement than a question, but Huet was not fooled. The smile on his face growing wider as he let us puzzle over what we were tasting a few seconds longer.

'1947,' he finally said. 'It is probably the greatest wine I ever made.' He said it with affection and pride, almost as if he were describing a favorite child.

As we swirled the wine, a heavenly bouquet of honey and apricots soared from our glasses. We asked Huet, then in his eighties, if he had ever tasted anything better. Although our question was almost rhetorical, Huet paused and turned serious.

'Only once,' he replied. 'It was when I was a prisoner of war in Germany during World War II.' And he went on to tell us one of the most amazing stories we have ever heard, a story about courage, loneliness, despair and, in the end, how a tiny bit of wine helped Huet and his fellow POWs survive five years of imprisonment. 'I don't even remember exactly what it was I drank,' said Huet. 'It was no more than a thimbleful, but it was the only wine we had in five years, and it was glorious.'

Glorious for him, intriguing for us. Until we heard Huet's story, we had never thought about 'wine and war.' We soon learned that the connection goes back a long way. In the sixth century B.C., Cyrus the Great of Persia ordered his troops to drink wine as an antidote to infection and illness. Julius Caesar and Napoleon Bonaparte were believers too. Napoleon even hauled wagonloads of champagne on his campaigns, most of the time anyway. The reason he lost the battle of Waterloo, some say, was that he did not have time to pick up any champagne and had to fight on Belgian beer alone.

Perhaps with that in mind, French soldiers in World War I were issued cases of champagne to keep close beside them in the trenches to keep their morale up. When World War II broke out, the French government sent utensils and recipes for making hot wine to the front. As one official explained, 'A ration of hot wine is not expensive, and very helpful in preventing epidemics and comforting soldiers.'

But wine's apogee as a military tactic may have occurred three hundred years earlier when it was used to save Germany's beautiful walled city of Rothenburg from destruction during the Thirty Years War. According to wine authority Herbert M. Baus, 'Rothenburg was at the mercy of the victorious Tilly's 30,000 men when that field marshal, in a moment of mercy, promised to spare the city if one of its aldermen could empty a three-and-a-half-litre goblet of wine in one draught. Burgermeister Nusch proved equal to the challenge, and the site of his epic feat is called to this day Freudengässlein, or Lane of Joy.'

For us, the joy of wine has been as much in the sharing of it as in the drinking. One of the greatest wines we have ever tasted was a 1905 Grand Vin de Château Latour. It was exquisite, absolutely mind-boggling, but what made the experience even more special was being able to share it with Gertrude de Gallaix, a dear friend who lived in Paris during World War II and who was born in the same year that the wine was made.

There also was a bottle of rosé we once drank that, in all honesty, was not much of a wine, but sharing it with friends on a warm summer's day made that day special and the wine as unforgettable, in a way, as the 1905 Latour.

André Simon, the noted French wine authority, described wine as 'a good counselor, a true friend, who neither bores nor irritates us: it does not send us to sleep, nor does it keep us awake . . . it is always ready to cheer, to help, but not to bully us.'

Yet the fascinating wines we tasted did 'bully us' at times into asking questions. Gaston Huet's story had piqued our interest and aroused our curiosity. Over the next few years, we met other winemakers who told us their war stories, some of them funny and some that touched the heart. As we listened, we gradually realized that these stories, like a good bottle of wine, were things we wanted to share. They were stories that deserved to be told and remembered – in a book.

Collecting the stories was not always easy. Some people were afraid and refused to talk about a time tainted by those who collaborated with the enemy and tried to make money from the war. 'It's much too sensitive,' said one person who declined to be interviewed. 'Better to let the dead rest in peace and the living live in peace.'

Many papers dealing with collaborators were sealed under a French law aimed at protecting the personal privacy of individuals. Other papers were destroyed at the end of the war on orders from the German high command.

Other problems we encountered included faded memories and the fact that many people have passed away. On several occasions, we received a note or call saying the person we were scheduled to interview had just died.

Although it was, literally, a race against time, sometimes we had to go slowly. People from the generation that had fought in the war were not always ready to talk about it. Their first reaction was 'Oh my, that was such a long time ago. I'm not sure . . .' and then their voice would drift off and silence would settle in. But then, suddenly, he or she might say, 'But there is one thing

I remember . . .' and then we would find ourselves listening to a wonderful story.

Younger people we approached were sometimes hesitant too. 'Please, I was only a child,' they would say, 'I don't remember anything.' But often they did, and their stories were among the most revealing, giving us very clear snapshots of a complicated era.

For instance, Jean-Michel Cazes, owner of Château Lynch-Bages and Château Pichon-Baron in Bordeaux, showed us that the barometer of the war was on the playground as well as on the battleground. In the fall of 1940, when he and his friends returned to school, Cazes, who was then eight, recalled how they all wanted to play at being Germans. 'The Germans seemed so strong and clever that we all wanted to be them in our games,' he said. Two years later, with the face of France already altered by the German occupation, the interests of the children had changed too. 'By then,' said Cazes, 'we all wanted to be the Maquis, the underground, fighting the Germans. It was much more romantic.' As more time passed and the Germans tightened their grip on Bordeaux, romance gave way to realism. 'We used to peek out at the Germans marching and then they seemed not just strong but also very frightening.' When the fortunes of the Germans began to change in the last years of the war, so too did games on the playgrounds. 'We all wanted to be Americans then,' said Cazes. By the end of the war, the change of heart was complete; the children in the playgrounds of France were playing at cowboys and Indians.

Many of the people we interviewed belonged to families that had been making wine for generations. Not only did they know what wine was about but they also knew what war was about. They had lived through it, some more than once, and they were acutely conscious of what it takes to survive. For the Rothschilds of Château Lafite-Rothschild in Bordeaux, it meant fleeing the country before the Germans took over their property. For Henri Jayer of Vosne-Romanée in Burgundy, it meant trading his wine for food so his family would have enough to eat. For Prince Philippe

Poniatowski of Vouvray, it meant burying his best wines in his yard so that he would have something to restart business with after the war.

Survival, however, did not always require desperate measures: sometimes people just got lucky. For René Couly of Chinon, it was a flat tire that saved him. 'My father had just been called up by the army and was made a truck driver, since he had lots of experience driving our trucks,' his son told us. 'He was in his truck following his company to the front when he had a flat tire. While he stopped to fix it, the rest of the troops continued on and marched right into an ambush. Every single person was taken prisoner.' Everyone, that is, except Couly. 'After changing the tire, my father turned around and went home to his vineyard.'

Although most of the information we gathered came from interviews, occasionally it was the wine itself that did the 'talking.' A 1940 La Tâche we tasted with Robert Drouhin, one of Burgundy's most respected winemakers and *négociants*, spoke volumes about the wartime difficulties winemakers had to overcome in order to make good wine. Most Burgundies that year were decimated by rot and mildew because the Germans had requisitioned all metals including copper for their industrial war machine. Without copper, winemakers had no copper sulfate for treating their vines. The La Tâche from the Domaine de la Romanée-Conti, however, was one of the survivors and a fitting climax to a wonderful dinner with Drouhin. Of the wine, our notes said: 'Good color, spicy bouquet, fading a little but still elegant and charming.'

Another bottle we shared with Drouhin on another occasion told an entirely different story. It was a white 1940 Clos des Mouches, extremely rare and one of the first white Clos des Mouches Robert's father ever made. Alas, the wine was undrinkable. It was dull brown and totally maderized. 'No good,' said Madame Françoise Drouhin, frowning slightly and putting her glass down. Her husband's reaction was a little different. 'Interesting,' he said. And he was right. We could literally sense, almost taste, the problems the

Drouhins faced when they made the wine. There was a hint of fungus and a touch of death on the nose.

And there was something else we noticed. The bottle it came in was pale blue-green instead of the usual brownish green, a color Burgundians describe as *feuilles mortes*, or dead leaves. 'This wine was probably bottled in 1942,' said Drouhin, 'when everyone had to recycle their bottles or get them wherever they could, which meant bottles were made with any sort of glass composition that could be had.'

But wherever we went and whomever we talked to, the point that was always stressed – the one we could never ignore – was how important wine is to France. It is not just a beverage or commercial product to be poured from a bottle. It is much more than that. Like the flag, the *Tricolore*, it goes to the country's heart and soul. 'Wine makes us proud of our past,' said one official. 'It gives us courage and hope.' How else to explain why *vignerons* in Champagne rushed into their vineyards to harvest the 1915 vintage even as artillery shells were falling all around? Or why King Louis XI in his first act after conquering Burgundy in 1477 confiscated the entire vintage of Volnay for himself? Or why a priest in a small village in Champagne not long ago admonished his parish to remember, 'Our champagne is not just about making money. It is about bringing joy to people.'

And perhaps something spiritual. 'Our wines evolve slowly and nobly, carrying with them hopes for a prolonged life,' explained one winegrower. 'We know our land was here before we came and that it will be here long after we are gone. With our wine, we have survived wars, the Revolution and phylloxera. Each harvest renews promises made in the spring. We live with the continuing cycle. This gives us a taste of eternity.'

Recently the French government commissioned a study of what makes the French 'French,' or, as one scholar put it, 'to assess what makes up French historical memory and identity.' It was a vast work, in seven volumes. Part of it was a survey in which people were asked to define the qualities that made them French. Places one through three were what you might expect: being born in France, defending liberty and speaking French. But right behind them in fourth place was wine, specifically knowing and appreciating 'good' wine. This came as no surprise to the survey's authors, who concluded, 'Wine is part of our history; it's what defines us.'

In 1932, a year before Adolf Hitler became chancellor of Germany, Hubert de Mirepoix, president of the French Winegrowers Association, gave a speech at the organization's annual convention in which he described how wine 'contributed to the French race by giving them wit, gaiety and good taste, qualities which set it profoundly apart from people who drink a lot of beer.'

Although this is a book about wine and war, it is not a wine book, not really, nor is it a book just about war. It is about people, people who indeed exude wit, gaiety and good taste, and whose love of the grape and devotion to a way of life helped them survive and triumph over one of the darkest and most difficult chapters in French history.

ONE

To Love the Vines

It was late August 1939, and French winemakers were fretting about the harvest. Two months earlier, the outlook had been bright. The weather had been good and there was the promise of an excellent vintage. Then the weather changed. For six straight weeks it rained, and temperatures plummeted.

So did the mood of winegrowers attending the International Congress of the Vine and Wine in the resort of Bad Kreuznach, Germany. The weather was all they could think about – that is, until the next speaker was announced. He was Walter Darré, the Minister of Food Supply and Agriculture for the Third Reich. Winegrowers had been jolted when they first walked into the convention hall and discovered a large portrait of Darré's boss, Adolf Hitler, dominating the room. Like the rest of the world, they had watched with growing alarm as Hitler annexed Austria, carved up Czechoslovakia and signed a military agreement with Italy's dictator, Benito Mussolini. Many, fearful that full-scale war was just one step away, felt sure Darré would have something to say about the latest events.

But when the Reichsminister took the podium, he did not speak about the war. He did not even talk about wine. Instead, he called for the Congress delegates to go beyond the concerns of wine and winemaking and work instead to 'advance the mutual understanding of peaceful peoples.' Those in the audience were thoroughly confused.

What they did not know was that at almost the same moment Hitler himself was giving a very different kind of speech – this one to his high command – in another German resort, Berchtesgaden, the favored vacation spot of the Nazi leadership. The Führer was telling his generals what was coming next and exhorting them to remember, 'Our opponents are little worms . . . What matters in beginning and waging war is not righteousness but victory. Close your hearts to pity. Proceed brutally.'

Within a week, his forces invaded Poland. The date was September 1, 1939. French winegrowers at the conference were promptly summoned home. Two days later, France, along with Britain, Australia and New Zealand, declared war on Germany.

For the second time in little more than a generation, French winegrowers faced the agonizing prospect of trying to get their harvest in before vineyards were turned into battlefields. As in 1914, the government mounted an extraordinary campaign to help. Winegrowers were granted delays in being called to active duty, military labor detachments were sent to the vineyards and farm horses of small growers were not to be requisitioned until the harvest was completed.

Memories of that earlier war, 'the war to end all wars,' still haunted them – the brutality, the hardships and especially the staggering loss of life. Out of a population of 40 million, nearly a million and a half young men were killed, men who would have entered their most productive years had they survived. Another million lost limbs or were so badly wounded that they could no longer work.

It was a bloodletting that left almost no family in France untouched: not the Drouhins of Burgundy, the Miaihles of Bordeaux, the de Nonancourts of Champagne, the Hugels of Alsace, nor the Huets of the Loire Valley.

Gaston Huet's father returned home an invalid, his lungs permanently scarred after his army unit was attacked with mustard gas.

Bernard de Nonancourt's father also suffered the ravages of trench warfare and died of wounds soon after the war.

The mother of Jean Miaihle lost her entire family when German troops attacked their village in northern France.

The Hugel family, which had lost its French heritage and nationality when Alsace was annexed by Germany after the Franco-Prussian War of 1870–71, sent their son away so that he could escape being drafted into the German army.

Maurice Drouhin, a veteran of trench warfare, escaped physical injury but not the nightmares which haunted him for years afterward.

Like nearly everyone else in France, these winemaking families watched with trepidation as the specter of another war approached. Although France had been the winner earlier, it had paid a terrible price. Could it afford another such victory? Many in France doubted it, especially Maurice Drouhin, who had witnessed the horrors of war close up.

Thoughts of his family and vineyard were all that comforted him as he huddled with his men in the muddy blood-soaked trenches of northern France, peering at the enemy across a strip of no-man's-land. Although the winter of 1915 still had that part of the country in its grip, Maurice knew that back home in Burgundy, the vines already would be stirring and workers would be busy pruning. If he closed his eyes, he could almost picture it, the men with their secateurs working their way slowly down the long rows of vines; and he could almost hear the church bells that called them to work each day.

Those bells were the first sounds Maurice heard each morning when he awoke in his home in Beaune. For him, they were the background music to life in the vineyards. They rolled across the villages and wheat fields, they sent children racing to school and mothers scurrying to markets for the freshest produce of the day. They heralded lunchtime and dinnertime, and they called people to worship, and to celebrate. But as World War I ground on, they were calling more and more people to mourn.

Now, on the battlefields of northern France, the sounds that surrounded Maurice were artillery and machine-gun fire and the agonized cries of the wounded. In the heat of one battle, he saw a German soldier crumple to the ground, unable to move after being shot. With German troops too frightened to venture into the storm of bullets to retrieve their comrade, Maurice ordered his men to cease firing while he raised a white flag. Then, in impeccable German, he shouted to the Germans, 'Come get your man. We will hold our fire until you have him.' The Germans moved quickly to rescue their fallen comrade. Before returning behind the lines, however, they halted directly in front of Maurice and saluted him.

Later, in a letter to his wife, Pauline, Maurice described the incident. Pauline was so moved that she passed the story on to the local newspaper, which published it. Headlined 'The Glorious Hours,' the article said, 'The glorious hours sound not just for heroic action on the battlefield but also for those activities that occur in daily life, for it is when war is over that a soldier's heart and character are also revealed.'

Maurice was highly decorated for his military service. Among his awards was the Distinguished Service Medal from the United States government, a medal for which he had been nominated by Douglas MacArthur. But as proud as Maurice was of that medal and his life in the military, it was his life in the vineyards that held even greater meaning for him – one that beckoned him home when the 'war to end all wars' had finally ended.

That life was one of legend and myth, a life which, in many ways, had changed little since the Middle Ages. 'It was a simpler time in the vineyards,' Maurice's son Robert recalled years later. 'We had a way of living, a way of making wine that was natural and *très ancienne*.'

It was made the way their grandfathers and great-grandfathers had made it. There were no experts to rely on, so everyone followed the traditions they knew and had grown up with. Plowing was done with horses. Planting, picking and pruning were done according to the phases of the moon. Older people often reminded younger ones that the merits of pruning were discovered when St Martin's donkey got loose in the vineyards.

It happened, they said, in 345 A.D. when St Martin, dressed in animal skins and riding on a donkey, went out to inspect some of the vineyards that belonged to his monastery near Tours in the Loire Valley. He was a lover of wine and had done much over the years to educate monks about the latest viticultural practices. On this occasion, St Martin tethered his donkey to a row of vines while he went about his business. He was gone for several hours. When he returned, he discovered to his horror that his donkey had been munching the vines and that some had been chewed right down to the trunk. Next year, however, the monks were surprised when they saw that those same vines were the very ones which grew back the most abundantly and produced the best grapes. The lesson was not lost on the monks, and as centuries passed, pruning became part of every winegrower's routine.

Days began early and lasted until the work was done. There were no fixed hours. As they pruned, checked for maladies, tied back shoots that had come loose – day after day, week after week, month after month – workers came to know each vine personally. There was an almost mystical connection as they let the vines set the rhythm and pace of life.

After picking, grapes were crushed with bare feet. The must, or grape juice, was then poured into giant vats, followed by a process called *pigeage*, in which naked workers plunged themselves into the frothy liquid. Holding tightly to chains that had been fastened to overhead beams, the workers would then raise and lower themselves over and over again, stirring the must with their entire bodies so as to aerate the mixture and enhance the fermentation. It was a dangerous exercise. Hardly a harvest went by without some workers losing their grip and drowning, or being asphyxiated by the carbonic gas given off by the fermenting juice. Victims were almost always men, since women, in some parts of France, were barred from the *chai*, or winery, during harvesttime. Their presence, according to superstition, would turn the wine sour.

Yet harvesttime was always the happiest time of the year. When the last grapes were picked and loaded onto a horse-drawn wagon, workers would gather wildflowers to decorate the cart and to make a bouquet for the lady of the house. She would hang the bouquet above the entry to the *cave*, where it would stay until the next harvest to bring good luck – and good wine – to the house. Others would even scatter grape leaves on the floor to encourage the 'good spirits' not to leave.

Time, then, was almost magical; it felt never-ending, Robert Drouhin recalled. During walks through the vineyards, he and his father often stopped for long, rambling conversations with the workers.

'People seemed to have more character then. They never hesitated to tell my father what they thought or how they believed things should be done, and my father was always ready to listen. Those were the moments when I learned to love the vines.'

Unfortunately, those vines were in miserable shape. The years between the wars had brought mostly misery to winemakers, who suffered through a string of horrible vintages – and not just because of the weather. Battles that had raged during World War I had rendered vineyards, especially those in Champagne, practically lifeless. They had been sliced up by trenches and blown apart by artillery and mortar shells, which left enormous craters in the ground. Worse were the chemical shells that leaked into the soil, poisoning the vineyards for years to come.

World War I had arrived just when winegrowers were beginning to recover from another crisis. Phylloxera, a tiny insect that attacks the roots of grapevines, had invaded France in the middle of the nineteenth century, reducing vast areas of vineyard to what one winegrower described as 'rows of bare wooden stumps – resembling huge graveyards.' Over the next thirty years, the disease would spread to every vineyard in the country, prompting the government to offer a 300,000-franc prize to anyone who could find a cure. All kinds of ideas were suggested, ranging from the bizarre – planting a live toad beneath each vine – to the hopeful – watering vineyards with white wine. Some growers flooded their vineyards with seawater; others sprayed their vines with a vast array of chemicals or simply burned them. Nothing seemed to work.

The remedy, as it turned out, was something totally un-French. Growers discovered that by grafting their vines onto American rootstocks, which were naturally resistant to the root-eating louse, they could save their vines. It was a long and costly process. Vineyards had to be uprooted and replanted. Then growers had to wait several years for their vines to begin bearing fruit, and even longer for them to reach full maturity.

Just when things began looking up after World War I, disaster struck again. This time it was the Great Depression, and the effect on the wine industry was devastating. In Champagne, major houses could no longer afford to buy grapes from their growers. In Alsace, huge numbers of winegrowers went bankrupt. Those in Bordeaux were forced to accept prices that were below the national average – the first time in history that had happened. In Burgundy, wine production fell 40 percent as nearly half the vineyards went uncultivated. Even the great Domaine de la Romanée-Conti was floundering, but the family which owned it was determined to hold on to it. 'My father felt it was like a beautiful jewel a woman has in her jewelry box,' Aubert de Villaine recalled. 'She would not wear it every day, but she was determined to keep it so she could pass it on to her children.'

To do that, de Villaine's father did what many other winegrowers were forced to do to survive: he took on another job. It was his third. He was already managing the family farm and running Romanée-Conti; now he started working in a bank as well. 'My father was constantly busy; he never stopped,' de Villaine said,

'but that is how much he loved Romanée-Conti and he spent every
spare moment working there.'

Although the Domaine de la Romanée-Conti would not begin
showing a profit until 1959, it was still considered the standard-
bearer of great Burgundy, a property that never cut corners or
sacrificed quality for the sake of making money. That was something
Maurice Drouhin admired and deeply respected.

With no one making much money anyway, Maurice decided to
take a huge risk and create a business that concentrated on one
thing only: great Burgundy wine. 'My father had a vision of quality,'
Robert said, 'a desire to create wines that were a pure reflection of
the *terroir*.'

Maurice had inherited a *maison du vin classique*, which meant he
sold a little bit of everything and made a little bit of wine himself,
but that was about to change. 'From now on,' he declared, 'not one
drop of anything but Burgundy wine in my house.' And he insisted
that all those drops be good ones. He looked at the great wines being
made by the struggling Domaine de la Romanée-Conti and thought,
'This is the future.' So, in the mid-1930s, Maurice began buying 60
percent of the domaine's production each year and distributing it.
At the same time, he pushed his winemakers to improve the quality
of wines of his own house, Maison Joseph Drouhin, adopting the
philosophy of Monsieur de Villaine at Romanée-Conti, who believed
that the winemaker was no more than an intermediary between the
soil and the wine and that he should interfere as little as possible.

In opting for quality at that moment, Maurice had, unknowingly,
placed himself at the forefront of a movement that would herald
major changes in French winemaking. Until then, winemaking
had been haphazard, more instinctive than scientific. There were
few rules – no limits, for example, on the use of sugar, which
winemakers usually added to boost the alcoholic strength of their
wines when grapes failed to fully ripen. Too often, however,
winemakers used it as a crutch for picking their grapes too early.

Quantity, not quality, was their motto and the surest way, they believed, to make money. They planted high-yielding vines that produced inferior grapes and, predictably, inferior wine. To cover up faults, they dumped in sugar and syrup, which resulted in huge beefy wines more suitable for chewing than drinking. Often, a good Burgundy was not Burgundy at all because it had been 'arranged,' or mixed with wines from the Rhône Valley and Algeria.

Some, including Maurice Drouhin, decided that was no longer acceptable. The solution, they decided, rested with three words: Appellation d'Origine Contrôlée, or 'controlled place of origin.' That meant wine should be what it says it is. Burgundy should be made only from grapes grown in Burgundy; the same was true with Bordeaux and wines from other regions. They should not be mixed.

But AOC embraced much more than geography. It also stipulated which vines could be planted, how they had to be pruned, what fertilizers and chemicals could be used and when harvesting could begin. Rules were also laid down for vinification, or winemaking.

None of this happened overnight. As Remington Norman, a Master of Wine who has written extensively about Burgundy, points out, the AOC system 'did not spring ready-made from the mind of some enlightened law-givers, but evolved over nearly four decades before being progressively codified from the 1920s onwards.'

Effective enforcement was the biggest headache. With only a few dozen inspectors, it was virtually impossible to keep watch over thousands of winemakers who labored creatively, if not scrupulously, in their cellars, blending a little of this with a little of that. As the famous French wine writer André Simon pointed out, blending 'is to some extent like kissing – it may be quite innocent, but it may lead one away from the narrow path of duty and propriety.' That was particularly true in Bordeaux, where, in some years, only a third of the wine sold with a 'Bordeaux' label was actually made in that region.

To curb such practices, in 1935, Drouhin and other winemakers created the Comité National des Appellations d'Origine, forerunner of the Institut National des Appellations d'Origine, or INAO, the governing body of French wine. Many growers, however, even those who were inclined to support the INAO, resisted at first, fearing it could work to their disadvantage by forcing them to pay more taxes or set their prices too high. No one wanted to drive off their customers, especially not then, but advertising for new ones was anathema. 'Advertising is wrong,' one winemaker said. 'We should never advertise. If our wine is good, people will come to us.'

Such a philosophy may have worked in Burgundy, where vineyards were small and most of the wine produced was consumed locally, but it would never have worked for producers in Champagne, who depended heavily on international markets and knew they had to advertise. They had learned from bitter experience how quickly the fizz can disappear. They saw, for instance, how tastes changed rapidly when Parisians discovered cocktails during the Roaring Twenties. They also saw how suddenly markets dried up, first in Russia when the czar was overthrown during the Russian Revolution, and later in the United States when Prohibition reared its head.

Marie-Louise Lanson de Nonancourt, however, had more urgent concerns: her family. Her husband had died of wounds after World War I, and she had been left with three sons to raise, one of them a baby named Bernard.

'My mother felt lost; she did not know what to do,' Bernard recalled. Nevertheless, she was about to demonstrate that she was another of Champagne's strong-minded and talented widows, like the famous Veuve Clicquot and Veuve Pommery.

Marie-Louise had spent her entire life in Champagne and, as part of the family which owned Lanson Père & Fils, one of the oldest champagne houses, she knew the business inside out. When she looked at Lanson, however, she saw a business with too many heirs. Two of her brothers, Victor and Henri, were in charge of running it, but there were some ten other brothers and sisters in the family as well as twenty-six or twenty-seven nephews and nieces. Under France's inheritance laws, Lanson would be broken up into tiny pieces with each member of the family getting shares. 'It will never be enough to support all of us,' Marie-Louise thought.

Like Maurice Drouhin, she was confronted with a difficult economic situation and decided to take a chance. In 1938, Marie-Louise found a run-down champagne company, Veuve Laurent-Perrier & Cie, whose owner had died some years earlier without heirs. It was in extremely bad shape and on the verge of bankruptcy. There was little equipment and even less champagne. Out of 100 houses, it was ranked almost at the bottom, number 98.

Marie-Louise was not discouraged. On the contrary, she was thrilled. 'It is exactly what I have been looking for,' she said. To the shock of everyone, especially her brother Victor, she poured her life's savings into buying it.

'Have you lost your mind?' he exclaimed. 'Everyone is struggling! How do you, a woman alone, hope to make any money, especially from a place like that?'

Marie-Louise believed the answer was standing right in front of him, her three sons. They were tall, strong young men who had already started to learn the champagne business. She had insisted they learn all aspects of it, starting at the bottom by packing cases and loading trucks.

'That's not enough,' Victor warned. 'Don't you realize there's a war coming? Your sons could be called up at any moment, and you of all people ought to know what that means. My God, you can already hear the sound of it in the distance!'

Indeed, Marie-Louise had heard the sounds. She shivered when Hitler, after annexing Austria earlier that year, vowed 'to smash Czechoslovakia by military action'; she watched as he carried out that threat, taking over the Sudetenland and then marching his troops into Prague.

Nevertheless, Marie-Louise was convinced she was doing the right thing. As her son Bernard later said, 'My mother always believed that if war happened, France and its allies would win.'

But she did have qualms. By the spring of 1939, she along with everyone else realized that the Munich Conference had been a failure. Hitler had not been appeased when Britain and France ceded the Sudetenland in Czechoslovakia to him; it merely whetted his appetite. When Hitler's forces marched into Prague, Britain, in response, launched the first peacetime draft in its history. French industries went from a forty- to a forty-four-hour workweek (German ones were already working sixty), while French Prime Minister Daladier called on the United States to send fighter planes. In Washington, President Franklin Roosevelt, his hands tied by the U.S. Neutrality Act, sent Hitler a list of twenty-six countries, demanding that their territorial integrity be respected. Hitler delivered his answer in Berlin. The Führer read the letter to the Reichstag, his voice dripping with sarcasm and his hand going up and down like a hammer as he ticked off the countries one by one: Hungary, Albania, Yugoslavia, Poland . . . As each name was read, the audience roared with laughter.

Five months later, Hitler sent his army into Poland. Two days after that, war was declared against the Third Reich.

It was a grim backdrop to yet another crisis unfolding in France's vineyards. The harvest of 1939 had just begun and it was as bad as everyone feared. In Burgundy, Robert Drouhin remembered a '*vendange sous la neige*,' or a harvest under a blanket of snow. In Bordeaux, the problem was rain, which resulted in thin, diluted wines, prompting one grower to complain, 'This isn't wine, it's dishwater.' In Champagne, Marie-Louise de Nonancourt did not have any grapes to pick. She had put her new domaine *en sommeil*, literally 'to sleep,' deciding it was better to leave her new firm in a state of dormancy than try to begin operating in the midst of war. Those Champenois who did pick had to do so with inexperienced women and children because most of the young men had been mobilized. The grapes they collected were largely unripe. The region worst hit was Alsace, where one grower described the grapes as 'complete rubbish.' Our best wine, he said, had only 8.4 degrees alcohol, nearly four degrees less than normal. 'We might as well have poured it down the drain.'

To most, it seemed as if the peasants' legend about war and wine was coming true. To announce the coming of war, the Lord sends a bad wine crop, the peasants said. While war continues, he sends mediocre ones. To mark its end, he sends a fine, festive crop.

In 1939, as war loomed on the horizon, winegrowers faced a harvest that almost everyone would eventually call the worst of the century.

As it turned out, winegrowers need not have worried about completing their harvest before the battles began. After war was declared on September 3, nothing happened. There were no battles, no threats of retaliation from Berlin, nothing except a few German planes which flew lazily over Paris. French forces launched a halfhearted thrust toward the German front but quickly drew back to more secure positions behind the Maginot Line, confident that this series of concrete fortifications which ran from Switzerland to the Luxembourg and Belgian borders would provide all the protection necessary. Considered unbreachable, it had been constructed between the two wars to deter a German offensive into France. It was also a symbol, a static reminder of French defensive thinking.

For the next eight months until the spring of 1940, France would languish behind the Maginot Line in what Janet Flanner of *The New Yorker* described as a 'curious form of lethargy,' waiting and wondering what Germany might do and behaving as if it were business as usual. The period of inaction was called *le drôle de guerre*, or Phony War.

'This is a queer war so far,' she wrote. 'Were it not for the existence of war, the knowledge, for example, that it is against the law to go onto the street without your gas mask, this Sunday would just be a beautiful Indian-summer day . . . Certainly this must be the first war that millions of people on both sides continued to think could be avoided even after it had officially been declared.'

Maurice Drouhin, however, had no such illusions. In the years following World War I, he had stayed in close touch with his army friends, including some in the United States such as Douglas MacArthur. Occasionally, he was asked by the French government to accompany an army delegation to the States to prod Washington to end its policy of isolation. Those trips were something he feared German intelligence might be monitoring.

As a precaution, Maurice had begun teaching his wife, Pauline, a code he learned in World War I. It involved making tiny pencil dots around letters or words in a book to create messages. 'Whatever happens,' he told Pauline, 'do not leave Beaune. If war comes and I have to leave suddenly, stay here; I will always find a way to contact you. The places that are deserted are the most vulnerable, the ones that will be looted first.'

Throughout the country, winegrowers like Maurice were beginning to worry about the vulnerability of their stocks of wine. With tens of thousands of bottles in his cellar, Maurice decided he had to try to protect at least some of it, especially his complete stock of Romanée-Conti from 1929 through 1938, which he felt represented the family's security.

Maurice's cellar was made up of a labyrinth of caves under Beaune, some of which had been carved in the thirteenth century. All the odd twists and turns made them perfect for hiding large quantities of wine. In one section, he decided to build a wall and hide his most valuable bottles of wine behind it. 'Not a word to anyone else about this,' he told his family. Building the wall was a family project and one that Maurice's son Robert, who was eight years old, found terribly exciting. 'While Papa laid the bricks, my mother, my sisters and I ran around the cellar collecting spiders to put in front of the wall. The spiders would then spin webs and make the wall look older.'

Similar efforts were underway in Champagne, only on a much larger scale. With miles and miles of limestone caves underpinning the region, producers secreted away not only huge amounts of champagne but also hunting rifles, furniture and even cars.

At Laurent-Perrier, Marie-Louise de Nonancourt did not need much space since she did not have much to hide, only 400 *pièces*, the equivalent of about 100,000 bottles, merely a drop for most champagne houses but all she had been able to afford when she purchased the domaine. Unlike other champagne houses, however, Marie-Louise not only built a wall; she also called on some extra help: her namesake, the Virgin Mary. After sealing up her champagne, Marie-Louise brought in her own personal devotional statue of the Virgin and cemented it into a niche of the wall where it was clearly visible.

'Now it is in her hands,' she told her sons. 'There is nothing more I can do to protect our future.'

In Alsace-Lorraine, an air of fatalism prevailed. 'Here we go again,' people thought.

The disputed provinces, on France's eastern border with Germany, became French territory in the late seventeenth century. Between 1870 and 1945, however, they changed hands four times, passing from France to Germany, to France, to Germany and back to France.

Among those who witnessed each change were the Hugels of Riquewihr, a family of winegrowers in Alsace since 1639. 'We are specialists in war and wine,' said Johnny Hugel. 'In 1939, we were just sitting down to celebrate our family's three hundredth anniversary in the wine business when something happened: war was declared.' The party was canceled.

The Hugel story, in many ways, is the story of Alsace. 'My grandfather had to change his nationality four times,' Johnny's brother André said. Grandfather Emile was born in 1869. He was born French, but two years later, in 1871, Alsace was taken over by Germany after the Franco-Prussian War, and he became German.

The end of World War I in 1918 made him French again. In 1940, when Alsace was annexed, he was forced to become German. By 1950, when Emile died at the age of ninety-one, he was once again French.

The constant swing between nationalities resulted in a kind of regional schizophrenia, a feeling of being part French, part German, but most of all Alsatian.

Selling wine under such conditions was often a struggle; it meant suddenly adapting to different economic situations. As Papa Jean Hugel once wrote, 'It is very easy on a map to change the line of the frontier overnight . . . but very often the new system was in direct contradiction to the previous one. The home market became the export market, out of reach through tariff restrictions and vice versa. Well-established connections were no longer available, and new markets had to be painstakingly won.'

In the fall of 1939, it seemed inevitable that the whole agonizing process was about to repeat itself. With the declaration of war, the French government, fearing an attack, ordered that the city of Strasbourg, which sat just across the Rhine River from Germany, be evacuated. A few weeks later, when nothing had happened, many of the city's 200,000 residents began trickling back, figuring it had been a false alarm.

The Hugels thought otherwise. They were convinced it was only a matter of time before the Phony War became a real war. They had seen how appeasement had failed at Munich the year before, how Hitler had played Prime Ministers Daladier and Chamberlain for fools. When Hitler signed a friendship and nonaggression pact with the Soviet Union in August 1939, the Hugels had little doubt war was just around the corner. They were proved right. 'At that moment, we felt that the only way Germany could be stopped was if the United States joined the war,' Johnny Hugel said. But those hopes were dashed when President Roosevelt, in October, reaffirmed his country's intent to remain neutral.

Throughout Alsace, there was a feeling of impending doom, a

sense of foreboding as threatening as the clouds that hung over the region during that cold gray November. The following month, as the holiday season drew near, the festive spirit that usually existed was nowhere to be seen. Most of Alsace's villages, which looked as if they had popped out of a Hansel and Gretel storybook, remained dark. There were no twinkling lights, no music and laughter, none of the things that normally accompany the Christmas season.

On Christmas Eve, the Hugels gathered together in Riquewihr as they always did, but it was a somber affair. In previous years, the house had always been decorated, everyone exchanged gifts and then sat down to a sumptuous dinner that included some wonderful wines. But not this year. No one was in the mood. Everyone feared that this would be their last Christmas as French citizens, and Grandpa Emile, an old man of eighty, did not want to die a German.

'My mother cried the whole night,' André recalled. With two of her sons nearly old enough to be drafted into the German army and one of her brothers living in Germany, there was no consoling her.

Gloom hung over another family as well.

It had been a bad year for the Miaihles, a prominent winemaking family in Bordeaux. With properties that included Châteaux Pichon-Longueville, Siran, Coufran, Dauzac and Citran, the Miaihles had been one of the biggest wine producers in all of France.

But not in 1939. 'All the men had been called to military service and there was a desperate shortage of labor in the vineyards,' said May-Eliane Miaihle de Lencquesaing, who was fourteen when war was declared. Unlike the Hugels, she and her family were optimistic when the Munich agreement was signed. 'We thought maybe everything would be all right, but we were wrong.'

One of their first clues came in the summer of 1939 when they received an unexpected visit from some Jewish friends from Italy, friends who were also in the wine business.

'They said the Italian government was chasing Jews away and that they didn't know what was going to happen,' May-Eliane said. 'There were two couples and three children, and we said why not stay here with us until we can figure out what to do?'

Ever since Hitler had come to power in 1933, a steady stream of worried and frightened Jews had been pouring out of Germany and Eastern Europe, some seeking refuge in Britain and France while others emigrated to the United States, Argentina and Palestine. In November 1938, the flow quickened when ninety-one Jews were murdered in Germany during a night of looting and burning known as Kristallnacht.

It was a tragedy May-Eliane's aunt Renée Miaihle could understand. She herself had been a refugee after being orphaned in World War I. As a result, when their Jewish friends from Italy arrived, she never hesitated. 'My aunt would turn no one away and the rest of the family agreed with her,' May-Eliane said. The two families were offered space in Château Palmer, of which the Miaihles were part owner. Still, the question remained: what to do next, and how long would the families be safe?

They had been there less than a month when German forces invaded Poland, engaging in an orgy of slaughter that claimed more than 10,000 civilian lives, including 3,000 Polish Jews, some of whom were forced into synagogues and burned alive.

Baron Robert de Rothschild, one of the owners of Château Lafite-Rothschild, had been watching the events with growing alarm ever since the early 1930s. As head of the consistory of the Great Synagogue in Paris, he was dismayed when others in the synagogue began complaining that too many Jewish refugees were flooding into France and that they should be turned away. 'You sit there with your Legions of Honor and French passports,' he angrily told them, 'but when the crunch comes, we will all be in the same sack!'

In an effort to ease restrictions on immigrant Jews, Baron Robert contacted an old friend of his from World War I, Marshal Philippe

Pétain, a war hero who was then serving as France's ambassador to Spain. He asked him to use his influence to persuade the government to change its regulations. Pétain refused to help.

'I think, by then, Pétain considered my grandfather to be an annoying Jew,' Eric de Rothschild later recalled.

By the winter of 1939, Hitler's march toward a Final Solution was well under way. What had started in the early 1930s with the expulsion of German Jews from their towns and villages continued with forced emigrations. Jews in Poland were expelled from their homes and forced to live in restricted areas, or, ghettos.

The nightmare that was unfolding was not lost on the Miaihles or their Jewish friends. There were moments, however, when they tried to put aside their fears. One of the Italians was a first violinist with the Trieste Symphony Orchestra and the others were musicians as well. Every day, there was chamber music, with the Miaihles joining in. 'I remember wonderful concerts of Schumann, Fauré and Bach,' said May-Eliane. 'They would be held from five to seven o'clock every day, even when the weather became cold.' Because there was little heating, those concerts 'made all of us feel warmer.'

For French soldiers on the Maginot Line, the cold winter months did little to lift spirits. Four months had passed since France had declared war and still nothing had happened. The front remained quiet. To kill time, some soldiers took up gardening and planted rosebushes along the Maginot Line. Others picked up binoculars and peered across the frontier, placing bets on German troops playing soccer.

The inactivity of France's 'fighting men' did not go unnoticed by folks back home. One of the soldiers, a shopkeeper in civilian life, received an irate letter from his wife asking him to deal with some paperwork. 'Since you don't have anything to do, *you* write to the customer. I've got my hands full.'

In Paris, meanwhile, restaurants were crowded and there were long queues in front of movie houses. 'Paris must remain Paris,'

explained Maurice Chevalier, 'so that soldiers on leave can find a
bit of Parisian charm despite all.'

Most felt sure that if Germany did attack, France was fully
prepared. 'Confidence is a duty!' newspapers said. But that was
not the only duty. The advertising department for a major store
discovered another one in that fall of 1939: 'Madame, it is your
duty to be elegant!' it proclaimed.

The government tried to present a confident face too. In March
1940, parliamentary debates over French military preparedness
were punctuated by great declarations of patriotism and bravado,
as well as rousing paeans to the virtues of *le vin chaud du soldat*,
or hot mulled wine for soldiers. The biggest applause was reserved
for Edouard Barthe, a government deputy and wine lobbyist, who
called for wine canteens to be established at every major railway
station where soldiers would gather. He also urged that 50 million
extra hectoliters of wine be distributed as rations for soldiers on the
front. 'Wine is the good companion of soldiers,' he said. 'It gives
them courage.'

But confidence was a thin veneer, and behind the scenes there
were deep misgivings. In the government, there were many who
felt that their leaders were spending more time playing politics than
preparing for war. Some, in the face of Germany's nonaggression
pact with the Soviet Union, felt France had targeted the wrong
enemy. 'Hitler is bad but Stalin is worse,' they said. Hardly anyone
had a good thing to say about French foreign policy, which one
historian said was torn 'constantly between defeatist panic and
aggressive overconfidence.'

Prime Minister Daladier – cautious to a fault – strongly believed
that a defensive strategy, symbolized by the Maginot Line, was
the best way to protect France. He rejected the views of a tank
commander named Charles de Gaulle, who argued that France's
hopes depended on the creation of a career army based on powerful
and mobile armored forces. De Gaulle's views, contained in two
books he wrote in the early 1930s, were dismissed by Daladier

and most of the military brass. Even when Daladier was replaced by the more aggressive-minded Paul Reynaud, de Gaulle's strategy was still largely ignored.

But others were paying attention. Young German military commanders had read de Gaulle's books from cover to cover and were swiftly incorporating his offensive-oriented strategy into their own army.

In some respects, the French government's reluctance to do so was understandable. As historian Robert O. Paxton said, 'Any Frenchman over thirty remembered the blind wastage of young men in 1914–18, which had made France a nation of old people and cripples. That stark fact was brought home daily by the sight of mutilated veterans in the street. It took on particular urgency in the middle 1930s with the advent of the "hollow years," the moment when, as demographers had predicted, the annual draft contingent dropped in half because so few boys had been born in 1915–19. One more bloodbath, and would there be a France at all?'

Such fears sometimes resulted in measures that seemed almost paranoid. Shipments of wine to soldiers, for instance, were considered a state secret. Officials feared that if the Germans discovered the quantity of wine being sent to the front – soldiers were entitled to a litre of wine a day – the enemy could easily calculate the number and exact location of troops there.

Of deeper concern was the continuing power struggle between Prime Minister Reynaud and the man he had replaced, Edouard Daladier, a struggle that infected the highest levels of government and induced a kind of paralysis in decision making. Both men had strong opinions on how the war should be conducted, Reynaud favoring a more aggressive approach while Daladier, who was now Foreign Minister, insisted on a defensive one. Unfortunately, both men also had mistresses who were equally opinionated and despised each other, and who were extremely adept at pillow talk when it came to telling their man how *they* thought the war should be fought. U.S. ambassador William Bullitt became so exasperated trying to deal with the French government that he fired off a telegram to President Roosevelt saying, 'Poison injected in the horizontal position is particularly venomous.'

It was now April 1940, seven months since the war had been declared. Winter had turned to spring and sidewalk cafés in Paris were filling up. It was beginning to feel like the summer of 1939 all over again, when, as Janet Flanner wrote, Paris experienced 'a fit of prosperity, gaiety, and hospitality.'

But it was all about to end.

On May 9, Hitler told his general staff, 'Gentlemen, you are about to witness the most famous victory in history.'

The following day, German forces, employing some of the very tactics Charles de Gaulle had advocated, breached the Meuse and plunged through the heavily wooded Ardennes, bypassing the Maginot Line. Eight months after France declared war on the Third Reich, the fighting had finally started.

The French army, powerful on paper, was overwhelmed. Though it had more tanks than the Germans, many were spread out thinly and ineffectually, 'ready, like a lot of small corks, to plug holes in the line,' one historian noted.

Nevertheless, French forces fought the invaders bravely. 'It's good that it's starting at last,' one soldier said. 'We can beat the Boches and have it over by autumn.'

In fact, it would be over much sooner, but not the way he expected.

TWO

Nomads

As the last rescue boats disappeared, so too did any hopes Gaston Huet had that he and his men might be saved.

It was May 24, 1940, and at the port of Calais on France's northwestern coast, tens of thousands of French and British soldiers were trapped by German forces, their backs to the sea. At that moment, Huet, a thirty-year-old French army lieutenant, would have given just about anything to be back in the Loire Valley, tending his vineyard in Vouvray.

It had already been a long war for Huet. A year and a half earlier, he had been among the first to be called up during the Munich crisis. Since that time, he had been home only once, for his daughter's first birthday. Now, with enemy forces closing in, Huet wondered when, or even if, he would see his family again.

Huet headed a transport company which had been dispatched to Belgium just before the invasion to fetch badly needed gasoline supplies for French forces. That mission became impossible, however, when motorized German infantry units backed by tanks and air support swept into France, overrunning Holland and Belgium as well.

'When we got to Flanders, we found that the Belgians had blown up the gas reservoir to prevent it from falling into enemy hands,' Huet said.

With communications down and the Germans moving at incredible speed, it was difficult to know which way to turn. Huet decided to push his company south and try to get back to France. The route, he quickly discovered, had been cut by German tanks, so he turned back north toward Antwerp, only to find virtually every road blocked by a crushing tangle of panic-stricken refugees. In desperation, Huet decided that he and his 200 men should make a run for the port of

Calais on the English Channel, where, Huet hoped, they could find
a boat that could evacuate them to England.

'About twenty miles from Calais, I ordered my men to begin
dispersing our trucks and supplies to keep them out of German
hands,' Huet said. Some of the trucks were driven into woods
while others were pushed into gullies, but not before a few essential
supplies were unloaded, such as food, water and thirty cases of
Vouvray, wine which Huet had brought from home 'to fortify the
men whenever necessary.' After stuffing a few bottles into their
packs, the company set off again.

The sight that greeted them at Calais was a nightmare. There on
the beach were thousands of British and French soldiers waiting –
hoping – to be evacuated. But no vessels were in sight, not even a
single fishing boat. Huet's heart began to sink. 'I did not know what
to do,' he said. 'There was absolutely no place for us to go. On one
side was the English Channel, on the other were the Germans.'

A massive evacuation was just beginning only twenty-five miles
away at Dunkirk but 'we knew nothing about it,' said Huet, 'and
even if we had, it would have been impossible for us to get there.'
All escape routes had been closed and now, suddenly, German
fighter-bombers had begun attacking troops on the beach. And
they were not the only ones; British planes were bombing them
too. 'They thought that the Germans had already taken over and
that we were Germans,' Huet said.

Amidst the fire and smoke, several small British navy boats
appeared. The masses trapped on the beach edged closer to the
surf, with some of the men plunging into the water, trying to swim
to the boats. The boats, however, were too small and could hold
only a few hundred people. With priority going to the British, Huet
and his men never had a chance. Someone from one of the vessels
shouted that they would try to return, but it never happened.

'I was stupefied,' Huet said. 'We were completely abandoned.'
So were thousands of other soldiers.

As the bombing grew more intense, Huet led his company to

cover in one of the concrete bunkers built as a line of defense along
the coast. From there, they could see the last of the rescue boats
slip out of sight. In despair and frustration, they stared at the huge
guns mounted in their bunker, all fixed in place and pointed out to
sea. According to Huet, 'Even if we could have turned them toward
the Germans, they would have done us no good. Their range was
too long; we would have just fired over their heads.'

Realizing it was only a matter of time – a short time – before they
would be captured, Huet and his men did the only thing they could:
they sat down and uncorked their last bottles of Vouvray.

As minutes passed, the bombing began to let up. Curious
about what was happening, Huet peered from the bunker and
was dumbfounded. At the bunker on his right, the French flag, the
Tricolore, was being lowered and a German one was being raised in
its place. Huet moved quickly to the other side of his bunker and
saw the same scene being repeated at every other bunker along the
coast. Only one French flag still flew, the one above his bunker.
With tears in his eyes and his men looking on, Huet approached
the flagpole and slowly lowered the flag. Ripping it into tiny pieces,
he then parceled them out to each of his men, stuffing one piece
into his own pocket. The rest, he burned.

Afterward, everyone sat back down, resigned to the fate that
awaited them. 'There was nothing else we could do,' Huet said.
'We were not armed to fight; we were a transport company. When
the Germans came, we had to surrender.'

Less than a month later, France itself formally surrendered –
but not before 10 million people, a quarter of the country's
population, had been turned into nomads, fleeing south, away
from the advancing Germans. It was the biggest migration of
people seen in Europe since the Dark Ages. 'They don't know,
nobody knows, where they are going,' one witness said. Under a
broiling sun broken only by fierce thunderstorms, children became
separated from their parents; hundreds of lives were lost in low-level

strafing by German fighter planes. But no one stopped; no one dared to.

'Nearly every Frenchman had been nurtured on stories of German atrocities during World War I,' according to historian Robert O. Paxton. One of them, Burgundy winemaker Henri Jayer, recalled how his father warned him, 'You must leave at once; the Germans are barbarians! They will cut off your hands if you don't do what they want.'

That same fear prompted the father of champagne maker Henri Billiot to insist that his family flee as well. Billiot's father, who had 'lost his health' in the earlier war, was convinced that the entire family would be massacred if they failed to leave. 'In the rush and confusion, one of my grandfathers became separated and panicked,' Henri said. 'He walked all day and night looking for us, but it was hopeless. Finally, he just gave up and returned home, where he suffered a stroke. I am sure it was the fear, his not knowing what had happened to the rest of us, that caused it.'

Many of the refugees were soldiers who once guarded the Maginot Line. Now, the only lines they occupied were those that stretched for miles, moving away from the frontier they were fleeing. 'It was a retreat without glory,' René Engel, a winemaker from Burgundy, said. Engel, who fought in World War I, recalled soldiers discarding their weapons as they passed his house, fleeing through the vineyards because roads were so congested. 'It was a sight that we, veterans of Verdun, watched with a heavy heart.'

For some, however, it was 'kind of exciting.'

Robert Drouhin, who was eight years old, remembers seeing people weighted down with food, mattresses, even birdcages. 'Sometimes, my sisters and I would stand and wave,' he said. 'We did not realize how dangerous the situation was.'

Or how dramatically life was about to change.

The Germans had moved amazingly fast. By June 12, they had overrun Champagne. Two days later, they entered Paris. Other units continued on, rolling down the highway past the vineyards of Burgundy's Côte d'Or. On June 28, their advance reached the Pyrénées and finally came to a stop. Their primary destination, however, was the port city of Bordeaux on the Atlantic coast, the commercial center of France's wine trade.

'The Germans swept in like angels of death,' said one resident, recalling how the sunlight glinted off their motorcycle goggles. Within hours they were setting up checkpoints, requisitioning homes and office buildings and taking control of the port. On hand to greet them was the French government which had fled Paris two and a half weeks earlier and turned the city into their temporary capital. Officials immediately entered into discussions about France's future.

Almost overnight, nearly everything about this ancient port city had changed. It bristled with gun emplacements; flags with Nazi insignias were draped everywhere. The port itself, a vital shipping point for Bordeaux wine producers for more than two hundred years, was now teeming with armed soldiers and being converted into a German naval base.

The most dramatic change, however, was the population. Earlier that month, it had been 250,000. Now, crammed with refugees who had fled the German invasion, it was nearly a million.

Like Robert Drouhin, Hugues Lawton found the unfolding drama incredibly fascinating. Hugues's father, one of Bordeaux's most prominent wine merchants, was a veteran of World War I and had told him stories about the war. 'I never dreamed I would ever see anything so interesting, so I was determined to see the action,' said Hugues, who was fourteen years old at the time. Fortunately, he happened to be looking out the window when the Germans arrived. 'I saw the first German tanks come in, and it was quite a thrill.' But even in his excitement, Hugues felt a tingle of fear. 'I remember seeing this German soldier go by on a motorbike; his nostrils were flared, he was so proud. I could not understand that.'

What many could not understand was how an army which even

some German generals considered the strongest in Europe could be defeated so quickly and easily. So staggering were the losses – 90,000 dead, 200,000 wounded, more than one and a half million taken prisoner – that when an old soldier from World War I called on his countrymen to lay down their arms, everyone was ready to comply and breathed a sigh of relief.

Marshal Philippe Pétain, the 'hero of Verdun,' had been serving as ambassador to Spain when Prime Minister Reynaud summoned him home to boost the country's morale. When Reynaud resigned on June 16, the eighty-four-year-old Pétain agreed to take over and form a new government. By noon the next day, he was on the radio addressing the people of France. 'With a heavy heart, I tell you that it is necessary to end the fighting.' Pledging to give himself to the country (*le don de ma personne*), the old Marshal said he would sign an armistice with Germany and that France, under his guidance, would return to its former glory. His logic was based on the belief that the country stood alone, that Britain would not survive a German attack and that France, by signing a peace treaty with Berlin, would emerge from defeat stronger and more united than ever in a new Europe dominated by Germany.

Pétain's assurances felt like a soothing balm and ninety-five percent of the public believed him. He was hailed as a male Joan of Arc, 'the leader who saved us from the abyss.' Among those who heard Pétain's June 17 broadcast was May-Eliane Miaihle de Lencquesaing. 'His words were just what we wanted to hear,' she said. 'We were all Pétainists.'

Those in the wine trade were especially enthusiastic. They knew Pétain owned a small vineyard on the Riviera. They also remembered what he had written about the role of wine during World War I: 'Of all the shipments to the armies, wine was assuredly the most awaited and most appreciated. To procure his ration of wine, the French soldier braved perils, challenged artillery shells and defied the military police. In his eyes, the wine ration had a place almost equal to that of ammunition supplies. Wine was a stimulant that improved his morale and physical well-being. Wine, therefore, was a major partner in the victory.'

Although there was no victory this time, most French took comfort in the belief that they had at least escaped the chaos another all-out war would bring. To further cushion the blow of defeat, Pétain argued that, under the Third Republic, the people of France 'had not been honestly led into war in 1939, but dishonestly misled into defeat.' It was finger-pointing at its very worst. As historian H. R. Kedward points out, 'No one admitted responsibility; everyone blamed someone else. Ordinary soldiers blamed their officers, the General Staff blamed the politicians, the politicians of the Right blamed those of the Left and vice versa, the government of Pétain blamed the ministers of the Popular Front, they in turn blamed the army, most people blamed the Communists, the Communists blamed the internal Fascists and the Fascists blamed the Jews.' There was, adds Kedward, 'enough fragmentation here to refloat French politics for a generation.'

What no one disputed was that this was a war France hoped to avoid. When it was declared, the reaction was a mixture of surprise, dismay and resignation. Although public opinion polls in the summer of 1939 indicated most people favored war if Germany attacked Poland, there was little overt enthusiasm when it finally happened – especially on the battlefield. Marc Bloch, a historian who was a staff captain in the French First Army Group, blamed the 'utter incompetence of the high command' and its passivity in the face of the German threat for France's defeat. He described how his own commander sat 'in tragic immobility, saying nothing, doing nothing, but just gazing at the map spread on the table between us, as though hoping to find on it the decision he was incapable of taking.'

It did not help that France had the wrong kind of tanks. Most were designed for supporting the infantry, not for the lightning warfare which Charles de Gaulle had advocated and which German forces used so effectively. The army was also hampered by an

antiquated communications system. One officer complained to
his superiors that a carrier pigeon system would have been more
effective. He was not only serious, but probably correct.

'No one who lived through the French debacle of May–June 1940
ever quite got over the shock,' says historian Robert O. Paxton. 'For
Frenchmen, confident of a special role in the world, the six weeks'
defeat by German armies was a shattering trauma.'

It was especially shattering for André Terrail, owner of Paris's famed
restaurant La Tour d'Argent. He was terrified that the Germans
would discover his wine cellar.

'For my father, that cellar meant everything and he was heart-
sick,' his son Claude said. 'It was his passion, his life's work,
his very soul.'

André Terrail had spent years putting together one of the greatest
cellars in the world, a cellar that contained more than 100,000
bottles on the eve of World War II, many of them from the
nineteenth century. So great was its reputation that even before
World War II, the rich and glamorous – from financiers like J.
Pierpont Morgan to movie stars to most of the titled nobility of
the world – were drawn to the Tour as much for the riches of its
cave as for its famous duck. The thought of losing that entire cellar
was more than André could bear.

He had already survived two wars, the Franco-Prussian in
1870–71 and World War I, in which he was wounded and taken
prisoner. When war was declared again, André was so depressed
he left Paris and placed the restaurant in the hands of his longtime
manager and friend Gaston Masson. André's son Claude, who was
with the French air force in Lyon, flew back to help.

'To be a Frenchman means to fight for your country *and* its wine,'
he said.

Claude arrived in Paris on May 12, 1940, just two days after the
Germans had crossed the Meuse River from Belgium. It was warm
and sunny, the kind of day that makes Paris the most beautiful

spot on earth. Indeed, there was almost a festive mood in the French capital. There were long queues in front of movie houses and most of the cafés were full. Claude must have been shocked by the Parisians' attitude. He knew how weak the French air force was, and he realized that the German breakthrough was a major blow.

With the military on high alert, Claude had only been granted a six-hour leave, and it was rapidly expiring. He and Masson already had agreed that the best way to protect the restaurant's wine in such a short time was to wall it in. With so much wine, however, it swiftly became apparent that they could not hide everything, so they resigned themselves to choosing 20,000 of the very best bottles, especially those from 1867, André Terrail's pride and joy.

The pace was furious, the mood almost frantic as Claude and Gaston, with help from the restaurant's staff, began sorting bottles. Cases of famous labels and vintages were hauled from one side of the cellar to another as one brick after another was slapped into place.

'We had only five hours left to do the job,' Claude remembered, 'but we got it done.'

A month later, on June 14, under skies heavy with soot from the oil reserves the retreating French government had ordered burned, forces of the Third Reich marched into the now nearly deserted city. With them came a special emissary from Hitler's chosen successor, Field Marshal Hermann Göring. The emissary's first stop was La Tour d'Argent. 'I want to see your cellars, the famous cellars,' he announced, 'and especially the bottles from 1867.'

Realizing what was at stake, Gaston Masson invited the officer in and tried to remain calm. Taking a deep breath, he informed his visitor that all the 1867s had been drunk.

'What? That can't be! Are you sure? I have been told about that wonderful wine,' said the German.

Masson apologized, but he was positive it was all gone. 'Of course, if you would like to check . . . ,' Masson said.

So, with a small contingent of his soldiers, the German followed

Masson into the elevator and down to the cellars five floors below. For more than two hours, they opened cases, turned bottles and checked labels. They searched every corner, every nook and cranny, all to no avail. Not a single bottle of 1867 could be seen.

When the Germans finally gave up and left, however, they did not go empty-handed. All 80,000 remaining bottles of wine were seized.

It was a small taste of things to come.

On June 22, a railroad boxcar was pushed into a small forest clearing in northeastern France and dusted off. It was the very train car in which Germany had been forced to surrender in World War I. Now, with Hitler and his generals looking on, France was forced to do exactly the same thing – sign an armistice that imposed many of the same harsh conditions that so humiliated Germany in 1918. The French army was reduced to 100,000 men; its once-proud troops were relegated to maintaining internal security; astronomical occupation costs were imposed; and more than half the country was placed under formal occupation. The *zone occupée*, which included the northern three-fifths of France as well as a strip of land running down the Atlantic coast to the Spanish border, contained most of France's industrial wealth and population. The unoccupied zone, or *zone libre*, was by far the poorest part of France, and it was where Marshal Pétain was told to headquarter his government.

Separating the zones was a Demarcation Line, an internal military frontier, which the Germans could open or close as they wished. Passes were required and travelers were subject to searches. In the first weeks after the armistice, the Line was open only to selected workers and administrators, those whom the Germans felt were essential to the recovery of basic industries and services in the north. Prevented from crossing were millions of refugees who had fled the invasion. It was a calculated move by the Germans. By forcing Pétain's government to keep the refugees for two or three months while they established an efficient occupation in the north, 'it allowed the Germans to appear organized and generous,' according to historian Kedward. Grievances about food and other problems, therefore, were directed against French rather than German authorities.

Still, at that early point, most French were not overly concerned about the division. It was a temporary situation, they thought, and the new government of Pétain believed so too. On June 29, when officials moved from Bordeaux to the health spa town of Vichy, one government minister told owners of the city's Hôtel du Parc, 'Don't worry about the heating, we'll be back in Paris by fall.'

The cheery optimism faded fast.

Marshal Pétain had believed that if he was a 'good collaborator' and co-operated with the Germans, Hitler would be pleased and the occupation would soon be lifted. He was wrong. Hitler was not interested in collaboration; he was interested in 'booty,' in milking France for everything he could.

'The real profiteers of this war are ourselves,' Hitler said, 'and out of it we shall come bursting with fat! We will give back nothing and will take everything we can make use of. And if the others protest, I don't give a damn.'

The fat Hitler alluded to included one thing above all, what former French Prime Minister Edouard Daladier called 'France's most precious jewel': wine. Its importance lay not only with marketplace profits; it was also a symbol of prestige, sophistication and power.

With the drawing of the Demarcation Line, most of France's best vineyards, the *grands crus*, came under German control, and authorities wasted no time in letting winegrowers know who was in charge. Less than a week after the Germans arrived in Bordeaux, the Miaihles, at Château Pichon-Longueville, Comtesse de Lalande, were told to find another place to live.

'About two hundred fifty soldiers suddenly showed up, and one of the officers told us he wanted us out along with all the furniture,' said May-Eliane. 'He was polite but firm and insisted we had to move immediately.' The château was furnished with a collection of Charles X furniture and artwork dating from the early nineteenth century that had been put together by the first Comtesse de Lalande. It took the entire Miaihle family to haul it to the château's attic.

One piece was deliberately left behind. It was a massive armoire that held kitchen supplies. The Miaihles decided to use it to protect their wine, pushing it from one side of the kitchen to the other so that it stood directly in front of the door that led downstairs to the cellar.

When the Miaihles finally left their château, German soldiers were already throwing straw pallets for sleeping on the parquet floors and hammering nails into the *boiseries*, the carved wood paneling, to hang their guns.

With the seizure of their home, the Miaihles moved to Château Siran in neighbouring Margaux, where May-Eliane's grandparents lived. They found Siran jammed with refugees from northern France, among them some distant cousins from Verdun. 'The place was overflowing but we really had no other place to go,' May-Eliane said.

They had been there only a couple of hours when the officer who had requisitioned Pichon suddenly arrived. 'He was furious and ordered us to come with him,' May-Eliane said. 'We were very, very scared.' The officer told them to get in their car and follow him back to Pichon. Upon their arrival the officer motioned the Miaihles into the kitchen. It was full of armed soldiers. In horror, they quickly discovered why: the armoire hiding the door to the wine cellar had been moved and the door was wide open.

'Do you think we are thieves?' the officer thundered. 'Did you think we would steal your wine?' Before the Miaihles could reply, he continued, 'Well, we are not thieves, and we will not touch a bottle of your wine!' He then sent the shaken Miaihles away.

Their fears, however, had just begun. The officer's tirade made them realize that something had to be done immediately about their Italian Jewish friends who were still at Château Palmer. 'We knew they were no longer safe there,' May-Eliane said, 'so we decided on a temporary measure and moved the two families into a small annex attached to the château.' An entrance connecting the two buildings was then walled up. In the rear of the annex, concealed by a thick hedge, was a tiny window. The Miaihles added a small trap-door so they could pass food, messages and other supplies to their Jewish friends.

But then something frightening happened: the Germans announced they were requisitioning Château Palmer.

'When I heard that, my heart dropped,' May-Eliane said. 'I really did not know what we were going to do. All we knew was that our friends couldn't stay at Palmer much longer without being discovered.'

The Miaihles were lucky in one respect. The officer who requisitioned their château kept his word: none of their wine was touched. Others, however, were not so fortunate. For two nightmarish months, wine producers throughout much of France suffered through an orgy of looting as the Germans gorged themselves on triumph and the delights of people's wine cellars.

In Burgundy, soldiers broke down doors of houses and pillaged the cellars of people who had fled.

In Champagne, nearly two million bottles were stolen and carted away. 'They stacked everything in the center of our village – food, clothing and, of course, champagne – then loaded it onto trucks,' remembers one resident. 'It left people in a very bad state.'

In the village of Le Mesnil-sur-Oger, seventeen-year-old Bernard de Nonancourt was working with his brother and several cousins at the Delamotte champagne house, packing and loading cases of champagne, when they heard trucks approaching. Minutes later, a convoy of fifteen vehicles pulled up and armed soldiers piled out. With them was a stern-looking officer who said he was there on behalf of Field Marshal Göring. 'Those who worked for Göring were always younger, rougher and more brutal,' Bernard said.

'They played the black market and never hesitated to circumvent rules when it suited them.' With their young commander in the lead, the soldiers marched into Salon, one of the most prestigious houses in Champagne, and began carrying out cases of champagne. 'It went on for several days,' Bernard said. 'Each morning, they would come back and take away more champagne. I particularly remember seeing cases of the 1928 Salon being hauled out.'

For most French, those first two months of the occupation were bewildering. Everything seemed out of control. Even the Germans seemed a little confused.

'One thing became clear at once,' wrote historian Philip Bell. 'German policy was not following a "blueprint." The speed of the victories took everyone by surprise – the German high command, government ministries, even Hitler himself. So far from there being any detailed program ready to be put into operation, nothing was prepared.'

In Bordeaux, Château Haut-Brion, which had been converted into a hospital for French soldiers by its owner, the American banker Clarence Dillon, was seized and turned into a rest home for the Luftwaffe.

The vineyards of Château Montrose were converted into a rifle range.

At Château Cos d'Estournel, decorative bells hanging from the towers of the famed wine estate suddenly began ringing. Soldiers were using them for target practice.

At Château Mouton-Rothschild, troops had no sooner moved into that jewel of a property than they began shooting at various paintings hanging on the wall. 'It was totally ridiculous,' said Baroness Philippine de Rothschild. 'I remember being told about this old cook, a woman, running around trying to remove the pictures before they were destroyed.'

Other times, however, the Germans were courteous and disciplined. Hugues Lawton's mother was just sitting down to tea when the maid entered the salon and announced, 'Madame, the

Germans.' On her heels were several officers. 'They were perfectly polite, but it was also perfectly clear they were taking over our house,' Hugues said.

In Burgundy, however, the Germans helped ruin the 1940 harvest when they prevented workers from entering the vineyards to treat vines for oidium and mildew. The problem was noted in the vineyard logbook of the Marquis d'Angerville of Volnay: '17 *juin 1940, Pas de travail aujourd'hui, occupation par les Allemands.*' (No work today, occupation by the Germans.)

At the Château du Clos de Vougeot, a landmark of Burgundy ever since monks planted vines there in the thirteenth century, soldiers moved in abruptly, turning the beautiful ground-floor salons into an ammunition depot and chopping wood on the floor, scarring the medieval monument permanently. They also had planned to chop up the château's magnificent fifteenth-century *pressoir* for firewood but were talked out of it at the last minute by two prominent winegrowers who pleaded that the grape press was a museum piece.

One of the worst incidents of German thuggery occurred in Sézanne-en-Champagne at one of France's most famous restaurants, the Hôtel de France. When troops arrived, they discovered the cellar was nearly empty and all of its most famous wines missing. They went on an angry rampage, breaking up the furniture, hacking at the artwork on the walls, smashing windows with their rifle butts and carting away what wine remained.

They no doubt would have been even angrier if they had known that the owner, only a few weeks earlier, had hidden his best wines behind the very walls they were bashing.

By the end of July, German authorities realized they had to find a way to control their troops. Not only were they stealing from the French; they were also stealing goods requisitioned by the Third Reich. At least 250 trainloads of goods destined for Germany had been looted. To put an end to it, authorities decided to make an example of two young soldiers who were arrested after breaking into the cellars of the Perrier-Jouët champagne firm in Epernay. The day after their arrest, a military court sentenced them to death. Although the sentence was later rescinded and the men instead were sent to the front, the message was clear: looting and pillaging would no longer be tolerated.

Field Marshal Göring, whose authority had been expanded to dictate economic policy for all occupied countries, was keenly aware that times had changed and that maintaining order was essential; but his instructions to the Occupation Authority also revealed a characteristic duplicity: 'In the old days, the rule was plunder,' he said. 'Now, outward forms have become more humane. Nevertheless, I intend to plunder, and plunder copiously.'

His first move was to sharply devalue the French franc, making the German mark nearly three times more valuable than it was before the war and purchases of fine wine or anything else tremendous bargains for the Germans.

For the French, it was a terrible blow. When some complained the franc would soon be worthless, Göring had a ready reply: 'Good, I hope it happens. I hope that very soon the franc will have no more value than the paper that one uses for a certain purpose.'

Göring's retort did not go down well, especially with a feisty little priest named Félix Kir (who bequeathed his name to that particular French aperitif). Shortly after the Germans changed the exchange rate, Kir spotted a merchant selling wine to German soldiers in Dijon. 'How much are you charging them?' he asked. The merchant said thirty francs. Kir shouted, 'Those guys just changed the exchange rate; charge 'em sixty! If they don't want to pay, don't sell.' The soldiers paid. Within an hour, the merchant was sold out.

Vichy was less outspoken. Its powers were only vaguely defined, set down in the armistice agreement which had been cobbled together in less than four hours by writers and translators who had to work by candlelight.

In theory, Vichy's administrative authority covered the entire country. It could negotiate prices, even argue about exchange rates, but it was subject to German interference and veto in the occupied zone. Only in the unoccupied zone, or *zone libre*, did Vichy exercise full executive power, but then only within the restrictions of the armistice which the Germans could interpret as they saw fit.

Clouding the picture even more was a bitter power struggle between Göring, who believed France should be treated like a conquered country, a milch cow, and plundered without mercy, and those in the Foreign Office, headed by Foreign Minister Joachim von Ribbentrop, who favored a more subtle approach, one that would enable Berlin to bring France into a German-dominated New Order as a subordinate power but one which might retain a limited amount of sovereignty. 'If France is to be treated like a milch cow,' argued one official, 'it has to be given some fodder.' A limited amount of fodder is about all Vichy ever got.

Yet most French, in those first six months, believed that the regime, ensconced in its sleepy setting and headed by a grandfather figure who professed only to want what was best for France, was just what the country needed. It extolled the traditions of old, provincial France, the need to return to rural life, and the sanctity of the family in which a woman's place was in the home. Under the motto '*Travail, Famille, Patrie*' ('Work, Family, Fatherland'), Vichy set out to rejuvenate France by promoting youth organizations, the pursuit of sports and a healthier, outdoor life. It also encouraged 'good works' and called for a greater role of the Catholic Church in education.

But there was a darker, more sinister side. Vichy was authoritarian, patriarchal and messianic. 'From the very beginning,' according to historian Kedward, 'it was a divisive and punitive regime, acting under the illusion that the widespread veneration for Pétain indicated a similar consensus for its political and social program.' Against the values of Liberty, Equality and Fraternity, Vichy preached a society in which people respected their place – and were kept there. Married women were prevented from holding jobs. Their real job was staying home and having children; it was practically a sacred duty.

For others, it was much worse. Within two months of coming to power, Vichy published the first of a series of decrees making Jews second-class citizens. Immigrant Jews were stripped of their rights, constantly harassed and threatened with deportation. Vichy's goal was to make France a unitary nation. 'France for the French,' they said. Communists and Freemasons were hunted down. Trade unions were abolished; local elected councils and mayors of larger towns were swept away, all of them replaced with pro-Vichy nominees. In that context, Vichy, according to Kedward, 'appeared as a force not of national integration but of political retribution.'

Although support for the government was about to fade, faith in the man who headed it remained high. For most French, there was a clear distinction: on one hand, there was Vichy; on the other, there was Pétain. Even the Marshal drew a distinction, saying he considered himself more as a moral tutor for the nation who shaped correct attitudes rather than policy. Crowds adored him and the Church worshipped him: '*La France, c'est Pétain, et Pétain, c'est la France,*' declared the French primate Cardinal Gerlier. On the road, peasants lined the rails when his train passed by; women held out their babies for him to touch. In one case, a woman hurled herself in front of his car to stop it so she might have a chance to touch his hand. According to an official report of the incident, the prefect turned to Pétain to apologize, but found the Marshal gently asleep (he was eighty-five), 'without,' said the report, 'losing his dignity or his sovereign bearing.'

The chaos of the first two months came as a rude awakening for most French, who traditionally viewed Germans as being disciplined and always 'correct.'

By August, however, most of the trouble had been brought under control, the clearest sign being in Paris, where soldiers were behaving much like tourists. They went sightseeing, saw movies and filled restaurants. Authorities had even created an organization called *Jeder einmal in Paris* (Everyone in Paris Once) to offer all the troops a holiday in the City of Light.

One officer, who said he considered France a 'second spiritual fatherland,' described Paris as 'even more brilliant during the occupation than before.' Hitler himself made a whirlwind tour of the city, his daylong trip highlighted by a brief visit to Napoleon's tomb.

For most Germans, however, the primary attraction of Paris was not historical monuments but gastronomic ones, restaurants which one soldier said 'allow you to live as God in France.' One of those restaurants was La Tour d'Argent, which a young officer named Ernst Jünger visited, later describing the 'diabolical feeling of power that came while dining on sole and the famous duck.'

Claude Terrail, who, three months earlier, had helped hide the restaurant's most precious wines, said the Germans who dined there always behaved correctly. 'They may have been killers outside but at night they came well dressed and behaved, and they paid for everything.' Where wine was concerned, the Germans always ordered the best. 'We tried to push the cheaper stuff,' Terrail said, 'but we didn't play tricks. It wasn't worth dying for.'

It was an attitude the Hugels of Riquewihr understood. Unlike the Terrails and so many others, they did not bother to hide their wine. 'We were Germany again,' André said, 'and the Germans were once again our customers, our only customers.'

Although there was no mention of Alsace in the armistice agreement, the region was annexed outright on August 7 and everything French was outlawed. Street signs were changed to German, Hugel et Fils became Hügel und Söhne and the wearing of berets was forbidden. 'If you even said *bonjour*, you could go to a concentration camp,' André's brother Johnny recalled. A cousin of the Hugels did, in fact, get sent to a camp when he refused to sign a statement saying he was of Germanic origin.

'You had to obey the rules, there was no alternative,' André said. 'In order to go on to high school, I had to join the Hitler Youth.' Brothers Johnny and Georges faced a grimmer prospect: they had to join the German army.

Georges was the first, because he was the oldest. It was not a happy moment, 'but I did what I had to,' said Georges. 'I was afraid my family might get sent to a camp. I saw some other guys run away and their families were sent to Poland.'

Unlike others, the people of Alsace had little confidence in Marshal Pétain. 'He was a weak man,' Georges said. 'Sure, he was the "hero of Verdun" and all that, but he was weak. The only reason soldiers liked him is that they thought there was less chance of being killed when he was in charge; that was because he never did much. A lot of officers felt he needed a good kick in the pants.'

Now that they were part of Germany again, the Hugels had to figure out how to keep their wine business running and, as Papa Hugel said, 'adapt to the new economic situation.' In one respect, it was not terribly complicated: Germany was the only customer. 'All of our wine, like everyone else's, was blocked by the Germans,' André said. 'We could not sell to our traditional customers like Great Britain; we could only sell to Germany and at prices the Germans set.' The Germans, he said, may not have stolen their wine in the usual sense, 'but they did steal it legally and massively. They emptied Alsace of its wine.'

Madame Marie Hugel, however, had more immediate concerns. Three weeks after the annexation, she was told to report to German headquarters. No one was sure why, although it was no secret that authorities were upset about Monsieur Hugel's refusal to join the Nazi Party. Letters and notices had been sent urging residents of Riquewihr to join, but Monsieur Hugel had steadfastly ignored them. Now there were rumors that their business might be closed and that the family could be deported.

'My mother was frightened,' André said. 'She did not know what to expect.'

When she arrived at headquarters, an officer informed her that her loyalty to Germany was in question. 'We are aware that you always speak French to your children,' the German said. 'Why do you hate Germans?'

Madame Hugel, momentarily taken aback, quickly recovered. 'What do you mean?' she asked. 'How can you say I hate Germans? My own brother is German, and I also have two sons who are about to fight for your Führer!'

Her response caught the officer by surprise, but he seemed satisfied. A few minutes later, he excused her. As she turned to go, the German stopped her and added a gentle warning. 'Madame, we are the Wehrmacht; we are not the bad ones and you shall have no further trouble from us, but once the yellows come, it will be awful.'

He was referring to the Gestapo.

No one, in those first few weeks, personified the pain of defeat more than Gaston Huet. When German troops arrived at his bunker, he and his men surrendered immediately. At gunpoint, they were ordered to stand up and start walking, 'but a very courteous officer told us not to worry, that we would be released soon,' Huet said.

He and his men were marched from Calais into Belgium. With each passing mile, more and more prisoners joined the column. At Bastogne, they were herded into railway cars used for hauling cattle to slaughter.

'We were completely exhausted,' Huet said. 'We had walked more than two hundred miles and had become just machines, no longer able to think.' There had been little food, just a bit of bread, and the water was tainted. Dead animals, killed in battles that had raged there, lay everywhere. 'We knew they would pollute the water in ditches, which was the only water we had to drink,' Huet said. Once in a while, he and his men found rhubarb along the road and mixed it in to make the water taste better, but 'there was always the smell of the stable.' Everyone became ill.

As they neared the German border, the size of their column had mushroomed. It now numbered in the thousands. 'I was stunned,' Huet said. 'The sheer number of French soldiers taken prisoner was amazing; it was something I never imagined.'

Although Huet still held out a flicker of hope Allied forces might rescue them, those hopes vanished when they crossed into Germany. On June 17, three weeks after their capture, they entered Oflag IV D, a prisoner-of-war camp for officers in Silesia, where they would spend the next five years.

'The moment I saw that place,' said Huet, 'I knew right away the war was over for me.'

THREE

The Weinführers

While the war was over for Huet and other POWs, it was only beginning on another front – the wine front.

Wine was the one commodity the German leadership was intimately connected with – personally, professionally and socially.

Men like Foreign Minister Joachim von Ribbentrop and former Vice Chancellor Franz von Papen, now ambassador to Austria, had come to Nazi posts directly from the wine trade. So had military leaders including Captain Ernst Kühnemann, commander of the port of Bordeaux and a wine merchant who had spent a great deal of time in the region before the war. General Moritz von Faber du Faur, the senior officer in Bordeaux, was a leading economist who also had a special interest in wine.

Others in the Nazi top brass such as Field Marshal Göring and Propaganda Minister Joseph Goebbels prided themselves on their knowledge of wine and possessed vast collections. Whereas Goebbels's tastes ran to fine Burgundy, Göring preferred great Bordeaux, especially Château Lafite-Rothschild. According to Albert Speer, an architect who served as the Third Reich's Minister for Armaments and Munitions, few things gave Göring more pleasure than sitting down late at night and uncorking a great bottle of Lafite-Rothschild. Speer said the only time he ever got close to Göring as a person was when the field marshal shared a special bottle of Lafite with him.

Foreign Minister Ribbentrop was a great lover of champagne, a taste he acquired when he represented the champagne houses of Mumm and Pommery in Germany. He had made a fortune in the wine trade after wooing, then marrying Anneliese Henkel, daughter of Otto Henkel, 'the king of German champagne.' (Henkel was Germany's largest sparkling wine producer, although the 'wine' he made reportedly was nothing more than apple juice 'juiced up' by a team of engineers in Hamburg.) With the fortune he made – and married – Ribbentrop had no trouble financing his political ambitions. To add a whiff of aristocracy to his lineage, he styled himself Joachim *von* Ribbentrop. His veneer of charm and elegance soon caught the attention of Hitler, who took him to meet President Paul von Hindenburg. Hindenburg, a real *von*, was not impressed. 'Spare me your little champagne peddler,' he told Hitler. But Hitler was impressed. He considered Ribbentrop 'greater than Bismarck,' and believed he was the ideal person to oversee the Armistice Commission, the body responsible for establishing Germany's economic policy for France.

About the only one in the top leadership who was not interested in wine was the Führer himself. After one taste of a great French wine, Hitler is reported to have pushed it away, calling it 'nothing but vulgar vinegar.'

Historians, however, are divided over the extent of Hitler's asceticism. While some say he did not drink at all, others claim he frequently drank beer and diluted wine. 'His asceticism,' according to Hitler biographer Robert Payne, 'was a fiction invented by Goebbels to emphasize his total dedication, his self-control, the distance that separated him from other men.'

This did not make for very enjoyable evenings when Hitler got his entourage together in front of the jade-green fireplace at the Führer's house at Berchtesgaden. As Speer wrote, 'To animate these rather barren evenings, sparkling wine was handed around and, after the occupation of France, confiscated champagne of a cheap brand; Göring and his air marshals had appropriated the best brands. From one o'clock on, some members of the company, in spite of all their efforts to control themselves, could no longer repress their yawns. But the social occasion dragged on in monotonous, wearying emptiness for another hour or more, until at last Eva Braun had a few words with Hitler and was permitted to go upstairs. Hitler would stand up about a quarter of an hour later, to bid his company goodnight. Those who remained, liberated, often followed those numbing hours with a gay party over champagne and cognac.'

Ascetic or not, when Hitler looked at the men surrounding him, he quickly understood how prestigious and profitable wine could be. He decided that Germany should obtain the very best of France's wines, and Göring quickly seconded the motion, telling occupation commissioners that France was 'fattened with such good food that it is shameful.' He admonished the Reich's soldiers in France to 'transform yourselves into a pack of hunting dogs, and always be on the lookout for what will be useful to the people of Germany.'

To get the best wine, however, the Nazi leadership did not want a pack; it wanted pointers, men who knew not only wine but also the people who made and sold it. So the Reich's economic planners turned directly to the German wine trade, creating a corps of what some called 'wine merchants in uniform.'

The French had another name for them: the weinführers.

Their job as *Beauftragter für den Weinimport Frankreich* (agents for importing wines from France) was to buy as much good French wine as possible and send it back to Germany, where it would be resold internationally for a huge profit to help pay for the Third Reich's war.

To do the selecting and buying, the Third Reich decided to send Otto Klaebisch of Matteüs-Müller, a sparkling wine producer and Germany's agent for several champagne houses, to Champagne. Adolph Segnitz, head of A. Segnitz and Company and Germany's agent for the Domaine de la Romanée-Conti, went to Burgundy. The most important of them all, Heinz Bömers, who headed Germany's largest wine importing firm, Reidemeister & Ulrichs, was assigned to Bordeaux.

German authorities, however, had made a mistake. The weinführers were, indeed, wine merchants and wine experts, but they were much more than that. They also were friends of many French wine producers and merchants. Their connection through generations of doing business together had long since transcended commercial matters; they had trained in each other's firms and spoke each other's language fluently. They were even godfathers to each other's children.

The weinführers also were keenly aware of something Maurice Drouhin stressed to his son at the beginning of the war: 'One day, whether in five months or in five years, this war will be over, and France will still be next to Germany. We will still have to live together.'

Heinz Bömers was late, and his children could hardly believe it. Their father was never, ever late, nor would he permit them to be, especially for family events like the regular Sunday afternoon game of croquet.

When Bömers finally emerged from the house, he apologized, explaining that he had been listening to the news on the radio. It was September 3, 1939, and he had just heard that Britain and France had declared war on Germany. Ushering his older son, Heinz Jr., away from the other children, Bömers said, 'I expect to be called into the army soon, and then I don't know if I will be able to speak to you again privately, so I will tell you today that we have lost this war. Don't speak about this with anybody, not with your brothers and sisters, and especially not with your friends at school. It would be dangerous for the whole family.' Before Heinz Jr. could reply, his father added, 'It is important to me that you understand how I feel. I want you to be prepared for what is ahead.'

Although Heinz Jr. was only thirteen years old then, he never forgot that moment. 'I have always had in my heart these words and his conviction that Germany would lose. My father told me the United States surely would come in to help the British. He felt that Germany, even though it was very powerful at that moment, could never defeat a country as big as the United States.'

At the time, the family was at its summer house near Bremen. Bömers looked around wistfully as they closed up the house that weekend to return home. 'I don't know if we will have the opportunity to come back here next year,' he said to his family. His concerns were well founded; they would not return for seven years.

When the Bömerses arrived home, an unexpected visitor was there to greet them. It was the headmaster of young Heinz's school. 'Please help me, Herr Bömers,' he pleaded. 'Your son is the only student in our school who does not belong to a Nazi organization. If you do not let him join one, there will be many problems for the school.' Bömers had consistently refused to sign papers enrolling his son in the Hitler Youth, so he asked what other Nazi groups were part of the school. The headmaster gave him a list, and Bömers noted the school orchestra among them. 'How often does the orchestra rehearse?' he asked. When he was told that it met three times a week, he said, 'All right. Heinz plays the flute, so he will join the orchestra.'

After the headmaster had left with the signed papers, Bömers told his son that he should go to practice only once a week. 'If anyone gives you trouble and says you must go more often, you tell them you are obeying your father and they must talk to me.' No one ever did.

The Bömers family already had a reputation for disagreeing with the Nazis, and especially with Hermann Göring. In 1930, Göring had been prime minister of the German state of Middle Saxony when Bömers's father was a senator from Bremen. Senator Bömers had made no effort to conceal his contempt for Göring and his politics, and when the prime minister came to Bremen, Bömers refused to see him. Göring was incensed and did not forget the slight.

Four years later, after Senator Bömers's death, Heinz Bömers was told he would lose the family business unless he became a member of the Nazi Party. Reluctantly, Bömers joined. 'He had to think of his family, to protect them,' Heinz Jr. said. 'He had to make compromises and I know he suffered from that. But he was always convinced the Nazi time was a temporary time, so you had to do all you could to survive.'

That is why when Bömers, forty-seven, who had been excused from active military duty for health reasons, received a cable in May 1940 from the German Ministry of the Economy offering him the job of *Beauftragter* in Bordeaux, he agreed to go. 'It was a job he could have refused, I think,' Heinz Jr. said, 'but I think he felt that this was someplace where he could help, could make things easier for everybody. He had many, many friends in Bordeaux.'

Bömers accepted the job on several conditions: that he not be paid by the Nazis and would pay his own way; that he be free to change as many marks into francs as he wished; that he not be required to wear a uniform; and that he have the authority to 'step in' if he felt the actions of German troops were inappropriate. 'He was afraid that some of these Nazis, like Göring, would like to have some very nice old Mouton-Rothschilds, and he could imagine that some of the soldiers would think they should just pick them up for him,' Heinz Jr. said.

Bömers arrived in Bordeaux just after the armistice was signed. In a way, it was like a homecoming. Prior to World War I, his family had owned Château Smith-Haut-Lafitte and made wine there until the French government confiscated it along with other German-owned property. In the years that followed, Bömers, working from his offices in Bremen, imported French wines and developed a close relationship with key producers.

So for many Bordelais, his arrival in 1940 posed a cruel dilemma: their old friend and business colleague now represented the enemy. To allay fears, one of Bömers's first acts as weinführer was to call wine people together and reassure them he was still their friend. 'Let us try to continue our business as normally as possible,' he said, 'but when I leave one day, I hope you will have better stocks of wine than you have now.' It was his way of telling them that he had their interests at heart and that when the war was over, he hoped to continue doing business with them.

'He came around and said hello to all of us,' said May-Eliane Miaihle de Lencquesaing. 'Of course, we all knew him from before the war, when he would come here, so we said to him, "As long as you are not wearing a uniform, you may come over in the evening and have dinner with us as usual."'

Nevertheless, many Bordelais were apprehensive. 'Bömers was a very powerful man,' said Jean-Henri Schÿler of Château Kirwan. 'If you did not want to sell him your wine, he could order you to do so.'

Even Daniel Lawton, who had trained in the Bömers firm in Bremen and who ran one of Bordeaux's oldest brokerage houses, got a taste of Bömers's temper. When he heard Bömers's demands for wine and the prices the Germans would pay, Lawton had no hesitation about standing up to Bömers and refusing.

Bömers was incensed. Glaring at Lawton, he warned, 'If you don't agree to sell us wine on our terms, there will be sentries with bayonets in front of all Bordeaux cellars tomorrow!'

'Go right ahead, do it,' Lawton replied.

It didn't happen. Bordeaux wine merchants, however, had little or no alternative but to deal with Bömers. 'We could no longer sell our wines to Great Britain or the United States,' said Schÿler. 'It was all closed up. We had a choice: we could sell our wines to the Germans or we could throw them into the Gironde River.'

Hugues Lawton, whose father had defied Bömers, agreed. 'You had to deal with a situation you did not want. Once you are defeated, you have to do what you are told.'

Although many Bordelais considered Bömers tough, even autocratic, they respected him. They had been worried he would go after Bordeaux's finest wines, treasures that one producer said constituted an 'inestimable museum of wine.' Another worried aloud, 'Will this integral part of French civilization be confiscated, pillaged, sent with the Renoirs, the Matisses, the Georges de La Tours to the other side of the Rhine?'

Bömers vowed that would not happen, even though his overlords in Germany were putting heavy pressure on him.

Instead, he did the Bordelais a favor: he relieved them of massive stocks of poor-quality wine that had accumulated after the harvests of the 1930s. One of his purchases alone amounted to the equivalent of a million bottles.

Bömers did most of his business with *négociants*, wine merchants who bought wine in bulk from growers, bottled it and then resold it. One of them was Louis Eschenauer, whose firm had specialized in exporting to Germany long before the war. 'Uncle Louis,' as he was called, was almost as famous for his close friendships with German leaders such as Ribbentrop as he was for his outstanding knowledge of wine. Eschenauer, who was seventy when Bordeaux was occupied, had done extensive business with all of the German leaders as well as Heinz Bömers during the prewar years and his business now, as a result, was flourishing. 'Eschenauer was one of my father's best friends,' Heinz Jr. said, 'and I know he worked with him a lot, tasting wines together and choosing wines to buy.'

But Eschenauer was only one of many *négociants* who were competing for Bömers's attention and trying to grab as much of his business as they could. According to Bömers's secretary, Gertrude Kircher, the behavior of the Bordeaux wine establishment ranged from 'absolute commercial cynicism to absolute toadyism. It was embarrassing how they bowed and scraped to him.' They threw big parties, one after another, and did everything they could to get the weinführer to attend. 'They would call up and tell me the names of all the other important people who had been invited,' Kircher said. 'They told me what they planned to serve, what was on the menu; they pretended they wanted to talk to my boss about German music and literature. Herr Bömers found it all ridiculous.'

Bömers had his own shopping list and list of suppliers. He preferred working with the old connections he and his family had established over the years, people like the Miaihles, who owned several châteaux and vineyards around Bordeaux.

'He was a very honest man,' May-Eliane Miaihle de Lencquesaing said. 'My parents used to tell me, "Thanks to Mr Bömers, we still have our wine." He tried his best to keep a good balance, not to make the Germans angry and to take care of his French friends.'

But it was sometimes a dangerous job. According to Jean-Henri Schÿler, 'Bömers had to walk a tightrope. It was a bit of a double game he had to play.'

Helping him play it was a merchant named Roger Descas, Vichy's representative to the German Economic Service Headquarters in Paris. Like Louis Eschenauer, Descas was an old friend of Bömers. He was also the man with whom Bömers negotiated wine prices and quotas. Descas, however, was at a disadvantage. If he set prices too high, he risked sparking inflation or even worse, retaliation from the German authorities. On the other hand, if prices were too low, French wine producers would be in an uproar.

Bömers understood, and sympathized. 'I have an idea,' the weinführer said in a phone call to Descas. 'Why don't you meet me for dinner. I'll explain everything when I see you.'

The two met that evening at La Crémaillère, one of Paris's top restaurants. There, as they dined on *filet de boeuf en croûte* and *turbot en sauce champagne*, Bömers outlined what he had in mind. 'It requires a bit of acting,' he said. 'You and I will meet here the evening before we are scheduled to appear at the economic offices; we'll work out all the details and decide then how much wine I can buy and what you should be paid for it. The next morning, however, when we present our cases, we'll pretend to get into an argument, one which hopefully will dispel any notion that we are in collusion.'

Descas did not have to think about it for long. 'Let's do it,' he said to Bömers.

When the two men arrived at the Hôtel Majestic, where the German economic offices were located, they went through the usual formalities. Each gave a short speech stating what he thought was fair. Then the real show started. Bömers accused Descas of trying to squeeze him and demanded that he lower his prices. Descas argued that the prices were fair and said it was the weinführer who was doing the squeezing. Bömers pretended to fly into a rage and the argument became more heated. Finally, by the end of the morning, the two reached an agreement on a set of figures. They were the very figures they had worked out the night before.

'This worked very well,' Heinz Jr. said. 'My father said the government representatives usually accepted his figures the first time and were satisfied he was getting the best deal.'

But not always. On several occasions, Bömers was called to Paris to answer complaints that he was being too friendly with the French wine merchants.

Those meetings, however, were nothing compared with those he faced when he was summoned, on three occasions, to Göring's office in Berlin. There, Bömers got the full brunt of the field marshal's fury.

'It was frightening,' Bömers later recalled. 'He said I was being too cozy with the French wine trade and practically accused me of treason. I told him, "If you are not satisfied with my work, I will finish and go home." But he knew I was an expert on Bordeaux wine and the best man for the job, so finally he did not do anything. But I cannot tell you how very disagreeable and even terrifying those meetings were.'

Twice a year, Bömers was given leave to return to Germany and spend time with his family. When he went back for Christmas in 1941, there had been a dramatic change: Britain's Royal Air Force was making nightly bombing raids over Germany and the United States had just entered the war. Even worse, Hitler had launched a 'war of annihilation' against the Soviet Union, an offensive he predicted would be over in six weeks. It had now been six months, and no end was in sight. The Russian winter had set in and German troops, stretched thin to begin with, were dying in the paralyzing cold.

These events convinced Bömers more than ever that Germany would lose the war, and he moved his family to Bavaria, where he hoped it would be safer. 'Every day you would hear that this young boy or that one, someone you knew very well, was killed,' Heinz Jr. said. 'It was terrible. Every night we heard the bombers going to Munich, where my two sisters were attending the university. Terrible, terrible. Even now when I try to explain this, well, it is something you just can't explain, but we had to live with it.'

The following summer, on his next visit home, Bömers was told that his brother-in-law, a Lutheran pastor, had been arrested after the SS discovered he was saying a prayer for Jews at the end of each service. 'My mother was distraught; she was very close to her brother, so she asked my father to try to help,' Heinz said.

Bömers went to the SS headquarters in Berlin to plead for him. The officer in charge told him to 'speak his piece.' When Bömers had finished, the officer said, 'Okay, are you done now? Because I want to tell you something. We know your brother-in-law is a good German; we know about all the medals he won in World War I. But he is not a good Nazi. He deserves the death penalty.'

Bömers returned from the meeting so badly shaken that he could not even remember what he had said to the SS officer. The officer, however, eventually agreed to release the brother-in-law, sending him to work in the post office and forbidding him to continue in his pastoral duties. 'You are lucky,' the officer told Bömers. 'I should have sent him to a concentration camp.'

'My father hated the Nazis,' Heinz Jr. said. 'He was absolutely anti-Hitler and considered him a criminal.'

But Bömers reserved a special loathing for Göring. He regarded him as a pretentious thug whose evil was matched only by his greed. It was Göring he was thinking of when he told the Bordelais that if any Germans, regardless of their rank or position, ever approached them and demanded their wine, they should call him immediately and he would come and put a stop to it. 'That happened, absolutely that happened,' Heinz Jr. said. 'He took his car and went out – I am not sure where this was – and ordered the troops to leave immediately. And they did.'

But Bömers could not be everywhere, and there were always those who conspired to get around the system. Working with French merchants who illegally cut their prices, some German officers, with no papers or official authorization, would drive their military trucks directly up to the vineyards and haul away massive amounts of wine.

Bömers suspected Göring was behind many of these incidents. He was sure the field marshal wanted to get his hands on as many bottles of great wine as possible. On one occasion, Bömers received an order from Göring for several cases of wine from Château Mouton-Rothschild. 'Mouton is too good for the likes of him,' Bömers thought, so he asked workers at the château, one of the few which did its own bottling, to help with a bit of deception. The weinführer sent them bottles of *vin ordinaire* and instructed them to glue on Mouton labels. The workers were only too happy to comply. The bottles of wine were then shipped to Göring's office in Berlin. Bömers never heard a word of complaint from the field marshal.

There was, however, a limit to how far the weinführer would go. When a group of *négociants* suggested the German leadership would never know the difference if he bought cheap wine from the Midi rather than their *grands crus* to fill orders, Bömers was furious. A few bottles to deceive his nemesis was one thing; a wholesale scam which could compromise his professional reputation was quite another. Most of the Bordelais seemed to respect that.

Hardly any of them considered him a Nazi. Bömers confessed to one producer that he was thrilled to be able to 'throw away his uniform' and do business in his usual way. 'He did as little as possible to harm the wine trade,' one merchant said. Even British wine authority Harry Waugh, who dealt extensively with wine producers in Bordeaux both before and after the occupation, described Bömers as 'sympathetic.'

Others went much further. 'He saved our wine,' May-Eliane Miaihle de Lencquesaing said. 'He made sure no one had to sell too much wine, and he made sure it was always paid for. After he came, no more wine was stolen.'

In late October 1940, shortly after arriving in Beaune, Adolph Segnitz, the newly appointed weinführer of Burgundy, received an unsigned note. 'Please be advised,' it said, 'that some here are trying to cheat you. They are hiding their best wines and selling you wines that are not so good.'

A few days later, Segnitz summoned winegrowers to a meeting. Holding up the note, he informed them, 'I have something here that I would like to read to you.' When he had finished, there was an awkward silence. Some in the audience squirmed nervously in their seats. After several seconds, Segnitz continued, 'Now I wish to tell you something. For me, this note means nothing. As far as I am concerned, it does not exist.' With that, he tore it up. The relief was almost tangible.

'He hated turncoats,' said Mademoiselle Yvonne Tridon, secretary for the Syndicat des Négociants en Vins Fins de Bourgogne. 'He didn't approve of French turning in French.'

Growers who had been listening to Segnitz considered him a man of honor with whom they could do business. 'He never threatened us or accused anyone of trying to cheat,' said Beaune *négociant* and winemaker Louis Latour. 'He was the only German we could talk to because he was from our world.'

Segnitz's family ran a wine firm in Bremen which had been importing fine French wines since its founding in 1859. A few years before World War II, Adolph Segnitz took over A. Segnitz and Company and began specializing in Burgundy. He was fascinated by the land, its history and culture, and he especially loved the wines that were produced there.

'He was a real Francophile,' recalled Mademoiselle Tridon. 'We never thought of him as a stranger or foreigner because he was always coming by. He worked well with people here and no one was afraid of him.'

Segnitz was in his sixties when Nazi officials offered him the job of *Beauftragter* in Burgundy. Like his friend Heinz Bömers in Bordeaux, he despised the Nazis and did not relish working for them. He agreed to do so, however, on condition that he be given a free hand to do his job and that Berlin would not interfere. 'My father was very clear about that,' his son Hermann said. 'He was determined to be completely independent.'

From the beginning, Segnitz tried to assure the Burgundy wine community that he understood their problems and sympathized with the hardships caused by the occupation. 'But let us work together and try to make the best of things so that we have something when this war is finished,' he said. Segnitz promised there would be no strong-arm tactics and that winegrowers could decide for themselves if they wished to do business with him. 'I am here to buy wine,' he said. 'If you wish to sell your wine to me, fine, but I shall not force you to sell.'

One of those who chose not to was Maison Louis Latour. 'My grandfather absolutely refused to deal with any German wine merchant after World War I,' said his grandson Louis. 'Germany had been a major market for us before that war but my grandfather was so upset that he vowed he would never do business with anyone from Germany again.' Grandfather Latour died shortly after Segnitz arrived but his son had the same attitude. 'My father liked Segnitz personally but he was just like my grandfather and refused to sell him any wine,' Louis said. Segnitz accepted it and did not try to force him.

Although Segnitz came to Burgundy 'with a lot of money in his pocket,' there was not much wine for him to buy. Harvests between 1939 and 1941 had been minuscule. The weather had been awful, with the early summers too dry, followed by days of heavy rain and sometimes hail. In 1939, which was mediocre at best, there were so few grapes to pick that the harvest took ten days instead of the usual two or three weeks. Even if the growing season had been perfect, the situation would have been difficult because most of the young men who picked the grapes had been mobilized into the army.

In 1940 conditions were even worse. This time, the harvest took only three days. Because grapes had not fully ripened, winemakers wanted to chaptalize, or add sugar to their wine to boost its alcoholic strength, but that was impossible because of a sugar shortage. It was also difficult for winemakers to clarify their wine – that is, to remove the particulate matter that often makes red wine cloudy. Normally clarifying, or fining, was done by adding egg white, which clings to the tiny particles and drags them to the bottom. Eggs, however, were even more scarce than sugar. As a result, many winemakers had to resort to what their fathers and grandfathers did. They used charcoal to fine their wines.

According to the Marquis d'Angerville, one of Burgundy's leading winemakers, 'Our wine was so bad in 1940 that we did not bother vinifying; we just poured it into the ground.'

The following year was not much better. Most able-bodied men who would have been working the vineyards were now in German prisoner-of-war camps. In addition, according to the government's *Revue de Viticulture*, chemical fertilizers were 'practically nonexistent' and rations of insecticides were 'inadequate.'

Consequently, what little wine Segnitz did manage to buy was mediocre at best. Some of the best, however, came from Maurice Drouhin. He and Segnitz had done business before the war and were good friends. In Drouhin's opinion, Segnitz not only understood wine but also was sensitive to people's feelings. He sympathized with their despair at being an occupied country and understood how they chafed under the shortages, curfews and other restrictions.

Yet the occupation of Beaune, initially at least, was 'not terrible,' according to Mademoiselle Tridon. 'Unpleasant yes, but we did what was necessary to survive.' Because mail was censored, Tridon, as secretary for the wine producers' syndicate, resorted to another delivery system: she stuck letters that she did not want the Germans to see behind the door of the women's toilet. 'The Germans were too dainty to go snooping there,' she said.

Because of the curfew, usually at 8 P.M., although the Germans could change the time on a whim, business and most other activity ended early. Bicycle lights were painted blue and residents were required to hang blackout curtains over their windows. 'It was so dark that even I, who have been here all my life, could get lost,' Tridon said.

More upsetting were the military patrols which moved constantly through the cobblestoned streets, checking people's identity papers and sometimes frisking them for hidden weapons. 'They would ask us questions but it was so ridiculous because none of them could speak much French,' Tridon said. 'Everyone laughed because whenever the Germans asked a question, we would reply with something entirely vulgar.'

Segnitz, who did speak French, was acutely aware of how despised the Germans were and did his best to fit in. Before World War I, his family owned two wine properties in Bordeaux, Château Chasse-Spleen and Château Malescot-Saint-Exupéry. When World War I broke out, the cellars of Chasse-Spleen were pillaged by local residents, who turned on the grape pickers, accusing them of working for the enemy. Both châteaux were then confiscated as enemy property by the French government.

Given that background, Segnitz was unfailingly polite and never wore his military uniform in public. Unfortunately, he still stuck out like a sore thumb. 'Segnitz would walk around town in a green loden coat, and he looked just like the German actor Erich von Stroheim,' said Louis Latour. 'He must have been a little bit frustrated, because he would always say, "How do people know I am German? I speak perfect French but everybody always says, 'Oh you must be that German.'"'

Although public opinion was intensely anti-German, most in Burgundy, as in other parts of France, were still pro-Pétain and supported the Marshal's program of close collaboration with Germany. Such was the reverence for him that the Burgundy wine merchants' syndicate decided to send the Marshal sixty-six cases of wine, some of which were bottled in 1856, the year he was born. Mademoiselle Tridon was dispatched to Vichy to make the formal presentation. Reading a letter from the syndicate, she said, 'We present this gift as a sign of our respect and as proof of our fidelity to your commands and to national unity.' Tridon later recalled that Pétain 'was very nice, but what I remember most about that day was how incredibly old he looked and how a doctor stood constantly by his shoulder.'

Shortly after their tribute to Pétain, wine merchants and producers were shocked to learn that Maurice Drouhin had been arrested. He was walking to a meeting in August 1941 at the Hospices de Beaune, the city's charity hospital, when a German patrol picked him up.

'The news came like a thunderbolt,' Louis Latour said. 'Everyone knew that Maurice and Segnitz worked closely together, so everyone here was very surprised when the Germans arrested him.'

About the only one who was not surprised was Drouhin himself. As part of the French army reserves, he had accompanied generals to Washington during the interwar years and had taken on periodic special assignments. 'My father never said what those assignments were but he often met with General Douglas MacArthur,' his son Robert said.

German intelligence closely monitored those trips and was convinced Drouhin was engaged in anti-German activity. When they arrested him, they said they had found a gun hidden in his house. It was a rusty old service revolver from World War I, which Maurice had left in a drawer and forgotten about. But it was all the excuse the Germans needed.

Maurice was imprisoned at Fresnes, outside Paris. Because he spoke German, he got along reasonably well with his guards. During one conversation, Maurice recounted some of his war experiences, including the incident in which he helped save a German soldier's life.

'Oh, so you don't hate Germany or Germans?' one of the guards asked in surprise.

'No, just your politics and government,' Drouhin replied.

Soon after his imprisonment, Drouhin's guard gave him a pencil so he could write to his wife, Pauline.

> *Aug. 14, 1941: My dear little wife, first of all I want to assure you that my health is fine. I suffer from only one thing, and that is being far from you and far from our dear children. No one as yet has interrogated me but I wait with impatience because I am sure I am here as a result of a simple error. Courage, my darling, the beautiful days will come again.*

But as days passed, Maurice grew increasingly concerned, not only about his own fate but about his wine business and how Pauline would fare in his absence.

> *Sept. 7, 1941: If I am not back for the harvest, rely on the advice of others. Be very careful around the barrels when the must begins fermenting; the fumes can be dangerous. Do not worry if we lose money while I am gone. It is best to put a brake on new business and just continue with our regular orders, especially with those customers who will help you get empty bottles we can use. Then start bottling little by little the 1938 Romanée-Conti. Begin with the best wines, and do everything you can to keep the staff.*

In a letter about a week later, Maurice told Pauline that he had just appeared before a military tribunal.

> *I was interrogated yesterday and I must pay tribute to the perfect loyalty of he who presided over my interrogation. I constantly felt I was in front of judges who were seeking nothing but the truth. I remain firm in the*

hope that my innocence will be recognized so that our separation will
be of a very short duration.

Well aware that the Germans were carefully reading everything
he was writing, Maurice repeated those sentiments in several other
letters to his wife.

Oct. 1, 1941: I was part of the War Council of my division in 1939,
so I know it is loyalty that motivates the military judges. I cannot
believe they would consider that unusable old revolver that I forgot
in my drawer to be a weapon and that they would punish me for a
simple act of forgetfulness. In any case, I am totally innocent and have
nothing to hide. At the end of each day, I say to myself that it is one
day less of this ordeal to live through.

But Maurice was frightened. That was something he could not
conceal from his wife, no matter how hard he tried to comfort
her.

Whatever you do, do not let yourself fall into melancholy or sadness
for me. You must make sure that nothing changes in the life of our
children, in their games, in their gaiety. You must do this for me, for
this will give me the courage to go on.

His moments of greatest comfort were when Pauline was allowed
to visit. On one of those visits, she told him that half of the Domaine
de la Romanée-Conti had been put up for sale, and that because
Maison Joseph Drouhin was the largest distributor of wines from
that famed estate, Maurice had an opportunity to buy it. As much as
he was tempted, Maurice shook his head. 'It would mean borrowing
money,' he said. 'I don't want to do that.' Borrowing money was
something winemakers rarely did in those days, and with his own
fate uncertain, Maurice was even more reluctant.

Sensing how worried her husband was and realizing full well the danger he was in, Pauline contacted the head of the prison and asked for an appointment.

'My husband is innocent,' she told him. 'Surely that old pistol your soldiers found when they searched our house doesn't make him a criminal. It doesn't even work.'

The German officer listened politely. He praised her devotion to her husband and then apologized. 'I'm sorry but there is nothing I can do,' he said. Pauline was distraught.

She was, therefore, surprised when not long afterward, she received a letter from him. 'As I told you, there is very little I can do,' he said. 'Even your noble spirit which I witnessed cannot be taken into consideration, as that would be against all the regulations. But I can tell you that this nightmare Monsieur Drouhin is living through will not last much longer. Please be patient. I will do everything in my power to make the course of these formalities as short as possible.'

Patience, however, was running out. At the Hospices de Beaune, which Drouhin headed as vice president, colleagues complained it was difficult to go on without their leader.

The Hospices was the cornerstone of life in Beaune and had been so since 1443 when Nicolas Rolin, chancellor to the Duke of Burgundy, founded a charity hospital of that name, ceding all his worldly possessions to the Hospices and endowing it with some of the region's choicest vineyards. Over the centuries, other pious Burgundians bequeathed their vineyards to the Hospices to support its work.

Now, officials warned, all that work was being jeopardized. Vineyards needed attention and so did the charitable institutions the Hospices ran, such as the hospital, an orphanage and a home for elderly men. In a letter to the head of the military tribunal, the board of directors said that Maurice's incarceration was crippling the entire organization. 'His absence is putting all the services we render into greatest difficulty. We beg that you do all that is possible to accelerate the solution of this affair.'

What few realized was that Drouhin's activities went far beyond the Hospices and his wine business. He was, in fact, deeply involved with the Resistance, something the Germans had long suspected but never had been able to prove. Even from prison, Maurice was continuing to direct its activities. With books such as *The Count of Monte Cristo* and others by Alexandre Dumas which Pauline sent to the prison, the two carried on a secret correspondence using the code Maurice had taught her. The correspondence contained messages for the Resistance about German troop emplacements and advice on how to sneak people across the Demarcation Line.

Just before Christmas, the Germans announced they were putting Maurice on trial. His friend and fellow *négociant* Louis Latour rushed to the prison to see if there was anything he could do. Their meeting was short, but it was long enough to convince Latour that Maurice was in serious trouble. 'He was terrified,' Latour said. 'He was afraid he was going to be executed.'

Pauline, desperate to save her husband, remembered the letter he had written to her during World War I in which he described how he helped save the life of a German soldier. She knew she had kept it, but where? Finally, she located it buried in a drawer containing other personal effects. Folding the letter into an envelope, she tucked it into a bag along with a copy of the newspaper in which the letter had been reprinted and headed to the prison.

There, she handed the envelope to the German commandant. He promised to read the letter and article and take them into consideration.

On February 13, 1942, the unexpected happened: the Germans freed Maurice. They gave no explanation. Undoubtedly, the letter and newspaper article helped, but many in Beaune were convinced that Maurice's friendship with weinführer Adolph Segnitz was also an important factor.

Although Maurice was relieved, he also realized the Germans were still suspicious and that it was probably just a matter of time before they would try to arrest him again. Upon returning home, the first thing he did was pack a small bag of clothes and other personal necessities and hide it under his bed. Then he turned his attention to restarting operations at Maison Joseph Drouhin, business he had told Pauline to 'put a brake on' during his months in prison. He also resumed his work at the Hospices de Beaune.

Maurice had been home for three months when the Hospices received a letter from the regional *préfet*, or administrator, in Dijon. The official wanted to know if the Hospices would be willing to donate a portion of one of its vineyards to Marshal Philippe Pétain.

Maurice summoned members of the Hospices board of directors to ask their opinion. Heads nodded and there were murmurs of approval. Everyone agreed that were it not for Pétain, France would have suffered a far worse fate at the hands of Germany than it currently faced. When the vote was taken, it was unanimous. They chose a prime section of vineyard on a slope overlooking Beaune, land that had been part of the Hospices vineyards since 1508. In honor of the Marshal, they decided to rename it Clos du Maréchal.

A few days later, vineyard workers, stonemasons and others converged on the site to build a stone wall around it. They also constructed an ornate stone archway carved with Pétain's symbol, a Frankish ax combined with a marshal's baton. As the arch neared completion, workers removed one of the stones near the base and hollowed it out. Inside, they placed a copy of the paper deeding the property to Pétain.

A week later, on May 29, 1942, a delegation headed by Maurice Drouhin arrived in Vichy to present the original deed to the Marshal in person. Pétain greeted them warmly and ushered them into his office. The old man, who was eighty-six, was beaming. Their gesture, he said, had touched him deeply. 'You have flattered a personal passion of mine, my love for the soil and my instinct as a winegrower,' he said. 'Thanks to you, I am now the owner of one of the best vineyards in Burgundy. If I don't give this gift more publicity, it is because I want to preserve the intimate character with which you have given it to me. I am especially grateful that you will be managing the vines for me. I think with pleasure of the first harvest to come.'

That was not all that was ahead. Each November following the harvest, the Hospices de Beaune staged a spectacular auction of its wines. Over the years, it had become one of the biggest celebrations of the Burgundian year with foreign dignitaries, wine buyers from dozens of countries and thousands of other wine lovers flocking to Beaune to take part in the festivities. There were wine tastings, lavish banquets and the auction itself.

In 1943, it was even more important. It was the 500th anniversary of the Hospices de Beaune. Unfortunately, there was a problem: no one wanted the Germans around. Because Maurice Drouhin was in charge of the program, it fell to him to tell the Germans they were not welcome. He was not looking forward to it.

In recent months, German soldiers in the area had become nervous and more aggressive. With losses on the snow-swept Russian front mounting, thousands of troops throughout Burgundy were being reassigned for duty there. Grim-faced soldiers, already dressed in white winter hats, moved sullenly through towns and villages as they prepared to leave. Those remaining in Burgundy were consolidated in more urbanized areas where German offi-cers believed they would be less vulnerable to attacks by the Resistance.

With understandable trepidation, Drouhin called Adolph Segnitz to say he had a matter of great urgency to discuss. The weinführer agreed to see him immediately. Maurice tried to explain, using words he hoped would not hurt his friend's feelings. 'It's not against you personally,' he said. 'The celebration, however, is a local tradition that does not involve politics; it is a kind of country fair that is primarily for French people.'

Segnitz took the news calmly. 'I understand what you are trying to say,' he said. Clearly, the weinführer was deeply disappointed.

He as much as anyone had been looking forward to the affair. Then he said, 'I must warn you that this may put me in an uncomfortable position with my superiors.' Segnitz could easily have turned down the request and Maurice would have had no choice but to accept it. Instead, Segnitz rose from his seat, extended his hand and said simply, 'I'll see what I can do.'

A few days later, Segnitz called on Maurice. 'I have some good news for you,' he said. 'You can have your celebration and no Germans will attend. You have my word.'

To the weinführer's surprise, Drouhin replied, 'You are wrong, one German will be present.' Then Maurice handed him a ticket. 'That's for you. You will be the only German there, but may I ask one more favor? Please make sure to come in civilian clothes and not military uniform.'

The 500th anniversary of the Hospices de Beaune was a success. Despite the occupation and the uncertainty of those days, writers, actors, religious figures as well as officials from Vichy showed up for the celebration. No one enjoyed it more than Adolph Segnitz.

Not long afterward, Maurice Drouhin received a thank-you letter from him. 'As you know,' he said, 'I am a great admirer of your culture and traditions, and each time I have entered the Hospices, I have been touched by the restfulness of spirit which we all need in this awful time of war. On this 500th anniversary, it is my wish to give the Hospices de Beaune a gift; perhaps you have a special need or there is something you have not been able to do for one reason or another.'

Attached to the letter was a check for 100,000 francs.

No region suffered more pillaging of its wine than Champagne. Nearly two million bottles were grabbed by German soldiers during the first weeks of the occupation alone.

It was, therefore, with immense relief that the Champenois learned that German authorities were sending in someone to oversee champagne purchases and, hopefully, end the looting and restore order. They were even more relieved when they found out who it would be: Otto Klaebisch of Matteüs-Müller, a winemaking and importing firm from Germany's Rhineland. 'We were so happy we got someone from the wine trade, and not a beer man,' Bernard de Nonancourt said. The de Nonancourts knew Klaebisch well because he had been the prewar agent in Germany for a number of champagne houses, including Lanson, which the family of Bernard's mother owned.

Brandy, however, was Klaebisch's original background. He was born in Cognac, where his parents had been brandy merchants before World War I. When France confiscated all enemy-owned property during the war, the Klaebisch family lost its business there and returned to Germany.

Otto, however, retained his taste for the finer things in life, especially great champagne. He pursued a career in the wine and spirits industry, putting his French background to good use.

That background made Klaebisch's appointment as weinführer of Champagne easier to take. 'If you were going to be shoved around, it was better to be shoved around by a winemaker than by some beer-drinking Nazi lout,' said one producer.

Klaebisch began his 'shoving' almost immediately. Unlike Heinz Bömers in Bordeaux, who had rented a small apartment, Klaebisch wanted something more impressive. A château, for instance. He found what he wanted when he saw where Bertrand de Vogüé, head of Veuve Clicquot-Ponsardin, lived. After one look, Klaebisch issued orders for the château to be requisitioned. An angry de Vogüé and family were sent packing.

'Klaebisch was very happy to be here,' de Nonancourt remembered. 'He did not like combat and the last thing he wanted was to be sent to the Russian front.'

Given his family connections and professional contacts, Klaebisch landed the soft assignment without difficulty. His brother-in-law was none other than Foreign Minister Ribbentrop, whose father-in-law, Otto Henkel, was a good friend of Bordeaux's Louis Eschenauer.

Eschenauer, in turn, was a cousin of German port commander Ernst Kühnemann. Eschenauer was also part owner of Mumm champagne, another property that had been confiscated from German owners in World War I. He had hired Ribbentrop to represent that marque in Germany.

Only a wine genealogist could unravel the complicated family and professional tree that entangled winemakers and merchants throughout France and Germany. It went a long way to explain how Klaebisch became weinführer of Champagne.

Klaebisch, however, was different from the other weinführers. He enjoyed the trappings of military life and almost always wore his uniform. He was also impressed with titles. When he first met Count Robert-Jean de Vogüé, the man with whom he would be negotiating champagne purchases, he was deferential to the point of being obsequious, or, as one producer put it, 'too anxious to please.'

De Vogüé, head of Moët & Chandon, had a complicated family tree of his own. He was related to many of Europe's royal families as well as to many of France's leading wine producers. He even had connections with the Vatican. He also happened to be the brother of Veuve Clicquot's Bertrand de Vogüé, whom Klaebisch had just kicked out of his house.

Klaebisch ran into problems almost from the moment he moved in. The 1940 harvest was disastrous. The yield was 80 percent below average. Aware that Berlin expected him to supply a certain amount of champagne every month, Klaebisch visited the houses he had done business with before the war and asked them to make up the difference from their reserves.

De Vogüé thought that was a bad idea. He feared that other houses would be angry and jealous. With international markets cut off and sales to French civilians prohibited, those firms might easily go out of business.

Even the houses Klaebisch wanted to do business with were unhappy. Yes, their market was 'guaranteed' but they also had to accept what the Germans were willing to pay, and it was not much.

Producers feared that the huge quantities of champagne Klaebisch was demanding would soon deplete their stocks, leaving them stuck in the same economic morass they had been in during the 1930s.

Those years, more than anything, defined the almost militant mood that still prevailed in Champagne when Klaebisch arrived. In 1932, champagne houses had managed to sell only four and a half million bottles of the 150 million that were in their cellars. The mood among growers who sold their grapes to the houses was sour too. In 1933 and 1934, they were paid no more than one franc a kilo for their grapes. In 1931, they had been paid eleven francs, a loss of income that severely jeopardized their businesses. The picture improved in 1937 and 1938, but quickly turned bleak again when war was declared in 1939. In desperation, producers began walling up their champagne and shipping other stocks to the United States and Great Britain for safekeeping.

Now they faced massive requisitioning. Pol Roger, the house that made Prime Minister Winston Churchill's favorite champagne, was ordered to send huge quantities of its 1928 vintage to Berlin each month. 'It was such a great vintage,' said Christian de Billy, president of Pol Roger, who was born in that year. 'We never had a lot and tried to hide what we could, but it was so wonderful and so well known that it was impossible to keep it out of German hands. Klaebisch knew it was there.'

As German demands for champagne escalated – at times Klaebisch was demanding half a million bottles a week – De Vogüé feared, more than ever, that houses like Pol Roger would not survive. On April 13, 1941, he called together producers and growers to set up an organization that would represent the interests of everyone in the champagne industry. 'We are all in this together,' de Vogüé told them. 'We will either suffer or survive but we will do so equally.'

The organization they created was called the Comité Inter-professional du Vin de Champagne, or CIVC, which still represents the champagne industry today. At the time, the goal of the CIVC was to enable producers to present a united front and speak with a single voice. De Vogüé, it was decided, would be the point man. 'He had the courage and enough audacity to represent the interests of Champagne and to be the one and only delegate to the Germans,' said Claude Fourmon, who was de Vogüé's assistant. 'He never doubted the Allies would win the war, so his goal was to keep everything at an acceptable level. He wanted to make sure that everyone had something to start over with when the war ended.'

Klaebisch was unhappy about the CIVC and did not want to deal with it; he preferred to stick with his prewar contacts. He knew that was how Bömers operated and he wanted to emulate the Bordeaux weinführer by taking complete control of the champagne business. Klaebisch summoned de Vogüé to his office in Reims.

There, he got right to the point. 'Here are the ground rules. You can sell to the Third Reich and its military, and also to German-controlled restaurants, hotels and nightclubs, and a few of our friends like the Italian ambassador to France and Marshal Pétain at Vichy. The Marshal, by the way, likes to have a good quantity for his own personal use.'

De Vogüé listened without interrupting as the weinführer outlined the conditions. 'Nobody gets any free samples, there are no discounts no matter how large the order, and no full bottles of champagne may be sold unless empty bottles are first turned in.' Then Klaebisch told de Vogüé how much champagne he wanted each month and what he was willing to pay for it. 'You can spread the order out any way you wish among the major champagne houses just as long as I get my champagne,' he said.

De Vogüé was taken aback. 'There is no way we can meet those demands,' he said. 'Two million bottles a month? How do you expect us to do it?'

'Work Sundays!' Klaebisch shot back.

De Vogüé refused. To their credit, each man seemed to have an innate sense of how far they could push the other. After more heated exchanges, de Vogüé said champagne producers would work longer days to meet their quotas but only if the weinführer extended the number of hours they could have electricity. Klaebisch agreed.

De Vogüé, however, was not the only thorn in Klaebisch's side. In Berlin, Field Marshal Göring was demanding ever greater amounts of champagne for his Luftwaffe. The navy was also making huge demands. Buffeted from all sides, the weinführer went back to de Vogüé. This time, he was more conciliatory. 'We've had our disagreements,' he said, 'but I've got a problem with Berlin and I hope you will see fit to help me.' Klaebisch described how Göring was pressuring him to supply more champagne. He then proposed that if the CIVC would keep the champagne coming, he would make sure producers had all the supplies they needed such as sugar for their *dosages*, fertilizer for their vineyards, even hay for their horses.

De Vogüé said it was a deal.

It was an especially good deal for Pol Roger. Not long afterward, a spokesman from Pol Roger contacted the weinführer's office to say they were doing some repair work in their cellars and needed cement. Klaebisch arranged for its immediate delivery. Pol Roger used the cement to wall up and hide some of its best champagne from the Germans.

'The champagne houses did their best to perform a little sleight of hand,' admitted Claude Taittinger, head of Taittinger Champagne. 'Most tried to preserve their best wines and palm off the inferior blends on the enemy.' They knew, for instance, that bottles whose labels were stamped 'Reserved for the Wehrmacht' and often had a red bar running across it were unlikely to fall into the hands of their regular customers. As a result, most of the houses did not hesitate to use them for their worst *cuvées*. 'What they forgot,' said Taittinger, 'was that Klaebisch was a connoisseur and capable of cracking the whip now and then to show he was not always fooled by our tricks.'

One day at lunchtime, Klaebisch called up Roger Hodez, secretary of the Syndicat des Grandes Marques de Champagne, an association representing the major champagne houses, and invited him for an aperitif. 'We've never had a drink together,' the weinführer said. 'Why don't you drop by my office and we'll have one.' Hodez felt he could not refuse.

When he arrived, Klaebisch invited him to sit down and poured him a glass of champagne. Then he poured one for himself. The weinführer seemed to be in a good mood and Hodez began to relax. Then, suddenly, Hodez's nose wrinkled as a ghastly odor rose from his glass. Bravely, he took a sip. The taste was only slightly better than the smell. There was no sign Klaebisch had noticed Hodez's discomfort. 'What do you think?' he asked affably. Before Hodez could reply, the weinführer suddenly leaned across his desk and put his face inches away from Hodez's. 'Let me tell you what I think,' he snarled, his voice rising in crescendo. 'It smells like shit! And this is what you want me to give the Wehrmacht to drink? I want the house that made this crap struck from the list of firms supplying champagne to Germany. I wouldn't dare send their stuff to Berlin!'

Hodez shrank back in his chair, fumbling for words as he tried to pacify Klaebisch. 'I'm sure it was only an accident,' he stammered, 'a case of dirty bottles perhaps, or maybe . . .' Before Hodez could say anything else, however, he was excused from Klaebisch's office.

The shaken trade representative went straight to de Vogüé and told him what happened. De Vogüé immediately contacted the champagne house and warned officials of what Klaebisch had said. The head of the firm shrugged, saying he did not care. 'We're not making much money from the Germans anyway. We'll be better off selling a little of our champagne on the black market and holding the rest until after the war.'

De Vogüé shook his head. 'That's not the point,' he said. 'We're all in this together and you have to provide your fair share.' He instructed the firm to send its portion of champagne to several other houses, which agreed to bottle it under their own labels.

Klaebisch, however, was more suspicious than ever that champagne producers were trying to trick him. He began conducting spot checks of champagne bound for Germany, pulling out bottles, popping their corks, sniffing their contents and then tasting them. That is how François Taittinger ended up in jail.

François was twenty years old when he was brought in to help run the family firm after his uncle had become totally deaf. Like others, he underestimated Klaebisch's knowledge of champagne and thought he could outfox the weinführer by sending him champagne that was distinctly inferior in quality. When Klaebisch discovered it, he ordered François to his office.

'How dare you send us fizzy ditch water!' he yelled.

François, known for his quick temper, shot back, 'Who cares? It's not as if it's going to be drunk by people who know anything about champagne!'

Klaebisch threw François into jail. In the same cell were a number of other champagne producers who had also tried to pass off bad wine.

A few days later, the eldest of the Taittinger brothers went to Klaebisch's office to plead François's case. Guy Taittinger was a former cavalry officer and a born diplomat. He regaled the weinführer with stories about his days in the French army. He described how he once had to 'drink a bottle of champagne that had been decapitated with a saber and poured into a backplate of armor.' Klaebisch was amused, so much so that finally he shook his head, put up his hand and said, 'Okay, you win. Your brother can go.'

Most people in Champagne saw Klaebisch not as a Nazi diehard but more as an arbitrator between the French wine community and Berlin. Never was that more evident than when Vichy launched a forced labor program, Service du Travail Obligatoire, or STO, to supply Germany with workers for its factories and industries. In one week alone, Pol Roger had ten of its workers hauled off to Germany; the next week, seventeen more.

'There's no way we can continue like this,' de Vogüé warned Klaebisch. 'We don't have enough people for our regular work, let alone for the harvest. If you do not get some of our workers back, you will have no champagne next year.' The CIVC itself tried to keep the houses functioning by rotating experienced workers from one champagne maker to another. Still, the companies were falling far short of their imposed quotas.

The weinführer, who prided himself on his efficiency, quickly contacted authorities in Berlin. Faced with a choice between less champagne or less labor in their factories, the Germans chose the latter and allowed some of the more experienced and older workers to return to their cellars.

Each concession from Klaebisch, however, seemed to generate another edict. From now on, he said, a German officer must accompany every worker going into the *caves*. Producers thought it was ridiculous and completely impractical. When the weinführer backed off, there was a huge sigh of relief, for the chalk cellars, the *crayères* of Champagne, were being used by the Resistance, both as a place of refuge and as a place to stockpile arms and supplies.

In fact, the Resistance was doing a great deal more. It had picked up on the fact that champagne shipments were providing significant military intelligence. Through them, they could tell where the Germans were preparing a major military offensive. They first became aware of this when the Germans, in 1940, ordered tens of thousands of bottles to be sent to Romania, where, officially, there was only a small German mission. Within a few days, Romania was invaded by the German army. Afterward, bottles of bubbly were distributed to all the troops, a way of saying to the soldiers that 'the Führer thinks of his men first.'

From that time on, the Resistance, with help from the major champagne houses, kept meticulous track of where large shipments of champagne were going. Alarm bells went off toward the end of 1941 when the Germans placed a huge order and asked that the bottles be specially corked and packed so that they could be sent to 'a very hot country.' That country turned out to be Egypt, where Rommel was about to begin his North African campaign. The information was relayed to British intelligence in London.

As the war continued, relations between Klaebisch and de Vogüé deteriorated. Klaebisch felt more and more as though he were being taken advantage of and being 'sandbagged' by de Vogüé. He was annoyed that de Vogüé always referred to him as Klaebisch, never Herr Klaebisch or Monsieur Klaebisch or even Captain Klaebisch, just Klaebisch.

But that was a mere irritation. Far more serious was that Klaebisch and other German authorities were becoming more and more convinced that de Vogüé and his colleagues at Moët & Chandon were actively helping the Resistance. Their suspicions were correct.

In the early days of the occupation, Moët & Chandon had been pillaged more than any other champagne house. The Chandon château on the grounds of Dom Pérignon's abbey had been burned down and many other buildings belonging to Moët were taken over to house German troops. To add insult to injury, the company had also been ordered to supply the Third Reich with 50,000 bottles of champagne a week, or about one-tenth of all the champagne the Germans were requisitioning.

'Under those conditions, I and others at Moët, the entire top echelon, couldn't help but resist,' said Moët's commercial director, Claude Fourmon.

De Vogüé himself headed the political wing of the Resistance in the eastern region of France. In the early stages of the war, he had argued against an armed resistance that could endanger innocent lives. As the war ground on, however, his feelings began to change and he welcomed the Resistance into Moët's twenty-four kilometers of cellars. 'At the very least,' said his son Ghislain, 'my father turned a blind eye to sabotage and subterfuge, and to tampering with champagne and its shipment.'

On November 24, 1943, Robert-Jean de Vogüé asked his cousin René Sabbe to serve as translator for a meeting he and Claude Fourmon were scheduled to have with Klaebisch. Because the

recently completed harvest had been so small – and so good –
they were hoping to persuade Klaebisch to reduce the amount of
champagne he was planning to requisition.

Shortly after they arrived, the telephone rang in an office next
to Klaebisch's. A young officer interrupted the meeting to tell the
weinführer that the call was for him. Klaebisch excused himself.
Within minutes he was back and sat down at his desk, crossing
his arms over his potbelly.

'Gentlemen,' he said, 'that was the Gestapo. You are all under
arrest.' On cue, several officers with pistols drawn burst through
the door and took the three men into custody.

'We were completely stupefied,' Fourmon later recalled. 'De
Vogüé had just persuaded Klaebisch to let houses sell more champagne to French civilians. I don't know exactly what triggered the
call but I think the Gestapo wanted to take de Vogüé out of the
line of command.'

De Vogüé's first reaction was 'Let Fourmon go; he knows
nothing.' He also pleaded for the release of Sabbe, saying he was
there only to translate. De Vogüé's appeals were to no avail.

All three were charged with obstructing the trade demands of
the Germans and imprisoned. Sabbe was released a few days later
because of his age, but Fourmon was sent to Bergen-Belsen, a
concentration camp in Germany.

De Vogüé was sentenced to death.

The sentence sent shock waves through Champagne. For the first
time in history, the entire industry – growers and producers, labor
and management – went on strike. Klaebisch was stunned and, at
first, did not know what to do. He branded the strike an 'act of
terrorism' and warned that force would be used unless it ended
immediately. The Champenois ignored him and stepped up their
protest.

In the face of such unprecedented action, Klaebisch seemed
paralyzed. Calling out troops, he feared, could result in even
greater unrest and force the Germans to take over the production

of champagne, something he knew they were ill prepared to do.

There was something else Klaebisch feared as well: the spotlight. The last thing he wanted to do was to call attention to himself, especially now when everything seemed to be falling apart. To make matters worse, his brother-in-law and mentor, Joachim von Ribbentrop, had fallen out of favor, and Klaebisch could all too easily picture himself suddenly freezing with other German soldiers on the Russian front.

After more fruitless appeals to the Champenois to end their protest, Klaebisch and the Germans gave in. They agreed to 'suspend' de Vogüé's sentence but said they were only doing so because he had five children. Instead, he was put in prison.

Despite his clashes with de Vogüé, this was not what Klaebisch had expected or wanted. 'I can well imagine Klaebisch was uncomfortable with my father's arrest,' Ghislain de Vogüé said. 'I suspect he was just obeying orders he had been given.'

But punishment of the champagne industry had only begun. Champagne houses which had supported the strike were hauled before a military tribunal and given a choice. They could pay a heavy fine, 600,000 francs (about one and a half million francs in today's currency), or the head of each house could spend forty days in prison. Nearly all paid the fine.

Moët & Chandon suffered the worst. 'They decapitated Moët,' Claude Fourmon later said. Nearly all of the top management was sent to prison or concentration camps.

Hoping to discourage further disobedience and justify their crackdown against Moët, Klaebisch and other German authorities produced a propaganda film. It showed faked cases of Moët & Chandon champagne being seized and opened, all of them filled with rifles and other weapons. The film was distributed to movie theaters throughout France and Germany. The Germans also forced French newspapers to run an article saying de Vogüé had been helping 'terrorists.'

Within a few months, the German Occupation Authority had completely taken over the running of Moët. The man they put in charge was Otto Klaebisch.

In many ways, the weinführers accomplished exactly what the Third Reich wanted. They helped stop the pillaging, restored order and supplied Germany with an extremely lucrative product. More than two and a half million hectoliters of wine, the equivalent of 320 million bottles, were shipped to Germany each year.

More important, the weinführers mitigated a situation that could have resulted in far worse consequences for France. They served as a buffer for a battle that raged within the German leadership over how to deal with France, between Nazis like Göring who wanted to 'smash and grab' and treat France like a conquered country and those who favored a less ruthless approach, incorporating France into a German-dominated new Europe and 'providing it with a little fodder' so it could be milked for all it was worth.

Above all, the weinführers recognized the economic and symbolic importance of France's wine industry and did all in their power to make sure it survived. It was for their benefit too, for they realized that when the war ended and they returned home to their businesses, it was essential to have someone – namely, the French – to do business with again.

While the war continued, however, and especially as it began turning against Germany, most people in France became convinced that the best guarantee of survival was to rely on themselves, not on the weinführers and certainly not on Pétain's Vichy government, which was becoming more fascist by the day. That meant finding unconventional methods and having the courage to bend or break established rules.

As Janet Flanner predicted when the war first began, 'Owing to the Germans' mania for systematic looting – for collecting and carting away French bed linen, machinery, Gobelin tapestries, surgical instruments, milk, mutton, sweet champagne – the French will have to become a race of liars and cheats in order to survive physically.'

FOUR

Hiding, Fibbing and Fobbing Off

S tationmaster Henri Gaillard was sweating.

For nearly a year he had put up with the German occupation, and it had caused him one headache after another. His salary was late; money for his staff never got to the station of St Thibault on time; one package after another was getting lost. He dutifully filled out the forms the Occupation Authority in Dijon sent him, and answered their never-ending questions about what his train station was doing.

But now he faced a lot more than a bureaucratic headache: his job was on the line – and maybe more than that.

This morning, when he came into work at his station in Burgundy, he heard the bad news. A train had derailed in his section because a switch had been thrown the wrong way, and now the entire contents of that train were missing. And not just any contents. The train had been filled with the best wines of Burgundy, all of it destined for Germany and for people Henri shuddered to think about – Göring, Himmler, maybe the Führer himself. What was he going to do?

Only days before, Henri had confidently asked his German boss in the Occupation Authority, the commandant of the 3rd Arrondissement of Dijon, for a pass to cross the Demarcation Line to visit his daughter in Lyon, who was about to have a baby. He had hoped to get permission so he would be there right after the baby's birth. It was his first grandchild, after all, and he had reminded the commandant that he still had one week of vacation remaining. He also pointed out that he was a World War I veteran who had been decorated (perhaps not the best thing to say to someone who was on the losing side of that conflict).

What would the Germans do now? Henri wondered. Would he get to Lyon? Lose his job? End up in prison?

Dipping his pen in the official brown ink, Henri Gaillard nervously began his report:

STATIONMASTER'S LOGBOOK, ST THIBAULT STATION, CÔTE
D'OR. BURGUNDY: I have the honor to inform you that there
has been an accident on the St Thibault railroad line. This is
the first time anything like this has ever happened since I was
placed in charge several years ago. I have absolutely no idea what
could have happened to the contents of the cars. I apologize
most humbly for the inconvenience and sincerely hope this will
not reflect badly on my character or career. Your most respectful
servant, Henri Gaillard.

If Gaillard did not know what had happened to the wine, he was
probably the only one who did not. All along the railroad lines of
France, farmers, winegrowers, and especially railroad workers, or
cheminots, were systematically stripping railway cars full of goods
bound for Germany.

'It was almost a sport,' said Jean-Michel Chevreau, a Loire Valley
winemaker. 'Our favorite amusement was cheating the Germans.'

Chevreau's 'cheating' began in July 1940 after a troop of German
soldiers, passing through his village, insisted on spending the night
in his wine cellar. The next morning, after they were gone, Chevreau
discovered that more than a hundred bottles were missing. He
decided to get even.

A few nights later, he and some friends armed with jerry cans
and rubber hoses slipped out after curfew and made their way
to the railway station in nearby Amboise where the Germans
were loading barrels of wine destined for Germany. When the
guards were looking the other way, they quickly and quietly
siphoned all the wine from the barrels, an exercise they repeated
over the course of several weeks until authorities in Berlin began
complaining that the barrels arriving there were empty. Officials in
Amboise promptly posted more guards around the loading area of

the train station. They also put floats in the barrels so they could tell if they were full.

But that did not stop Chevreau and his friends. 'We continued siphoning, then filled the barrels with water,' he said, laughing.

STATIONMASTER'S LOGBOOK, ST THIBAULT STATION:
Please let me know what you would like me to do with the large container of wine barrels that has arrived here. The barrels are all empty. I remain your most respectful servant, Henri Gaillard, stationmaster.

Chevreau and others throughout the country were engaged in a special kind of resistance – not *the* Resistance but one that Janet Flanner called 'hiding, fibbing and fobbing off.' Not only were enormous quantities of wine hidden from the Germans, but the French, according to Flanner, also 'patriotically lied about the quality of the stuff they delivered to the enemy who ordered vintage Burgundies and ignorantly accepted *piquette* (thin, tart wine unfit for sale).' They also 'fobbed off' watered-down wines and brandy to their conquerors, selling them diluted *grands crus*, watery champagne and '60-proof eau-de-vie in place of the 80-proof cognac they had paid for.'

In Champagne, producers bottled their worst wines and marked them 'Special Cuvée for the Wehrmacht.' They then added insult to injury by using poor-quality corks that normally would have been thrown away. When the Germans arrived to investigate a firm they thought was cheating them, the management, according to writer Patrick Forbes, 'would be terribly, terribly sorry, but a pipe had burst or the river Marne had risen, and not wishing to mess up their beautiful shiny jackboots in a flooded cellar, the Germans – with luck – would go away. Not that they ever displayed much enthusiasm for visiting the enormous chalk and limestone caves where champagne houses stored their wine: they were afraid of meeting the fate of Fortunato, the hero of Poe's "The Cask of

Amontillado," who was walled up alive in the eerie catacombs of the Montresors.'

Much of the 'hiding, fibbing and fobbing off' was the result of lessons learned from earlier wars. After the battle of Waterloo, Prussian troops pillaged cellars throughout Champagne. Before they left, some scratched their names and a few *dankeshön* as well as some less polite graffiti on the walls.

In World War I, it happened again, but this time the Germans were not the only culprits. French troops en route to the front also helped themselves to numerous cases of champagne. Among them was a young soldier who would later become one of France's most famous performers. When Maurice Chevalier later recalled that moment, he laughed about it. 'It was almost a patriotic act,' he said. 'We felt, "That's a few less for the Prussians!"'

Often, the Germans made it easy for the French to cheat. 'They were incredibly sloppy when they placed orders for wine,' chuckled Alsace's Johnny Hugel. 'We'd get a piece of paper saying send ten thousand bottles to such and such a place, but they never designated precisely which wine they wanted, so we would always send our worst, like the 1939, which was absolute rubbish. If the Germans hadn't arrived, we would still have that vintage unsold in our cellars.'

Some winegrowers and producers deliberately misread and misdirected orders so that the Wehrmacht's wine, for instance, ended up in Homburg instead of Hamburg.

STATIONMASTER'S LOGBOOK, ST THIBAULT STATION: I
have the honor to inform you that I have received several large
wine containers with unreadable labels. Although the destination
appears to be St Thibault, it does not specify *which* St Thibault.
No merchant in the area recognizes the name of the sender.
Waiting for a useful response from you, I am your servant, Henri
Gaillard, stationmaster.

One of the most unusual examples of how winegrowers tried to protect their wines from the Germans during World War I took place in Bordeaux. The owner of a château, upon learning that the Kaiser's troops were heading in his direction, elected to hide his precious bottles in a pond on his property. All went smoothly until the following morning, when one of the officers billeted at the château decided to go for a stroll around the pond. Peering across the ornamental water, he suddenly stopped, his eyes widening in amazement. There, on the surface of the water, was a sea of floating labels.

By World War II, French winegrowers had come up with a few new twists. André Foreau, a winemaker from Vouvray, buried his best bottles under the beans, tomatoes and cabbages of his vegetable garden. Foreau's brother-in-law Gaston Huet used the natural caves of the Loire Valley to hide his stocks of wine. Then he planted weeds and bushes in front of the caves to conceal their entrances.

Nevertheless, the winemakers of Vouvray were worried when they learned a contingent of German troops was headed their way and planning to spend the night. But Mayor Charles Vavasseur, himself a winegrower, had an idea. He went to an artist friend and asked him to try his hand at forgery. Together, they produced some very official-looking papers, saying all the wine of Vouvray had been 'reserved for the Wehrmacht.' When a representative of the Occupation Authority arrived to make the arrangements for the German soldiers, Vavasseur showed him the 'official' documents and explained that the only places large enough to hold all the troops were the wine *caves*. 'Of course you can put them there,' Vavasseur said, 'but, well, I cannot guarantee that the soldiers will not touch the Wehrmacht's wine. I can only hope they will emerge sober in the morning.' The German official decided it was best to find another place for the men to sleep.

Such foresight did not prevail in Aloxe-Corton, where another contingent of soldiers stayed overnight. 'They helped themselves to a lot of bottles from my cellar,' recalled Daniel Senard, a Burgundy winegrower, whose house had been requisitioned by the Germans. Senard had hidden most of his better wines but purposely left a few in plain sight. 'We couldn't hide everything,' he said. 'If we did, the Germans would have become suspicious. As it was, they probably would have taken more of my wine if they hadn't discovered something else.' That 'something else' was a cache of stoneware bottles filled with a clear liquid, which the soldiers thought was gin, bottled in the traditional Dutch manner.

'They began consuming it with great enthusiasm,' Senard recalled with a chuckle, for it was not gin the Germans were drinking, but purgative water, eau-de-Santenay, a powerful laxative. 'It was the sort of thing everyone's grandmother kept on hand "to clear the system."' That night, the courtyard was unusually full of soldiers coming and going, exchanging the goose step for the green-apple quick step.

According to an American writer who was in France at the time, the Germans 'had the feeling that they were constantly being tricked and laughed at.'

In Alsace, for instance, when the Germans heard that the Hugels owned a pig named Adolf, they dispatched several soldiers to the family's house. When the soldiers arrived, they found the gardener at work and the pig dozing nearby. The officer in charge approached. 'You,' he said menacingly, 'what were you thinking about when you named this pig Adolf?' The old gardener, however, was not intimidated and did not miss a beat. 'Why do you ask?' he replied. 'What are *you* thinking?' The officer, embarrassed, was at a loss for words. He turned and led his men away.

Even in Paris, when the Germans went out to dinner in the poshest restaurants, they often felt something was being put over on them. Were they getting what they ordered? Was that vintage bottle of wine the real thing? Although the Germans were suspicious, they had no way of knowing that a number of restaurants had indeed hatched a deal to disguise their wine. It was done with the help of a very special carpet company.

Chevalier's was a chic carpet firm that had been in business for generations. It bought and sold only the finest carpets, such as antique Aubussons and high-quality Persians. When a valuable carpet needed cleaning, even one from a museum, it usually went to Chevalier's. Although no one seems to remember who came up with the idea, someone decided the dust was too good to throw away. Some of it came from carpets that were centuries old and had never been cleaned. Before long Chevalier's was bundling up sacks of ancient dust and distributing it to some of Paris's best restaurants. There, it would be sprinkled on bottles of cheap young wine to make them look old and rare. The bottles would then be presented to German clients who thought they were getting something extraordinary.

Like restaurant owners in Paris, Madame Gombaud of Château Loudenne in Bordeaux was determined that the Germans would not get what they wanted. When she learned that the Germans were planning to use part of the château for a brothel, she was furious. She rushed outside to the farm buildings and began gathering rat droppings, which she then distributed liberally throughout the château, particularly in the bedrooms.

A few days later, a German inspection team arrived to make a final assessment. It did not take long for them to decide that the brothel idea was not a good one, and it was soon dropped.

'We knew certain things were going on,' one German officer later recalled. 'We knew, for instance, that winemakers were building walls and hiding their wine behind them. We absolutely knew they were being built, but we didn't have time to check everyone's cellar.'

Clearly, they did not have time to knock down the cobwebs that disguised the new wall in Maurice Drouhin's wine cellar. Nor did they have time to dismantle the woodpile that concealed the freshly built wall at the Domaine de la Romanée-Conti. And it certainly would have been impossible for them to pore through all the papers and documents that obfuscated the true ownership of certain wine properties.

No one did a better job of clouding the picture than the Bartons, an Anglo-Irish family with interests in Bordeaux since the 18th century and which owned Châteaux Langoa- and Léoville-Barton. When World War II broke out, Ronald Barton, who ran the two estates but had never taken out French citizenship, realized he was living on borrowed time. Nonetheless, he was determined to look after his interests as long as possible. Every night when he sat down for dinner, Barton made it a practice to drink one good bottle of Langoa or Léoville, his own private toast echoing that of Maurice Chevalier. 'Here's one less for the Germans if they win, one less for my heirs if we do.'

When Marshal Pétain signed an armistice with the Germans that June, Barton, who was British, knew he had to flee and barely managed to catch the last ship out of Bordeaux. It was an emotional departure, with Barton wondering aloud to friends 'whether he would ever see his beloved Langoa again.'

His fears were well founded. Soon after Barton arrived in England and joined the British army, the Germans announced they were seizing his châteaux and vineyards as enemy property. But then something unusual happened. Barton's business partner, Daniel Guestier, went to the Germans in Bordeaux and argued that the seizure was illegal because Barton was Irish. He reminded the Germans that Ireland was neutral in the war and that, therefore, the Germans had no right to confiscate the property. Barton's sister in Dublin, who was, in fact, a true citizen of the Republic of Ireland, launched a letter-writing campaign. Friends, business associates, even total strangers bombarded German authorities with mail, all bearing Irish stamps and postmarks and stressing Ronald's Irish background. Even the Irish ambassador to Berlin joined the conspiracy, underscoring Ireland's neutrality and claiming that Ronald Barton was indeed Irish.

The ploy worked. Although the Germans did use Châteaux Langoa- and Léoville-Barton to billet their troops, they did not confiscate the two properties as they had intended.

The Bartons were not the only ones to thwart the Germans in this respect. France's Vichy government surprisingly played a role as well.

It was no secret that Field Marshal Göring was a lover of the great wines of Château Lafite-Rothschild and had long coveted the famous estate. Hitler reportedly planned to grab Lafite as 'spoils of war' and present it as a gift to his chosen successor. To prevent that from happening, Vichy, which had no desire to see choice French property fall into German hands, employed a piece of legal cunning and sequestrated the château and its vineyards. With Lafite now officially the property of the French State, the Germans were unable to confiscate it as a Jewish asset.

But, as with Langoa-Barton, the Germans did set up a headquarters in the château and housed some of their troops there. That made Lafite's book-keeper, a woman named Gaby Faux, very nervous. Madame Gaby, as she was called, lived at Lafite and had agreed to do her best to watch over the property after the Rothschilds fled France. She had even accepted the most sacred objects of the Paris's Great Synagogue from Robert de Rothschild, who was head of the Consistory of the synagogue, and hid them under her bed and in her bathroom to protect them. She was sure the Germans would never enter the private quarters of a single lady. But she was not so sure about Lafite's wine cellar.

Just before the troops arrived, Madame Gaby enlisted the help of several other people who worked at Lafite and began moving some of the more precious bottles, including the classic 1797s, to the cellars of neighboring châteaux who agreed to hide it among their own wine. As an added precaution, she did something even more extraordinary: she began 'cooking the books.' Night after night, she sat in her little apartment on the Lafite premises, carefully transferring ownership of Lafite's wine away from the older generation of Rothschilds, which had escaped from France, to the brothers Alain and Elie. The two Rothschilds, who were in the French army, had been taken prisoner when the Germans overran France. She knew that because they were prisoners of war, their property was protected under the Hague and Geneva Conventions and could not be touched by the Germans.

STATIONMASTER'S LOGBOOK, ST THIBAULT STATION: *You contend that there was cattle missing from my last shipment. Were they bulls or cows? Your servant, Henri Gaillard.*

The Germans sensed the stalling and subterfuge but could do little about it except to step up their security and surveillance. Even Henri Gaillard felt the pressure. As wine, food and cattle continued to mysteriously disappear from trains passing through his station, Gaillard was bombarded with posters from German authorities reminding him that he was being watched closely. 'The Country Has Its Eyes on You, *Cheminot*,' warned one. Gaillard was ordered to hang the poster in his office and keep it there for one month.

But subterfuge and obfuscation were not what worried the Germans most. It was the increasing sabotage, especially along railway lines. In retaliation, the Germans began forcing the French themselves to help improve security. What they failed to realize was that many of the people they enlisted to help them were the very ones causing the problems, people like Jean-Michel Chevreau, who had been siphoning their wine.

'It was a time of high drama relieved by moments of high jinks,' Chevreau said.

Some of those high jinks occurred during nightly patrols that Chevreau and others were forced to conduct. 'We had to go out every night between our village and Amboise and report any incidents,' he said. 'The Germans also gave us wooden sticks which we were supposed to poke at suspicious objects.'

In an effort to make sure Chevreau and others did their work, authorities in Chevreau's village of Chançay would stamp their papers, noting the time they began; the papers would be stamped again in Amboise to note when they had finished. 'But we never did any work,' Chevreau said. 'All we did was calculate the time it would take to walk along the tracks between our village and Amboise; then we would get on our bikes and go to Amboise and hang around for a while before getting our papers stamped there. Then we rode home.'

STATIONMASTER'S LOGBOOK, ST THIBAULT STATION: I am responding to your query as to the whereabouts of a missing wine shipment. There has been no wine shipped by my station this month. Your respectful servant, Henri Gaillard.

Gaillard was not surprised to receive another poster, this one admonishing him to remember the slogan of Marshal Pétain's National Revolution: 'Work, Family, Fatherland.' It was a slogan Gaillard and many French were becoming increasingly cynical about. Work? That was for the benefit of Germany, people scoffed. Family? With one and a half million Frenchmen now prisoners of war in Germany, many families were without fathers, husbands and sons. Fatherland? Nothing more than a milch cow for the Germans.

Despite Pétain's promises, most French realized that a peace treaty with the Germans was not about to be signed, that prisoners of war were not coming home and that the occupation was not going to end anytime soon.

With each day that passed, the occupation, with its rationing, roadblocks and curfews, seemed to infect another aspect of French life. Authorities routinely opened private mail to check on public opinion. Cinemas were required to show German-made newsreels. American films were banned and listening to American jazz was prohibited. But as rules and restrictions increased, so did genuine resistance.

It manifested itself in subtle ways at first with what historian H. R. Kedward called 'minor gestures of defiance, made to look accidental or unthinking: knocking over a German's drink, misdirecting a German tourist, pretending not to hear or understand orders given in the street, or wearing combinations of clothes which made up the forbidden tricolor of blue, white and red.'

The wife of one winemaker remembers walking down the street of her town on July 14, Bastille Day, arm in arm with her mother and sister-in-law. All celebrations of France's national holiday had been forbidden by Vichy, but the women had their own way of celebrating right under the noses of the authorities. She wore a blue dress, her mother was in white, and her sister-in-law wore red.

In Champagne, a young manicurist also found a way to protest the German presence. Seeing an officer who came regularly for a manicure enter the shop where she worked, she got up, put on her coat and walked out. 'I couldn't bring myself to touch his hands,' she said.

Such 'gestures of defiance' followed a speech almost no one heard. On June 18, 1940, just a day after France agreed to surrender, a 49-year-old French army general went on the radio from London to urge his countrymen to fight on. His name was Charles de Gaulle. De Gaulle said France had not lost the war, only a battle. 'I call upon French men and women everywhere to resist and continue the struggle.' Very few, at first, answered his call.

Within a few weeks, however, an underground pamphlet entitled *Advice to the Occupied* urged people to obey the curfew as this would enable them to be at home in time to listen to the BBC. Everyone, it said, should 'display a fine indifference but keep alive the flame of your anger; it will become useful.'

Many heeded the advice and listened to the BBC, not to receive secret messages or commands but to obtain accurate news to counter the official German and Vichy propaganda. 'There was a special aura about it and whispering all the news,' said May-Eliane

Miaihle de Lencquesaing. 'When the broadcasts were finished, everyone re-set their radios to a French station or Radio Vichy. It was something all of us did automatically just in case the Germans came snooping.'

On November 11, 1940, there was a special bulletin: students in Paris had clashed with German police at the Arc de Triomphe while trying to commemorate France's victory over Germany in World War I. According to the broadcast, shots were fired and students fell bleeding to the pavement. When their comrades rushed to pick them up, police with riot batons charged.

The clash sparked a 'palpable change' in the atmosphere. 'Only a short time ago, public opinion was weak and soft, prepared to agree to anything,' wrote one French diarist. 'Vichy and Berlin have now contrived to make the entire country aware of this servitude.'

And awareness gave way to biting cynicism.

'If we had been "occupied," to use the polite term, by the Swedes,' commented one Parisian, 'we would at least have been left with a dance step, a taste for blue and yellow ribbons; if it had been the Hottentots, or the Italians, or the Hungarians, we would have had a song, a smile, a certain way of shaking the head . . . But as for them, everyone knows only too well that they'll leave us nothing. Not a melody, not a grimace. Even street kids wouldn't dream of imitating the goose step.'

Despite his fears of repercussions, stationmaster Henri Gaillard was also becoming annoyed, and his messages to German authorities in Dijon reflected it. They had become clipped and more cynical. Most telling, he was no longer using the formal, stylized endings – the so-called *patisseries*, or pastries, beloved by the French – to close his communications with the Germans. Gaillard was now merely signing his name.

STATIONMASTER'S LOGBOOK, ST THIBAULT STATION: You would do well to remember that wine shipments cannot arrive as quickly as your demands do. You will not get your shipment

until you send me the correct papers. I've told you this before.
There is one additional matter as well. My toilet is broken. It
would be nice to have it fixed before winter, especially since it is
now leaking into my wine cellar! Henri Gaillard, stationmaster.

By 1941, Gaillard's disillusionment was shared by nearly everyone in the country. Clandestine newspapers calling on the French
to defy the Germans had appeared. So had active Resistance groups
in both the occupied and unoccupied zones.

One of the first groups was *Combat*, started by a group of
French military officers and reservists. Jean Monmousseaux, a
winegrower and *négociant* from the Touraine, was one of its members. Monmousseaux had served in de Gaulle's tank regiment and
was one of the few who had heard his broadcast from London.
He was extremely moved. 'My father found it very hard to accept
France's defeat,' his son Armand said.

Monmousseaux met frequently with his former army buddies,
saying, 'We ought to be doing something, but what?' One day,
the answer appeared at his door in the person of one of his old
comrades. 'Come along Jean, we are going to need you,' he said.

Because Monmousseaux lived close to the Demarcation Line, he
had become a familiar sight to the Germans as he crossed from one
zone to another with his barrels of wine. Those barrels, his friends
pointed out, were big enough to hold a man. Jean understood
immediately, and enthusiastically agreed to help.

Putting a person in a barrel, however, is not easy. Wine barrels
are made to be watertight. Both ends of the barrels are firmly sealed
and fixed beneath the curved ends of the staves, and each of the
staves is made to fit perfectly to its neighbors. Putting someone in a
barrel requires first removing the metal rings around the barrel and
then taking it completely apart, stave by stave, and finally putting
it back together again in the same way, around the person. 'That
is the only way,' Armand said. 'You can't just pour him through
that little hole.'

Jean and his cooper, the barrelmaker, tried a few dry runs. The best time they could make on each end of the run was two hours, two hours to take the barrel apart, get a man into it, and then put it back together again around him. Then there was the trip itself and the wait at the Demarcation Line, which could take hours more. It was a long time for a man to be confined in such a tiny, nearly airless place, but it was possible.

'It's worth the risk,' Monmousseaux reported to his colleagues. 'Let's do it.'

So, over the next two years, Monmousseaux conducted a traffic in human beings, ferrying Resistance leaders in and out of the Occupied Zone in his wine barrels. As each mission was completed, he would put his barrels back together, fill them with wine and return home. The Germans never discovered what he was doing.

By now, incidents along railway lines had become an almost daily occurrence. Cars were derailed, shipments of wine, food and other goods bound for Germany disappeared or were being destroyed.

Nearly every week, stationmaster Gaillard had to notify his German bosses in Dijon that another shipment of goods was missing. One week, he reported that a crate of wine arriving in his station weighed substantially less than it did when it was first loaded onto the train. The following week, Gaillard's report was even worse. 'I am returning to you a case of wrapped but totally empty food packages,' he wrote. 'They were supposed to contain 37 kilos of foodstuffs, but they do not. Also missing is one 50-kilo sack of salt.'

Incidents of stealing and outwitting the Germans had become so frequent that those involved sometimes found themselves tripping over each other. In Bordeaux, for example, a local Resistance group spotted a train loaded with wine for Berlin and decided to liberate its contents. 'They pillaged it neatly,' one Bordelais remembered.

Once home, all were thrilled to discover that the bottles they had swiped came from some of the best vintage years and greatest châteaux. Immediately, they began uncorking a few of the bottles

to celebrate their success. Then, one by one, their faces fell. The
wine was ghastly. Bordeaux *négociants* had beaten the Resistance to
the punch, gluing high-class labels on bottles that were filled with
nothing but plonk.

STATIONMASTER'S LOGBOOK, ST THIBAULT STATION: A
large container of wine bottles has just arrived at my station.
Please tell me what you would like me to do with them. They are
all empty. Waiting for a useful response. Henri Gaillard.

Defying the Germans was a dangerous game. In Bordeaux, a
man was shot and killed when he raised a clenched fist as German
soldiers were staging a parade. Another was executed for cutting
telephone wires.

Even the Hugels of Alsace, who 'fobbed off' poor-quality wine
on the Germans whenever possible, realized they had to be careful.
'If we got an order from the Platterhof, the guest house of Hitler,
we always sent our best wine,' Georges Hugel said. 'We usually
received two orders a year from the Platterhof and most of the
time those orders were very precise. There were a lot of people
there, not Hitler, though, who appreciated good wine. We didn't
dare cross them.'

Others, especially those who were young like 17-year-old Gerald
Boevers, were more daring. Boevers, who lived in the champagne-
producing village of Louvois, was bored. It was July 14, Bastille
Day, but Vichy authorities had banned all traditional celebrations,
fearing they might lead to anti-German demonstrations. Boevers
and three friends decided to celebrate anyway. They found several
metal containers and filled them with gun powder from hunting
ammunition they had hidden from the Germans. Someone then
struck a match while the others ran for cover.

'It was a pretty big explosion,' said Boevers, 'big enough to bring
the police and a bunch of soldiers down on us.' Boevers and the
others were taken immediately to Gestapo headquarters where, for

the rest of that day and night, they were interrogated and severely beaten. 'At one point,' said Boevers, 'a man from the Gestapo told me, "If you were 18, we would have shot you." It was the only time I was glad I was too young to join the French army.'

Another young Frenchman, Marcel de Gallaix, also decided to take some chances. Marcel was a lawyer who specialized in property rights. Despite his wife's fears, he agreed to represent winegrowers in Burgundy who wanted to challenge German requisitions and confiscations. To reach his clients, he often had to cross the Demarcation Line, an exercise that was both nerve-wracking and time-consuming. Trains could be held up for hours while passengers and cars were searched. By the time Marcel finally reached his destination, he discovered another problem: no one had any money. 'That's okay,' he said. 'You can pay me with wine.'

So on each trip, he went home with a satchel full of good Burgundies – all in unmarked bottles. 'That way he could tell the Germans it was merely some table wine he had picked up,' his wife Gertrude said. 'Maybe weeks or days later, we would get a packet of labels, sometimes in the mail, sometimes someone would bring them to the apartment. Goodness, did that wine ever do marvelous things for those awful wartime meals!'

By the winter of 1941, which was one of the coldest ever, conditions of life in both zones of France 'had declined from austerity to severe want,' according to historian Robert Paxton. With imports cut off, oil and coal supplies dwindled. According to Jean-Bernard Delmas of Château Haut-Brion, 'You got so cold you couldn't think of anything else.' Jean-Bernard was in grade school at the time. 'I will never forget how cold it was in our classroom. We wore our coats all day. The teacher would have us run around the classroom every few minutes just to warm up.'

STATIONMASTER'S LOGBOOK, ST THIBAULT STATION: I would like to remind you that it is now December and my toilet is still not fixed. I am also attaching my list of missing freight

for this week: seven packages of groceries, weight 210 kilos.
Please follow up on this as quickly as possible. Henri Gaillard,
stationmaster.

Food had become everyone's overriding concern. German requisitions had created desperate shortages, not only for ordinary people
but also for those in the Resistance who were hiding in the woods
and hills.

Fortunately, there were people like Jean and Madeleine Casteret,
vineyard-workers-turned-cattle-rustlers. The Casterets lived in St
Yzans, not far from Château Loudenne, which the Germans once
considered using as a brothel. Now they were raising cattle and
growing food for their soldiers there.

'We did our rustling at night after the Germans had gone to
bed,' Jean said. 'The Resistance would send us a coded signal over
the radio and we'd set off.' They would sneak over to Loudenne
and quietly herd as many animals as they could toward the nearby
woods where the Maquis would be waiting. 'It was dangerous
because you just never knew when one of the guards might spot us
and wake everyone up, but it was enormously satisfying to *narguer
les allemands* (stick it to the Germans).'

Even Henri Gaillard may have felt a tinge of satisfaction from time
to time.

STATIONMASTER'S LOGBOOK, ST THIBAULT STATION: I have
the honor to inform you that train 9305, which was due at
2:30 P.M., has been halted at kilometer 45 because of the arrival
on the tracks of two cows. It would appear that someone opened
the doors of several box cars and let the animals loose. Some
have disappeared. Henri Gaillard, stationmaster.

FIVE

The Growling Stomach

G ertrude de Gallaix was in a hurry. It was just after six in the morning, but she knew that long lines of women and children would already be forming at her neighborhood market.

Grabbing her shopping basket and book of ration tickets, Gertrude rushed from her third-floor Paris apartment down the spiral staircase to the street below. In her basket was an egg carrier (no merchant had cartons) and a *filet*, a crocheted string bag, to hold any vegetables she could buy. There were also two empty wine bottles, ones she and her husband Marcel had finished off during the week. Because of a bottle shortage, Gertrude knew that no merchant would sell her more wine unless she had empties to return.

Gertrude turned left from her apartment building and headed south down the street, rue Boissière, toward Place d'Iéna, two blocks away. Although there was only a hint of dawn, the streets were already busy. A street sweeper wielding a twig broom opened a fire hydrant to flush litter he had swept from the sidewalk into the gutter. A knife sharpener, standing by the curb with his cart and whetstone, rang a bell, crying, 'Knives, scissors, anything for sharpening? Very cheap!'

As Gertrude continued along Boissière, she glanced to her right. On rue du Bouquet de Longchamp, two German soldiers were standing guard. Gertrude gave a little shudder. That was where the Commissariat de Police was located and where she, an American, was required to register at least once every day. Though married to a Frenchman, the Germans considered her an enemy alien and insisted on knowing her whereabouts at all times.

Gertrude had nearly reached the intersection at Place d'Iéna when she realized something was wrong. Although it was the biggest market in the 16th Arrondissement, there were no lines, no queues of frantic shoppers trying to get their marketing done before children had to be taken to school, no old grandmothers or grandfathers holding a place in line for their sons and daughters. No one. As she got closer, she discovered why. There was no food. By 6:05 A.M., whatever had been brought in that day from the country had already been picked over and was gone.

More shocking, there was not a drop of wine. The space where the wine merchant usually set up his stand was as empty as the bottles in Gertrude's basket.

'Food was one thing, but a wine shortage? In France? That is something I never thought I would see,' Gertrude later recalled.

The wine shortage, which was being felt throughout France by 1941, was but one of many caused by the Nazis in their drive to make Germany self-sufficient and independent of imports. By requisitioning most of France's raw materials, finished products, especially its food and wine, Hitler believed Germany would be in a stronger position to win the war. The Führer put his heir apparent, Field Marshal Hermann Göring, in charge of requisitions. Göring, who weighed nearly three hundred pounds and was called 'Fat Stuff' behind his back, could not have been more pleased. 'The French are so stuffed with food that it is really a disgrace,' he said. 'This is the secret of their wit and gaiety. Without this wealth of food, they would not be so happy.'

Immediately, Göring began systematically stripping France of her bounty: wheat from the Ile de France, cheese and vegetables from the Loire Valley, fruit from the orchards of Normandy, Charolais beef from Burgundy and, most of all, trainload after trainload of wine, thousands of bottles of which found their way into the field marshal's personal cellar.

As head of Economic Planning for Occupied Lands, Göring had virtual economic omnipotence. One of his first moves in his new job was to bar the French from Paris's luxury restaurants, which he had exempted from most wine restrictions and whose wine cellars he kept stocked to meet the demands of their German clientele. 'It's for us that Maxim's and La Tour d'Argent must make the best cuisine,' he said. 'Three or four first-class restaurants reserved for German officers and soldiers will be perfect, but nothing for the French. They don't need that kind of food.'

Had he stopped there, it might have been seen as just a slap in the face. Instead, he delivered a kick to the stomach, declaring French people would have to make do on 1,200 calories a day, half the number an average person needs to survive. Older people, those the Germans considered less productive, were given ration books limiting them to 850 calories a day.

Göring's moves sparked deep resentment, especially among winemakers, winegrowers and others connected with France's wine trade. Léon Douarche, vice president of the French Winegrowers Association, complained that Göring was snatching wine away from those who need it most. 'The old and ill need wine,' he declared. 'It's an excellent food for them; it's easily digested and a vital source of vitamins and minerals. It's the best elixir for guaranteeing a long life that has ever been invented.'

Douarche's message struck a chord. Medical doctors throughout the country called on German and Vichy authorities to provide for a more equitable distribution of wine in order to compensate for the loss of calories. Those engaged in 'intellectual work,' they said, should be entitled to half a liter of wine a day; manual laborers should have at least a liter and, in some cases, a liter and a half (two full bottles) as long as it was consumed with meals; women should receive one-third less than men.

To underscore how desperate the situation was, the doctors cited a visit they made to a nursing home where they found several elderly patients pretending to be near death. 'We asked them why they were doing that. We said, "Don't you want to get well, don't you want to go home?" They replied, "No, here if the staff thinks you are dying, they give you wine with your lunch twice a week."'

The doctors concluded their report with a warning: 'It would be a mistake to refuse wine to those who are truly ill. It can lead to a lack of equilibrium.'

Their warning and recommendations were ignored.

For the first time since the siege of Paris in 1870, signs of severe malnutrition appeared in France. Although France still produced more food than any other European country, it was now the worst-nourished, and everyone felt it. 'We were obsessed with food,' said Gertrude de Gallaix, 'it was all we could think of.'

Gertrude threw out her geraniums and began growing vegetables on her balcony. 'Some of my neighbors raised chickens and rabbits on theirs. One even had a goat tethered to the railing so she would have milk for the baby.'

In the countryside, the situation was slightly better. At Château Siran, for instance, there had always been a vegetable garden, but as food shortages grew worse, it took on much greater importance, according to May-Eliane Miaihle de Lencquesaing. 'In addition to the vineyards, our lives increasingly revolved around the garden. Our first concern was always the garden.'

We arise every morning at 6:30, not one minute later she wrote in her diary. *After making our beds and before having breakfast, we water the vegetable garden. Our everyday life is marked by a total lack of basic goods, little heating, a very restricted diet with no sugar, little bread, almost no meat, butter does not exist . . . We live according to the rhythm of the seasons. The harvest of plums for jam made with very little sugar; it is bitter and does not keep long. We grind corn to make a rough flour which serves as a base for most of our food. We roast barley to make fake coffee.*

It was the kind of diet and lifestyle that prevailed throughout Bordeaux. Many winegrowers planted corn and millet between their rows of vines so they would have something to feed their animals. To feed themselves, some ripped out vines to make room for bigger gardens. But the gravelly soil, which was perfect for vines because it provided good drainage and forced the roots to grow deep, was inhospitable to vegetables. Whereas vines grew best when they were made to suffer, vegetables needed to be pampered.

One day, Grandmother Miaihle decided that her family, which had been putting in long days in their vineyard and garden, could use a bit of pampering as well. She announced they were going on a picnic. She had picked some tomatoes and radishes that morning and had saved some corn bread from the night before, and now she packed it in a basket with a bit of jam as well. May-Eliane and the other children could hardly wait to get started.

Hopping on their bicycles, they headed off down a meandering dirt road that took them past vineyards and through shaded pine woods toward Château Cantemerle, three miles away. It was a pleasant ride. The sun was shining, birds were singing and, best of all, no Germans were in sight. When they reached Cantemerle, one of the oldest properties in Bordeaux, a half hour later, everyone was in high spirits. The château was an ideal spot for such an outing, surrounded by tall oak trees and a large, lovely park. Adults chattered about the weather, their vineyards and the war, while the children played *cache-cache* (hide-and-seek) and other games. Even lunch was a kind of game.

We began running around chasing after frogs. That is what we ate: frogs. We just ran around and picked them up off the ground.
(Diary of May-Eliane de Lencquesaing.)

Some games were more serious than others. In the summer of 1940, France was invaded a second time, this time by potato bugs called *doryphores*. The 'invasion' was especially acute in Burgundy, where huge potato fields were under attack. The Germans, who were shipping French potatoes back to the Fatherland, were irritated that France had not yet eradicated the pest. To solve the problem, schoolteachers were ordered to send their pupils into the fields to

collect bugs. Robert Drouhin remembers his teacher handing him
and his classmates jars, saying, 'See who can collect the most.'
For the children, it felt like a holiday as they scurried out of
their classroom into the field and began picking bugs off the
potatoes. 'At the end of each day, our teacher had to turn the
bugs we had collected over to a German soldier,' Robert said.
'I don't know what the Germans would have done if we hadn't
collected enough bugs.'

Before long the French, who called Germans *les Boches*, or
goons, had a new nickname for their oppressors: *les doryphores*.
'*Ja*,' sneered one soldier who heard the pejorative name, 'we're
the *doryphores* all right. We will eat the potatoes and you will eat
nothing.'

Or next to nothing. By 1942, said one historian, the real voice
of France had become 'the growling stomach.'

To assuage the beast, nearly everything became fair game. In
Bordeaux, a reporter from a local newspaper was cutting across the
city's Square Laffite on his way to work when he suddenly stopped.
It seemed awfully quiet. Where were the pigeons? He began to
count. Later, he wrote in the newspaper, 'The pigeon population
has plummeted from 5,000 to 89.' *Pigeon rôti* had become a staple
on many Bordelais' tables.

And that was not all.

'We were so hungry that we ate the goldfish in the pool,'
remembered a young American who arrived in France in 1940.
Varian Fry, who was thirty-two, had been sent to the port of
Marseille on the Mediterranean coast on a mission of mercy. His
assignment from the Emergency Rescue Committee of New York
was to help artists and intellectuals flee the Nazis.

Word of his operation with its promise of false identification papers and escape abroad spread quickly, and people began
lining up on the stairs outside his office. But smuggling people
out of the country took time, and soon Fry had a houseful of
people to feed and care for until the necessary arrangements

could be made. Among his 'guests' were Marc Chagall, Marcel Duchamp, André Breton, Hannah Arendt and Max Ernst. There would be more than 1,500 in all before Fry too had to flee France.

'What helped a lot was wine,' he said. 'As food grew scarcer, we drank more and more of it. Occasionally on Saturday evenings, we would buy ten or twelve bottles of Châteauneuf-du-Pape, Hermitage, Mercurey, Moulin-à-Vent, Juliénas, Chambertin, Bonnes Mares or Musigny and have an evening of drinking and singing.'

Over the next thirteen months, however, the situation deteriorated. 'For several days, we had no bread at all, and practically no meat,' Fry wrote in a memoir. That is when they remembered the goldfish in the pond. 'But the worst of it was that it also became harder and harder to find wine,' he lamented.

That was true even in Bordeaux, the largest fine-wine district on earth. 'The Bordelais have stopped drinking their wine!' exclaimed one newspaper. They did not have much choice. With so much wine being requisitioned, many restaurants limited the amount they served to customers. Some stopped serving wine altogether, prompting one patron to complain, 'We have to drink so much water these days that it feels like Noah's Ark here!'

But German requisitions were only part of the reason for the wine shortage. Many growers were no longer able to get their wine to market because the Germans had seized their trucks. Those who still had vehicles could not drive very far because gasoline was severely rationed.

New laws also cut into the amount of wine available. Growers were ordered to distill part of their wine into fuel and industrial alcohol, which the Germans needed as solvents and antifreeze for their motor vehicles as well as a basis for their explosives. Those producing more than 5,000 hectoliters of wine a year were ordered to distill one-half of their harvest.

Those regulations, coupled with unfavorable weather, lack of labor and a shortage of chemicals to treat vines guaranteed that wine production would drop, and drop sharply. In 1940, production fell nearly 30 percent. By 1942, production was barely half of what it had been in 1939.

Wine Production and Yield During WWII (*in hectoliters*)

Year	Production	Yield per Hectare
1939	69,015,071	46.2
1940	49,427,910	33.6
1941	47,585,638	32.7
1942	35,022,362	24.4

Among those severely affected were the Miaihles, who owned five vineyards in Bordeaux: Châteaux Siran, Palmer, Pichon-Longueville-Comtesse de Lalande, Ducru-Beaucaillou (until 1943) and Coufran. 'But there's an old saying here,' recalled May-Eliane years later. 'The more châteaux you own, the poorer you are. Certainly at that time, nobody had any money and that included us.'

Even before the war, the Miaihles' vineyards, like so many others, were already in terrible condition because of the recession in the 1920s and the poor-quality harvests of the 1930s.

In the spring of 1942, Edouard Miaihle, May-Eliane's father, informed the family that they could no longer afford to pay their workers and would have to sell one of their farms. He also warned they would have to uproot many of their vines because they were unable to take care of them.

But that was just the beginning. That year, the Germans requisitioned tens of thousands of farm horses – 30,000 from one wine region alone – for transporting soldiers and material to the front. Edouard's brother Louis was ordered to bring all of the Miaihle horses to the square in front of the town hall. He was upset but held his tongue. With two families of Italian Jews still hidden in one of their châteaux, the last thing he wanted to do was call attention to himself.

When he arrived, Louis found the square filled with horses

belonging to other winegrowers, the animals pushing and neighing their displeasure at being packed into close quarters. As disgruntled growers held the reins, Germans armed with pens and clipboards carefully examined the horses, checking their teeth, stroking their flanks, deciding which were worth taking. Some growers tried to trick the Germans by putting stones in their horses' hooves to make them limp.

Finally, Miaihle's name was called. 'These yours?' an officer asked, glancing at the six horses Louis was holding. Miaihle nodded. The German began circling, stopping at one point to lift one of the horse's hooves. After making a few notes, he remarked, 'They're good,' and signaled another soldier to take them away.

'It nearly killed Uncle Louis. He was so attached to his horses,' May-Eliane said. Her uncle had worked long hours with them, training them to walk a straight line through the vines and to pull with just the right force so that the point of the plow would bite deep enough into the rocky soil to clear weeds but not so deep that it would damage the roots of the vines.

While other winegrowers had mules or oxen to replace their horses, the Miaihles were left with only cows. It was a pitiful sight. The cows strained at their yokes, bellowing in protest, as they struggled to drag the plow between the vines. 'Oh, those poor cows, they had a terrible life, and they had to give milk too!' recalled May-Eliane.

Loss of their horses, however, was not the only problem the Miaihles had to face. There was no copper sulfate either. The powdery substance, sometimes called bluestone because it turned workers and vineyards blue when carelessly sprayed, was used to combat oidium and mildew, fungal diseases that attacked grapevines in wet years. The chemical had all but vanished from the marketplace after the Germans requisitioned France's copper and other metals for its war industry.

That was when Louis Miaihle asked his son Jean to drop out of school. 'I need your help,' he explained. 'I want you to stay home and work with me.'

Jean, sixteen, took a close look at his father, and saw a tired man who was aging too quickly, his heart condition exacerbated by the strain of two years of German occupation, two years of struggling to keep his family fed and the vineyards producing. As much as he loved school, especially his science classes, Jean knew he could not refuse.

'What do you want me to do?' he asked.

His father replied, 'Find a way to make copper sulfate.'

When the occupation began, the Germans had allowed *vignerons* to exchange copper products for copper sulfate. Growers scoured their homes and cellars for whatever they could find, copper wire, old pots and pans and finally even decorative ornaments they stripped off their walls. But that exchange system quickly became impractical, and the copper sulfate ran out.

Jean pored over books and publications looking for ideas. Most of what he came up with was laughable. 'Here is how to deal with your copper sulfate shortage,' said the *Bulletin International du Vin*. 'Treat vines less often, reduce the dose, avoid waste by directing sprays with greater care, let women and children do the work to make up for the lack of male workers.'

In frustration, Jean paid a visit to his old chemistry teacher, explaining that he needed to find a way to make ten tons of copper sulfate every four months. 'My teacher knew all kinds of formulas and was eager to try them out.' Before anything could be tried, however, they had to find copper. The Germans had confiscated all the metal they could get their hands on in Bordeaux, including a group of bronze statues commemorating the French Revolution which had stood at Place Quinconces. They were melted down and shipped to Germany.

Fortunately, Jean's family had a good friend in the Belgian consul general in Bordeaux. When Jean explained what he needed, the consul agreed to help. Belgium was still getting copper from its colonies in Africa. In exchange for wine, the consul agreed to smuggle some copper into Bordeaux on trucks that hauled wine and wine bottles to and from Belgium.

Jean and his chemistry teacher were now ready. They set up their 'very simple, primitive laboratory' at Château Coufran, where Jean's family lived. The old farm building they used was far enough from the main house to be safe from the curious eyes of anyone passing through.

It was a bad choice.

In 1943, Coufran suddenly became part of the *zone interdite*, a no-go zone the Germans set up along the Bordeaux coast as a defense against an Allied invasion. They ordered the Miaihles out of their château and moved German soldiers in. From now on, the authorities said, you will need a special pass to come on the property, even to work your vineyards.

But with the lab already built and all his supplies at Coufran, Jean decided to forge ahead anyway, sneaking past the German lines at night, or hiding at the end of the day and not leaving when work stopped in the vineyard. Working at night helped hide the smoke from the lab, and the lab itself was still far enough away from the house to keep the smell of sulfur from German noses, as long as the wind was in the right direction.

For a few months, all went smoothly. Hunched over test tubes and other equipment, Jean mixed nitric and sulfuric acid and applied it to the copper he had accumulated. Soon he had made an impressive amount of copper sulfate. His father was thrilled.

But then, abruptly, the Belgian copper supply was cut off. The consul told Jean it had become too dangerous, that the Germans were becoming suspicious and the smuggling would have to stop.

Jean did not know what to do – until one day when he spotted an itinerant scrap metal dealer on the street. The dealer admitted he was getting metal 'here and there' and would be happy to supply Jean with copper if Jean supplied him with wine. 'It was our little cash-and-carry deal,' Jean later recalled. 'I didn't ask any questions and we didn't exchange names.'

Their chief problem was getting the copper to the lab. The only way was by gazogene car, regular cars which, because of fuel shortages, had been converted to run on burning wood. 'We would get into our cars and start for Coufran from Bordeaux. Every hill, even little ones, we would have to get out and push the car,' Jean said. 'I don't know how many times on each trip we would have to stop and get out the pick to break up the charcoal that was blocking the engine. Those gazogenes were awful. They were so slow and we were always nervous and worried about being stopped and searched by the Germans even though we had passes to work in the vineyards.'

Although he was aware of the risks, Jean found making copper sulfate under the noses of the Germans exciting, even exhilarating. 'I really wanted to be involved in the war and that way I felt as though I was.'

But two things happened almost simultaneously that brought the reality of war to Jean's doorstep. While working at the lab one night, he received news from a friend that his scrap metal dealer had been arrested. It turned out that the copper the dealer had been supplying to Jean had been stolen from a German warehouse.

Jean was terrified, unsure what would happen next. Would the scrap metal dealer talk? Would the Germans come for him next? He had been arrested once for being out after curfew and was released only because a friend of his father's who was from a German family spoke up for him. 'It was a moment of absolute panic,' Jean said. 'I could not sleep for days I was so nervous.'

When weeks passed and nothing happened, he began to relax. But not for long. In the wee hours of the morning when he was still at the lab, Jean was startled by a burst of anti-aircraft fire, followed by a deafening crash. After quickly shutting down his lab, he stepped outside. There, in the middle of the vineyard, was the burning wreckage of an American plane. Minutes later, the sound of barking dogs could be heard as German patrols came out of the château and began searching for the downed fliers.

Jean dashed back to his lab and began dismantling it as quickly as possible, hiding pieces in the hayloft and wherever else he could, even burying parts in the vineyard. Then he quietly slipped back to Bordeaux.

Jean Miaihle's career as a chemist had come to an end.

> God made man—
> Frail as a bubble;
> God made love—
> Love made trouble,
> God made the vine—
> Was it a sin
> That man made wine
> To drown trouble in?
> —*Anonymous*

Now, there was not enough wine to even do that, and everything the Vichy government did only made winegrowers' troubles worse.

They increasingly saw Marshal Pétain's collaborationist regime as meddlesome and manipulative, more anxious to appease Berlin's thirst for wine than to meet the needs of its own people.

To stretch the dwindling wine supply, Vichy, under the guise of healthier living, launched an anti-alcoholism crusade. Certain days were designated 'alcohol-free,' and bars and restaurants were forbidden to serve alcoholic drinks on those days. Advertising alcohol was prohibited and, for the first time ever, a minimum drinking age was established in France; it was set at fourteen. When people complained, Vichy, unconvincingly, sought to justify its moves by pointing out that one of the reasons France lost the war was that it had too many bars, one bar for every 80 persons compared with one for every 270 people in Germany.

Under pressure to meet Germany's demand for more wine, Vichy

was trapped and in a terrible bind. At the very time it was trying
to persuade the French public to drink less, it was also struggling
to convince winegrowers to produce more. Growers were told they
could now make wine from 'undesirable' or 'prohibited' grape
varieties. They were also encouraged to water their wine. Those
committed to quality were appalled.

Equally upsetting was a new government revenue-raising scheme.
Desperate for money to pay occupation costs demanded by Germany, Vichy imposed a 20 percent tax on all wine that growers
sold. Stores had to add another 20 percent when they sold that
wine on to the man-in-the-street. Not surprisingly, less and less
wine was sold in shops because it was now too expensive for most
people. Wine merchants lost money, and winegrowers did too.

As a result, the wine began flowing in a new direction, toward a
flourishing black market where merchants and winegrowers could
sell their wine 'under the table.' French wine lovers jumped to take
advantage, and so, too, did the Germans. Between July 1942 and
February 1943 alone, the Germans, loaded with their overvalued
marks, bought more than 10 million bottles of wine on the black
market.

Vichy was furious about the black market activity and retaliated
by taking complete control of everything related to wine production.
From now on, warned officials, we will decide how, when and where
wine is to be shipped and distributed. Individual citizens will be
issued ration tickets while dealers and shippers will be granted
purchase certificates specifying which wines they can buy. To plug
any loopholes, officials also declared that growers would no longer
be granted a perk they had enjoyed from time immemorial: the right
to keep large amounts of wine for tax-free 'family consumption.'
That wine was usually sold to friends, giving producers a bit of
extra income.

The French wine trade was in an uproar. The harder Vichy pushed,
the harder winemakers and winegrowers pushed back. Black marketing actually increased. In response, the government unleashed its

'Fraud Squad.' Inspectors arrested dozens of winegrowers suspected of conducting fraudulent wine operations. Many others were placed under investigation. One grower alone was charged with falsely labeling 50,000 bottles of wine.

Claude Carrage, a grower from the Mâconnais in southern Burgundy, watched with growing dismay as the crackdown intensified.

Carrage owned a small vineyard near Vinzelles, an area best known for dry white wines, including Pouilly-Fuissé. It was here among the dips and rises of the region's chalky hills that the austere, intellectual monks of the Cluny monastery, in the twelfth century, first taught peasants how to plant vines and care for their vineyards.

In those days, the wines of the Mâconnais were unknown outside the region and nearly all of it was consumed locally. But about 1660, a bold and imaginative winegrower named Claude Brosse decided to change that. Loading a cart with two barrels of his finest wine, he set off from Mâcon bound for Paris, 250 miles away, on a route known as 'the highway of the ready sword, where a fight was to be had for the asking, and death often attended the dropping of a lace handkerchief.'

Brosse made it to Paris safely, and his arrival, after a monthlong journey, caught the eye of France's Sun King. Louis XIV was curious about a winegrower who would venture so far from home, and even more curious about his wine. When Brosse offered him a taste, the King willingly accepted. After a few sips, the King told Brosse the wine was very good, perhaps not as great as Chambertin, the *grand seigneur* of Burgundy, but nevertheless thoroughly enjoyable. 'Do you think you can get more of it to Paris?' the King asked Brosse. When Brosse said he could, the monarch placed an order for his cellars. After that, the wines of the Mâconnais became extremely popular and much sought after.

It was a story Claude Carrage knew well. How ironic, he thought; Brosse got his wine all the way to Paris and here I am, four hundred years later, not even able to get my wines to market in Dijon, only seventy-five miles away. Instead of highwaymen, I have the Germans to worry about.

To protect his wine, Carrage hid his best vintages in a tiny hut in the middle of his vineyard. 'No one could ever have imagined how much wine could be stored behind the tools and bundles of kindling in that little shed,' his nephew said. 'I assure you it seemed much larger inside than outside!' The wine was contained in seven casks, 'marvelous white wines, dry and cool,' the nephew remembered. 'They were a pale yellow and tinged with green. He made me taste every single one of them. And each time, we toasted: "Here's another one that Pétain won't give to the Boches!"'

But Carrage's bravado soon gave way to anger and despair. 'He was beside himself,' recalled his niece Lucie Aubrac. 'His Marshal Pétain, "victorious at Verdun," had betrayed him ignominiously.'

It happened when Vichy's wine inspectors arrived to requisition Carrage's stock of wine for industrial alcohol. 'When they finished, they poured a glass of heating oil into every barrel to adulterate the wine and make it unfit for consumption. That way, they ensured its delivery.'

Carrage was in tears. 'The wine, that's really nothing,' he said. 'But the casks! They've been here since my father's day. The older the cask, the better the wine. They're lost. That stinking oil leaves an odor that never goes away. They're good only for burning! And to think – all this just to send wine to be distilled for fuel for the Boches. They may have enough to go all the way into Russia but they won't have any left to come back – they'll all die. Ah – that Marshal's a fine man! He deserves to be shot twelve times!'

For Vichy and the Germans, that incident and others like it had unintended consequences. 'More than any rational argument, more than any patriotic explanation,' said Carrage's niece, 'those glasses of heating oil adulterating a fine Pouilly-Fuissé swung the winegrowers of the Mâcon hills to the Resistance.'

*   *   *

And not only those from Mâcon. Throughout France, on both sides of the Demarcation Line, Resistance groups sprouted like weeds in the vineyard.

So too did genuine hostility toward Pétain. Until then, public disapproval had been directed mainly against his government and the avidly pro-Nazi Prime Minister Pierre Laval. Now, scorn was being heaped on the old man himself. There were jokes about his womanizing. ('Sex and food are the only things that matter,' he had said.) His tendency to fall asleep during meetings was ridiculed as well. After his assignment to Spain, Pétain had been nicknamed 'the conquistador.' Now there were snide references to '*le con qui se dort*' (the asshole who sleeps).

Angered by the jokes and alarmed by a more militant Resistance, the eighty-six-year-old Marshal took to the vineyards of the Midi to upbraid *vignerons*. He accused them of breaking the law and defying his policies, warning that a 'cold wind' was blowing across France. His words had little effect.

People did pay attention, however, when German forces, in November 1942, crossed the Demarcation Line and occupied the entire country. Speaking on the radio, Pétain called on his countrymen to stick together. I am your guide, your true leader, he told them. Things will work out if you have faith in me.

But when people heard the next broadcast, what little faith they had began to wither and die. This time, it was Prime Minister Laval speaking. With the war going badly for Berlin – its aura of invincibility had been punctured, first in the skies in the Battle of Britain, then in the sands of North Africa and now in the mud and snow of Russia – Laval saw his opportunity and took it. He knew that German war industries were desperate for labor and that French people were anxious for prisoners of war to be returned. Over the radio, Laval announced he had made a deal: for every three workers who volunteered to go to Germany, one prisoner of war would be brought home.

Laval's plan was a total failure. Hardly anyone volunteered. 'I didn't want to work for the Germans,' said one winegrower, expressing the feelings of most. 'The last thing I wanted to do was go to work in Germany.'

Laval was stung, and Nazi leaders in Berlin were seething. Laval decided to play hardball. In early 1943, he announced the formation of forced labor battalions, a program called Service du Travail Obligatoire, or STO. Under the program, men between sixteen and sixty years of age would be ordered – not asked – to go to Germany. Anyone who resisted or tried to escape would be hunted down and punished severely. To back up his threat, Laval created a paramilitary police force called the Milice. Armed by the SS and styled after the Gestapo, it specialized in the capture and torture of resisters. Seeing their own countrymen dressed in khaki shirts, black berets and black ties inspired fear and hatred throughout the population.

Nearly 700,000 Frenchmen reported for STO when they were called up, among them a young man from Vosne-Romanée, Henri Jayer, who would become one of France's greatest winemakers. 'I had a wife and baby daughter. I was afraid of what would happen to my family if I did not report,' he explained. Jayer was sent to work in a submarine motor factory in Vienna. (He escaped after several months and spent the rest of the war hiding at a cousin's home near Vosne-Romanée.)

In the beginning, vineyard workers were granted exemptions from STO, but as Germany's need for workers grew and more and more people fled to the Resistance, the exemptions were eliminated.

That was when Bernard de Nonancourt, his brother Maurice and several cousins were urgently summoned by their uncle to his office at Lanson Champagne in Reims.

'We believe the government is about to call everyone up for STO,' he said. 'I am going to fiddle with your birth dates so I can make you all apprentices, too young to be called up.'

Twenty other workers at Lanson were not as fortunate. They were obviously too old to be turned into apprentices and were indeed ordered to report for STO. Bernard's brother Maurice, who was already involved with the Resistance, was determined to help them. Through his contacts, he learned of a train being sent to the south to collect meat. The *cheminots*, or railway workers, had agreed to turn off the refrigeration in some of the cars until the train had crossed the Demarcation Line.

Shortly before daybreak on the appointed day, Maurice shuttled the twenty champagne workers to the railway station, where the train cars were waiting. There beside the track, he gathered them together and quietly reassured them that everything was organized and that they were in good hands. 'The Resistance will be there and open the doors,' he said. 'They have already arranged for hiding places.'

The men quickly mounted the steps into the still chilly cars, but just as the train was about to depart, one of the workers panicked. 'No, I can't do it,' he told Maurice. 'What will happen to my family?' Maurice pleaded with him to reconsider, but soon the entire group had become unnerved. 'We have our orders for STO, we have to go,' they said. One by one, they jumped off the train, some stopping to apologize to Maurice, others so scared they ran for home.

Maurice was shaken. Word of the aborted mission was sure to leak out, and his entire family would be in danger. The only way to spare them and to save himself, he decided, was to make a run for it, go underground and hopefully escape to Spain. But the Gestapo was quicker. It picked up his trail almost immediately and arrested him.

'We never heard from my brother again,' Bernard said. 'All we know is that he was taken to a concentration camp in Germany where he fell ill and was sent to the gas chamber. I could never bring myself to tell our mother how he died, just that he died in the war.'

It was a decisive moment for Bernard; he knew then that he had to get into the fight against the Germans.

'Le Grand Charles already had inspired me,' he said. 'Maurice and I both heard de Gaulle's radio appeal from London,' the call telling the people of France in 1940 that the war had not been lost and that they should resist. 'But now I knew that I could not wait any longer. I had to avenge my brother.'

Bernard's goal was to get to London and join de Gaulle's Free French Forces. His mother, however, was distraught. Her husband had died as a result of World War I, then Maurice had been captured. The thought of losing a second son was more than she could bear.

'She begged me not to go, but after a while she realized that it was useless,' Bernard said. 'She gave me the address of some distant cousins, two very elderly maiden ladies, who lived just south of the Demarcation Line. She knew they would take me in and help me.' Once he got there, his plan was to proceed to Grenoble, from where, he was told, the Resistance could get him to London.

It was winter when he set off, first hidden in a truck carrying empty champagne bottles, and later traveling by foot, avoiding main roads whenever possible.

When Bernard finally neared the Demarcation Line, he heard a German patrol approaching. He plunged into the Creuse River to hide, but the current was stronger than he had realized. Grabbing a branch protruding from the bank, he struggled to hold on until the Germans had passed. Finally, when they were out of sight, he let go and cautiously made his way to the other side of the river. His pants and shoes, however, did not make it; they had been completely swept away. 'I was frozen and absolutely filthy,' Bernard said, 'but I had one thing left: the flask of cognac my uncle Victor Lanson had given me. I thought, "There'll never be a time when I need this more."'

Once fortified, he trudged on.

It was the middle of the night when Bernard reached the small town where his elderly cousins lived. 'The only person I saw was the village idiot, who was roaming the streets. Looking as I did, that was probably fortunate. I asked him, "Where is the home of the St-Julien sisters?"' With some effort, Bernard got the information he needed and made his way to the house on the edge of town. It was three o'clock in the morning when he began pounding on the door. 'The two old women came to the door, clinging together and trembling like leaves, they were so scared,' Bernard recalled. 'They thought I was the creature from the Black Lagoon.'

After letting him in and drawing him a bath, the women went to the attic to find something for Bernard to wear. All they came back with was a pair of their grandmother's bloomers. '"So this is the price of liberty," I thought, and I pulled them on.'

By dawn, the six-foot-six de Nonancourt was on his cousin's bicycle pedaling toward Grenoble, still garbed in bloomers.

For Georges and Johnny Hugel, joining the Resistance was never an option. With Alsace annexed by Germany, there was no way for the two brothers to escape the fate awaiting all Alsatian boys: induction into the German army. Those who tried to escape were caught and executed. The few who slipped through German hands saw their families arrested and deported to concentration camps.

'Neither of us wanted to be German soldiers, but our family was already in trouble with the Gestapo,' Georges said. 'We would never have done something that might put them in a worse position.'

The Hugels' troubles had begun in 1936, when the Summer Olympics were held in Berlin. Madame Hugel's father, Albert Zoll, whose company had sent him to work in Germany, marked the occasion by raising the French and German flags outside his home. No friend of the Nazis, he deliberately put the French flag on top. Within an hour, the Gestapo arrived, warning that unless the flags were reversed, they would take him to headquarters. Albert complied, saying no insult had been intended and that his actions were merely a gesture of welcome for Olympic guests. The Gestapo did not arrest Albert but noted in their files that this family of Alsatians was 'too French' and should be watched carefully.

Three years later, the Hugels came under greater scrutiny. This time, it was during a ceremony in front of the Monument aux Morts in Riquewihr, honoring those killed in World War I. The date was July 14, 1939, Bastille Day. France and Germany were not yet at war, but Hitler was already flexing his muscles, having overrun Austria and now threatening the rest of Europe. Some in Riquewihr had openly expressed their admiration for the Führer, complaining that the French Third Republic was weak and that France could use a strong leader. Such comments angered Grandfather Hugel, who was mayor of Riquewihr. When it came time to give his speech, he lashed out. Glaring at the crowd in front of the war memorial, he pointed toward the Rhine River and declared, 'For those of you who don't like France, the bridge is open!'

No longer were the Hugels merely seen as being 'too French'; now they were also considered anti-Nazi.

Even the weather seemed to be looking askance at them. That September, when picking began, it was apparent to the Hugels and nearly everyone else that the 1939 vintage would be disastrous. It had rained most of the summer, and the grapes, while abundant, had never ripened. Hauling them in for pressing was not easy because the Hugels had only one horse and no vehicles left. Their other horses and all of their trucks had been requisitioned by the French army, which was mobilizing to face the Germans.

Over the next two months, Jean Hugel watched his wine closely, recording its progress as it underwent fermentation in wooden casks. On December 21, he went into the cellar again to check on his wine. He was horrified. It was worse than he feared: the best cask had only 8.4 percent of alcohol, much less than the minimum standard of 11 percent and far below the desired level of 12.5 or 13. 'The wine was awful,' Johnny said. 'It was thin, diluted, the worst we ever made.'

When Alsace was annexed the following year, German authorities made life even more difficult for the Hugels by 'blocking' their wine, prohibiting them from selling it even to German wine merchants.

With the exception of a tiny amount they were allowed to sell to friends and local restaurants, all of the wine had to be held for the German army, navy or certain leaders of the Third Reich. Nazi officials, however, made no promises about when or even how much they would buy. 'If they told us to send a few cases to the Russian front, we had to send it,' Johnny said. 'But that's how we unloaded that awful 1939 vintage. The Germans were careless when they filled out their orders and did not always specify what vintage they wanted, so we always shipped the '39.'

That was the only wine they tried to sell. With other outlets closed and prices fixed so low that it was hard to break even, the Hugels decided to make an effort to hold on to their wine. 'We began making up excuses whenever we got an order from the Germans,' Johnny said. 'We'd say, "We have no corks," or "We've run out of bottles," or "We have no transportation."' Most of the time, the excuses worked.

The Germans, however, were not finished with the Hugels. When authorities dispatched Polish prisoners of war to Alsace to alleviate a labor shortage in the vineyards, the Hugels were left out. That left Johnny and his father to do most of the work. 'I was spending all my time in the vineyard working behind a horse and plow. On those hot summer days when the horse didn't want to move and the flies were all around, it was a nightmare.'

An even worse nightmare occurred when the Germans notified Johnny's father that their 300-year-old family wine firm was about to be closed down. No reason was given but it was no secret either: Jean Hugel had never joined the Nazi Party. The Nazis had sent letter after letter but Jean kept putting them off, hoping he could keep the family wine business running without joining the Party. He also wanted to preserve the firm for his sons. Now, however, two of them had been drafted into the German army.

Johnny tried to delay being called up by enrolling in medical school, but he was assigned to a medical unit in northern Italy.

Georges, who had been sent to officers' training school after his induction, was targeted for a more frightening destination, a place no German soldier wanted to go: the Russian front.

More than a million had already perished there and another three million were now bogged down in a costly war of attrition. Some who survived had warned Georges what to expect. 'My training was good, so I felt prepared,' Georges said. 'I was not afraid.'

His family, however, was terrified. On the eve of his departure, Georges's mother sobbed uncontrollably; his father was barely able to speak. Finally, Georges's grandfather rose from his chair. Moving slowly across the room to his desk, he opened the drawer and withdrew the tricolored sash he had worn as mayor of Riquewihr when he had delivered his denunciation of pro-German Alsatians. 'I have something I want to give you,' he said. Taking a pair of scissors, he cut off a portion of the sash with the blue, white and red colors of the French flag and said, 'This is the most important thing I have. Always carry it with you. In case of trouble, tell them you are French, not German.' The elder Hugel also gave Georges two gold coins. 'That is all I can do for you,' he said sadly.

Georges arrived in the Ukraine on July 15, 1943. Unlike the war in the West where conventional military rules applied, this was something completely different. Hitler had called it a 'war of annihilation.' Conquering Russia, he declared, would be easier than France. But he had underestimated the resolve of the Red Army.

'Hitler was crazy,' Georges said. 'There were a few fanatics in our group who believed in what he was talking about but most of us thought he was crazy. We weren't fighting for Hitler. We were just hoping to stay alive.'

From the day they arrived, Georges and his unit found themselves on the defensive, almost always retreating. Nothing was motorized and everything, including food and ammunition, had to be hauled by horses. Day after day they walked, much of the time in drenching rain which turned the vast plains of the Ukraine into an endless sea of mud. 'It was two feet deep, up to our knees,' Georges said. 'We could barely walk. Our horses and carts were always getting stuck.'

And all around them, nearly everywhere, lay the stench of death. Atrocities and scorched-earth tactics carried out by both armies had turned the landscape into a wasteland of decaying corpses. The worst atrocities were committed by the Einsatzgruppe, German commandos who followed in the wake of the German army's advance, methodically rounding up Slavs, Jews, Gypsies and Communists, and killing them. 'It was worse than you can imagine,' Georges said, 'the people, the animals lying there . . .

'You had to have something to hang on to or you would go mad.' For Georges, it was a motorbike his father bought him as a graduation gift when he finished high school in 1939. 'I tried not to think about home, my family, the vineyards; that was much too painful. Instead I concentrated on the motorbike and a trip I made with it in the Alps. I relived every kilometer, pictured everything I saw. The mountains, the forests, that was what I tried to think about.'

But nothing could block out the horrors that confronted him as he and his men slogged westward: the burned-out and abandoned villages, the bodies of victims dangling from trees or scaffolds where they had been hung by the SS. Those were the worst moments. If the bodies were not too high, Georges would order his men to cut them down.

'We didn't feel anything,' Georges said. 'We were numb, incapable of feeling any emotion. We had walked so far, more than a thousand miles, and we were beyond exhaustion.'

But conscious enough to hear the haunting cries of Russian partisans armed with loudspeakers calling them murderers and arsonists for burning their villages.

When possible, Georges and his men followed behind tanks, keeping to the paths that the armored vehicles cut through the mud. Georges cautioned his men not to follow too closely because the tanks were the targets the Russians trained their guns on. Despite Georges's warning, some soldiers were careless and paid with their lives.

September came and the warmth of summer fled. But not the rain.
Never the rain. If anything, it became heavier and the mud deeper.
Only one thing kept Georges and his men moving: the knowledge
of what would happen if they fell into Russian hands. 'Surrender
was never an option. We knew what they did to Germans they
captured,' Georges said.

One afternoon, Georges felt a burning sensation in his boots. He
tried to ignore it but when the pain persisted, he was forced to stop.
Removing his boots, Georges discovered they were full of blood. His
feet had been pierced by pieces of shrapnel and become infected,
and blood poisoning, caused by weeks of marching through water
and mud, had also set in. Unable to walk, Georges was left by the
roadside. His unit moved on.

'That was my most frightening moment. A wounded soldier
was of no use to the Russians and I knew if they found me I
was dead.'

It turned out to be the best piece of luck Georges ever had. A Red
Cross truck came by and stopped. The driver was lost and asked if
he knew where a certain town was, explaining that he had a load
of wounded soldiers he was taking to a field hospital. Georges said
he knew where the town was and would show the way if he could
hitch a ride. The driver agreed and lifted Georges into the already
jammed ambulance.

After a few weeks in a field hospital, Georges was shipped back to
Germany, where he spent the last months of his term as a German
soldier recuperating. He never returned to Russia.

Bernard de Nonancourt was excited; his role as a soldier in de
Gaulle's Free French Forces was about to begin. At least, that was
what he hoped. After two months on the road, the young champagne
maker from Reims had finally reached Grenoble.

Bernard looked around, trying to get his bearings. Before leaving
Champagne, some of his brother's friends had given him the name
and address of a priest who was a liaison person for the Resistance.

Not surprisingly, the priest had only one thing to say to Bernard. 'Go to confession, young man, but go to the Cathedral of Nôtre Dame and make sure you go to the confessional of Abbé Pierre Goundry.' The priest then gave Bernard a password to slip into the litany of confession.

When he arrived at Nôtre Dame, Bernard made a quick tour of the Gothic cathedral, confirmed he had found the right confessional and got into line behind several other people waiting to confess. How many of them, he wondered, are here for the same reason I am? Bernard repeated his password over and over in his mind, his excitement growing as he moved closer to the confessional. 'This is where it really begins,' he thought. 'In just a few days, I will be in England with de Gaulle.'

Finally his turn came and he slipped quickly into the tiny booth. 'Father, I have sinned,' he recited by rote, 'it has been six days since my last confession. . . .' And then the moment came and he slipped his password into the litany: 'We'll meet again.'

Abbé Pierre leaned closer to the screen and whispered to Bernard to meet him at his home that evening. He then surprised Bernard by continuing with the confession, leaving the young champagne maker groping for the right words and growing impatient for the ritual to end.

It was already dark when Bernard arrived at Abbé Pierre's home, the shadows of the evening making the moment seem even more exciting to Bernard.

The abbot, however, was a practical man, not given to the romantic fancies gripping de Nonancourt. 'All right,' he said, 'now, tell me what it is you want.'

'I want to go to England to fight with de Gaulle,' Bernard replied immediately.

'Hold on, not so fast,' Abbé Pierre said. 'What experience do you have? What is your background? What do you think you can do there?' On and on the questions went, and Bernard began to worry. Had he made a mistake? Was this the right priest?

Could he do anything to help him? Was he even part of the Resistance?

What Bernard did not know was that Abbé Pierre, who was to become one of France's leading humanitarian crusaders, had been part of the Resistance from the very beginning. He was one of its original organizers, plotting strategy, working to get people out of the country and recruiting new members.

'Look, I don't mean to discourage you,' the priest said, 'but you should understand that we need you more here in France. There's a lot of work to do and we need young men like you.'

It was a disheartening moment for Bernard. He felt the dream he had been nurturing since de Gaulle's speech from London was being shattered, but finally he nodded. 'Okay, what do you want me to do?' he said.

'That's simple,' the abbot replied. 'Fight Germans. We're going to train you to become a commando.'

SIX

Wolves at the Door

Once upon a time in Burgundy, the wolves ran free. They prowled the forests and, in times of famine, roamed the streets of towns and villages. In the tenth century, it is said, their packs were so enormous and so vicious that they drove the Dukes of Burgundy from their windswept capital in Auxerre to the safer climes of Dijon. It was the curse of the wolves, the Dukes declared; evil lurked wherever the beasts were found.

Nowadays, many scoff at such stories but old-timers swear the tales are true. Monsieur Le Brun, who lived in Auxerre just before World War II, said, 'The wolves used to bother us a great deal. It has always been so in the winegrowing districts. The wild animals learn to eat the food that is available, and so we have had to guard the grapes.'

That was especially true during times of famine. Over the centuries, the rocky winegrowing regions of France, whose soil was unsuited for other sorts of agriculture, were a frequent prey to famine and a prime attraction for hungry wolves that survived by eating the grapes. But people noticed something strange. According to Monsieur Le Brun, the grapes had an 'exhilarating effect' on the wolves. 'I suspect the stomach of the wolf is so constructed that the fermentation of the fruit juices proceeds rapidly after the animal has eaten the grapes. At any rate, intoxication is frequently the result.'

Such sights are rarely seen anymore since most of the wolves have been exterminated, but Monsieur Le Brun says he recalls seeing a drunken pack running by his home. 'They came right up this very street,' he said, pointing to the cobblestone lane that ran through the middle of the town. 'Few who saw that sight will forget it.

'The wolves were all intoxicated. That was what caused them to come into the town in the first place, and it was also what saved the townsfolk after they had come in. They were too drunk to remember that they were wolves.'

Residents, cowering in their cottages, watched in utter amazement as the beasts raced through the streets, howling and drooling, before collapsing in a stupor.

'They just lay down in the street, stupidly drunk,' Monsieur Le Brun said.

Then the townsfolk, hunting knives in hand, stepped cautiously out of their doors. When the wolves did not move, they killed them all. That, according to Le Brun, was the last wolf scare in Burgundy.

Except, perhaps, on stormy nights when rain walks across rooftops and the wind howls down chimneys. That is when older folk say they can still hear the howling of wolves as they creep ever closer to the gates of the cities and to the doors of those living there.

The door at 7, rue d'Enfer in Beaune shuddered. It was not yet six in the morning and the Drouhin family was asleep. When the pounding began, everyone came instantly awake; they knew who it was.

Maurice did not hesitate. Reaching under his bed, he grabbed a small suitcase. It had been packed two years earlier in fear of this very moment. There was no time for goodbyes. Maurice mouthed 'I love you' to his wife, who gave a quick nod, and then he fled from the room. He slipped quietly down the stairs, through the cold house and into the wine cellar.

His wife, Pauline, went to the window, threw open the panes and looked toward the street below. Several officers from the Gestapo accompanied by about a dozen soldiers were standing in front of the door. 'What is it?' she asked.

'We want to talk to your husband,' one of them shouted back. 'Open the door!'

'He's not here,' Pauline replied in all honesty.

'Well then, where is he? We need to see him immediately.'

'He's away on business. I think he said something about going to Paris,' Pauline said, trying to buy as much time as possible for her husband to escape. The Germans did not believe her and demanded again that she open the door.

Eight-year-old Robert, who had been sleeping in his parents' room, was listening to every word. When he heard what his mother had said, he crawled out of bed and, on hands and knees, edged his way along the wall of the bedroom, out the door and into his sisters' room next door.

The girls were already awake and straining to hear what was happening. Robert hurriedly related what had transpired. 'Mama told the Gestapo Papa has gone to Paris on business,' he told them breathlessly. Then, once again on hands and knees, he scurried back to his parents' bedroom and crawled into bed.

By this time, his mother had finally agreed to go downstairs and let the Gestapo in so they could search the house. 'Stay in bed,' she cautioned Robert.

The Gestapo marched through the house, searching every room, opening every armoire, pushing aside the clothes, tossing out linens, looking under beds and behind doors. When they got to the bedroom of the Drouhin daughters, they asked them where their father was. 'Gone to Paris,' they answered nervously.

Then they invaded the next bedroom, where Robert was pretending to be asleep. 'Where's your father?' one of them demanded, shaking his shoulder.

Robert sat up, rubbed his eyes and looked up at the men towering above him. In a small voice, he replied, 'He's gone to Paris on business.' The Gestapo were taken aback. A sleepy little boy just awakened surely would be telling the truth, they thought. The chagrined officer jerked his head toward the door. 'We're wasting our time, let's get out of here,' he said.

Downstairs, beneath the house, Maurice lit a candle and began navigating the labyrinth of tunnels that made up his wine cellar.

Centuries earlier, this huge underground maze, carved out of solid
rock, held the wines of the Dukes of Burgundy and the Kings of
France. Now, Maurice hoped, it would provide a way for him to
escape. Ever since he was released from a German prison in 1941,
he had been sure it was just a matter of time before the Germans,
who were convinced he belonged to the Resistance, would come
for him again. That moment had arrived.

Driven by the awful certainty that he would be killed if he were
caught, Maurice searched frantically for a small wooden door that
would lead him to safety. Even with his candle and his knowledge
of the vast cellars, the darkness made it difficult to find his way. On
one of the four levels of passageways that made up his cellar, he
finally found what he was looking for. Maurice brushed away the
cobwebs and eased himself behind the wine racks; then he gripped
the handle of the door and pulled. It opened easily. Stooping
slightly as he went through, Maurice quickly made his way up
several steps that led to the street outside, the rue de Paradis, or
Street of Paradise.

He paused there for several seconds, watching and listening
intently. Nothing moved. No Germans were in sight. Just the faint
glimmer of dawn as the first rays of light brushed the ancient tiled
roofs of the sleeping town. Maurice disappeared into the still of the
early morning.

The Miaihles shuddered to think what would happen if the Jews
they had hidden at Château Palmer were discovered. They knew all
too well that the Germans had set up a transit camp at Mérignac on
the edge of Bordeaux, and that trains packed with Jews of all ages
and nationalities were now running out of the Gare St-Jean directly
to Auschwitz.

They knew something else as well: time had run out. With
German soldiers occupying the main part of Palmer, they had to
get their friends out of the annex where they had hidden them just
before the Germans moved in.

Like most Bordelais, the Miaihles had hoped things would work out differently. They were relieved when, in 1940, Marshal Pétain took over as head of state and were comforted by his grandfatherly assurances that he would protect them by serving as a buffer between the French and the worst excesses of the Germans. Their hopes, however, were soon dashed when they saw Bordeaux's 5,000 Jews being forced to wear yellow Stars of David. They were further dismayed when Pétain's government stripped immigrant and refugee Jews of their rights and property and began deporting them.

But it was an incident in 1942 that illustrated just how perilous things had become. That July, the Germans, with help from the French police, launched their first massive roundup of Jews in Paris. Four thousand Jewish children were snatched from their parents and herded into a sports stadium in Paris, the Vélodrome d'Hiver. They were left there for five days without water, adequate food or sanitation. When church leaders, for the first time, protested Vichy's collaboration and begged Prime Minister Laval to intervene, he refused. The children's suffering had no effect on him. 'They all must go,' he said.

The children were deported from the transit camp at Drancy along with 70,000 other Jewish victims.

Thus far, the Miaihles and their Jewish friends had been lucky. The Germans had never suspected that just on the other side of Château Palmer's kitchen wall were two families, four adults and three children, in hiding.

Arrangements for their escape fell to Edouard and Louis Miaihle. The two brothers were a familiar sight to the Germans, especially Louis, who visited the property nearly every day to check on the wine and oversee work in the vineyards.

Now, however, they stepped up their visits and varied the times of them, ostensibly to check on the vineyard. In reality, it was to make sure the Germans became used to their comings and goings.

Often, Louis would walk up and down the rows with his secateurs pretending to prune the vines, stopping now and then to pick off caterpillars or check the grapes for signs of mildew. Edouard was usually close by, holding what German sentries presumed was a basket of vineyard tools. Under the tools, however, were food, clothing and other necessities for their Jewish friends. When the Germans were out of sight, Louis and Edouard would sneak through the hedge to the annex and slip the provisions to the Jews through a trapdoor.

They would also relay the latest news, and lately most of it had been bad. They explained what was happening to other Jews in Bordeaux and warned their friends to be extra careful, not to make a sound. The slightest cry from one of the children could give them all away. Edouard assured them that they were working on a plan to get them out of France but it would take some time. Try to hold on, he said.

Finally, one day, the Miaihle brothers had some good news. They had found someone to forge identification papers for their friends. They also had secured passage for them on a ship out of the country.

It had been arranged through the help of a neighbor, a helpless old man whose arthritis confined him to a wheelchair. Or at least that is what he wanted the Germans to think. In reality, General Brutinel, a retired French-Canadian army officer, was operating an escape network out of his home at Château Lascombes, helping British airmen whose planes had been shot down get back to England.

Edouard Miaihle had become acquainted with Brutinel shortly after the general acquired Lascombes in the early 1930s. Their mutual interest in wine soon led to a close friendship. Many evenings, the two would get together in the great library of Château Lascombes to compare wine notes and great vintages they had drunk. Almost always it was done over a special bottle of wine.

Often, however, their discussions ranged far beyond wine to include such subjects as art, politics, war and the latest news from the BBC. On many of those occasions, Edouard was accompanied by his daughter May-Eliane. She remembers listening with awe as General Brutinel, 'this brilliant highly cultured man,' described his philosophy of life and the cruelty with which human beings sometimes treat each other. 'Man often behaves like a wolf toward other men,' she recalls him saying.

'Can this be true?' May-Eliane whispered to her father. 'Yes,' he replied sadly.

The escape of the Italian Jews from Château Palmer took place at night. Louis, who lived at Château Coufran, met Edouard at Château Siran, where the rest of the Miaihle family was then living. Taking two cars, the brothers drove the three kilometers to Palmer and parked in the shadows some distance away from the château. The Miaihles then crept across the grounds to the annex and tapped on the trapdoor. The two families were ready. Quickly and quietly, they began passing their luggage out through the small opening before crawling out themselves.

Although German guards patrolled the perimeter of the property, none was in sight. With hand signals and whispers, the Miaihles guided the Italians across the grounds and through the vineyards to where the cars were parked. Speaking in hushed tones, the brothers quickly told their friends that their destination was the port of Bayonne near the Spanish border, where arrangements had been made for them to board the last boat to Argentina.

And then they were off, moving slowly and without headlights down a dirt path through the vineyard, away from Château Palmer.

'I'll always remember those two cars leaving, and disappearing into the night,' May-Eliane said. 'We thought they might not make it, that there was an eighty percent chance that Daddy and Uncle Louis would be caught and put in a camp.'

By the end of 1943, the 'wolves' were again edging closer to the vineyards. The Germans realized that the Resistance was becoming more militant and they were determined to crush it.

Unnerved by ambushes which seemed to lurk around every corner, they retaliated without mercy, not only against the Resistance
but against anyone suspected of supporting it. The war that France
had managed to avoid in 1940 had now come to the country. Farms
were burned, villages were razed and thousands were executed by
firing squad.

Even the vineyards were no longer safe. 'Every day as we
tended our vines, we listened for the click of the rifle,' said
André Foreau of Vouvray. *Vignerons* like Foreau, and most in the
countryside, had become thoroughly disillusioned with Pétain's
government and its broken promises. It had failed to ease the
harsh conditions imposed by the occupation and had done little to
control requisitions by an increasingly predatory German army. The
'heroic patience of the peasant' which Marshal Pétain once praised
had run out.

Winegrowers stepped up their assistance to the Resistance by
allowing their property to be used for nighttime parachute drops
of money, arms and supplies, items that became vitally important
as more and more Frenchmen refused to report for STO. Between
April and December 1943, about 150,000 men were on the run
from STO. Within the next six months, that number more than
doubled.

Many sought refuge with the Maquis, hiding in the forests and
hills. Many others were taken in by winegrowers and farmers who
hid them in their barns and cellars.

As the Resistance became more entrenched in the countryside,
the Germans began sending patrols into towns and villages that
had barely been touched by the occupation.

Jean-Michel Chevreau, the Loire Valley winegrower from Chançay,
noticed it immediately. In 1940 when the occupation first began,
the Germans rarely came through his village. When they did,
Jean-Michel and his friends would treat it like a game, sneaking
out after curfew and siphoning wine from trains bound for Germany.
'We loved trying to stay one step ahead of them,' Jean-Michel

said. 'Every time they thought they had us, we'd come up with something new.'

By 1943, however, everything had changed. Heavily armed patrols now regularly descended on Chançay and villages like it. 'These were not the same Germans we knew in 1940,' Jean-Michel said. 'They were ruthless, unpredictable.' Nearly every Frenchman knew someone who had suffered at the hands of the Germans, and a deep seated fear entered their lives.

The French finally realized that they were facing an all-pervading authority which was prepared to crush what it could not control. According to historian H. R. Kedward, 'With every week that passed, the reality of being a defeated *and* occupied country forced the French to reappraise their initial reactions to the Germans. Where it had been common to acknowledge that the Germans were well-behaved, the phrase expressing the fact, "*les Allemands sont correct*," rapidly became a joke in poor taste, and sullen resentment took its place.'

Resentment, and much more than that. There was now the conviction that one mistake, one false step, could result in torture or even death.

'We tried to live in the shadows,' Jean-Michel said.

That year, in the darkness of a December night, a solitary truck wound its way carefully over Champagne's Montagne de Reims (Mountain of Reims) toward the city of Reims. The driver, who knew the route well, relied on his darkened headlights as little as possible. It was well after curfew.

Suddenly, a light flashed in front of him. He blinked several times to see what was happening but the light was leveled directly at him. Then there came a shout in heavily accented French ordering him to stop. He slammed on his brakes.

A German soldier yanked open the door and pulled the driver out. Where are you going? What are you doing? The questions came fast and furious as other soldiers converged on the truck and began searching it. Before the driver could say anything, there was a shout from the rear of the vehicle. A soldier jumped down, holding an armful of weapons.

'What's all this?' the officer demanded. The terrified driver refused to talk. Slamming his fist into the driver's stomach, the German repeated his question. The driver, held upright by two other soldiers, said he did not know anything about the weapons. They dragged him to another vehicle and drove him to Gestapo headquarters in Reims. Other soldiers followed in the truck he had been driving.

Under torture, the driver said he did not know anything about the weapons but confessed that he had been sent by his boss 'to make a pickup' and that he was just following orders. His boss was the Marquis Suarez d'Aulan, who ran Piper-Heidsieck Champagne. The pickup consisted of a huge cache of arms, including rifles, pistols and grenades, that had been parachuted in for the Resistance. The weapons had been dropped into a vineyard Piper owned near Avize on the Côte des Blancs, about twenty miles south of Reims.

Like many other champagne producers, the marquis had turned his vast cellar into a place of refuge for the Resistance. He also had created an arms depot there, stockpiling weapons that were flown into Champagne by the Allies and which were to be handed out to the Maquis when the battle for the liberation of France began.

The Germans had long suspected what was going on but had never been able to prove it, thanks largely to the disciplined and highly secretive nature of Resistance organizations in Champagne. With the arrest and confession of the driver from Piper-Heidsieck, the Germans now had the evidence they needed.

Early the next morning, a convoy of vehicles carrying soldiers and the Gestapo descended on the headquarters of Piper-Heidsieck. They did not bother to knock; they pushed straight in, demanding to know where Monsieur Suarez d'Aulan was. A Piper employee replied that the marquis was not there, that he had gone mountain climbing in the Alps. The Germans began searching the premises.

They discovered a huge quantity of weapons hidden in the cellars, but no sign of Suarez d'Aulan.

Furious, the Gestapo sped to his home, hoping to catch other members of the family, but someone else from Piper had gotten there ten minutes earlier and warned the family what was happening. By the time the Germans arrived, everyone, including the marquis's wife, Yolande, was gone.

The Germans, however, were not about to give up. A few days later, when Yolande's mother died, the Germans sensed another opportunity. They decided to surround the church during the funeral service and arrest the family when they came out.

The service began as planned. As prayers were recited, soldiers took up positions around the church, guarding all the doors. When the service ended, however, only one member of the family emerged. It was Suarez d'Aulan's fifteen-year-old daughter, Ghislaine. The rest of the family had stayed away, suspecting the Gestapo might try something but believing they would not bother a young girl.

The Gestapo, however, was so angry that it grabbed Ghislaine as a hostage, warning that she would only be released in exchange for her parents. Ghislaine insisted she had no idea where they were. The officer said they would wait. The girl was thrown into the prison at Châlons-sur-Marne, where other Resistance figures from Champagne were being held.

The entire Champagne community was outraged. They besieged the Germans with letters of protest. Some braved immediate punishment and possible imprisonment by going to the Gestapo and voicing their complaints in person. Even the mayor of Paris, Pierre Taittinger, became involved by calling on the King of Sweden to intervene.

Three weeks later, in the face of increasing protests and with no sign of Ghislaine's family, the Germans finally let her go.

By then, her father, an experienced pilot, had made his way to Algiers and joined a French fighter squadron. Her mother found refuge with the Maquis, hiding out in the Vercours region of eastern France.

Their champagne house, however, was placed under direct German control. The person charged with running it was weinführer Otto Klaebisch.

Even small producers like Henri Billiot were feeling the pressure. Billiot owned about five acres of vines near Ambonnay, selling his grapes to the major champagne houses. With his father in ill health and his grandfather partially paralyzed by a stroke, Henri, who was seventeen years old, had to take care of the entire family. That included his five younger brothers and sisters, his parents, two sets of elderly grandparents and his aunt and her three children. His uncle, an officer in the French army, had been sent to a camp in Germany after refusing to work for the Germans.

'My youth was not a time of fun,' Henri said. 'I worked twenty-four hours a day trying to feed the family. I never had holidays or weekends.'

But he did have a horse. That was more than most champagne producers had, because most horses had been requisitioned by the Germans. The Billiots still had theirs only because of Henri's partially paralyzed grandfather. When the Germans came to requisition his horse, Grandfather Billiot had parked himself and his wheelchair in front of the stable and refused to move. Shaking his cane in the face of the German officer, Grandpa Billiot bellowed, 'You can't have my horse. Get the hell out of here!' The outburst startled the officer, who snarled back, 'You're too French!' Turning on his heels, he and the other Germans stomped angrily across the courtyard and slammed the big wooden door as they left.

Thanks to his grandfather's obstinacy, Henri was able to pool his resources with a neighbor who also had managed to keep one horse. With two horses, vineyard work became much easier. Other parts of Henri's life, however, were becoming much more complicated.

The Germans, who had opened an officers' training school near

Ambonnay, announced they were requisitioning part of Billiot's house to quarter some of their soldiers.

About the same time, Henri's sister Denise came to him and revealed that she had been working with the Resistance. Now, she said, the Resistance was wondering if Henri would be willing to get involved by joining the Service des Renseignements, or Information Service. In other words, become a spy. Denise told Henri the Resistance felt he was well suited, that he knew the vineyards and had spent long hours each day working in them or biking up and down the paths to check on the vines. It would be a simple matter, Denise suggested, for Henri to go just a bit further and also check on German comings and goings, and then, once a week, bike up the slopes of the Montagne de Reims and relay his information to a contact.

It sounded exciting. Like many of his friends, Henri wanted to become involved in the war and do something to help his country. Unlike them, he had not been able to run off to join the Free French Forces because of his obligations at home. The spy job seemed perfect. Henri eagerly accepted.

All went well until the winter of 1944. Heavy snows confined nearly everyone to their homes and prevented Henri from venturing outside to monitor German troops or meet with his contact. It was doubly depressing because four German soldiers had moved into Billiot's house.

Henri struggled to bide his time and concentrate on his champagne business. Like other growers, he had been thinking about making his own champagne. His grapes were of high quality and had always commanded a good price, so why not?

Before he could experiment, however, his sister appeared with another message from the Resistance. 'Go to Bouzy immediately,' she said. 'Your contact wants to see you.'

Despite the darkness and the deep snow, Henri got on his bike and pedaled several kilometers to the rendezvous point, a windswept patch of ground in the middle of a vineyard. There, he was met by his contact, a truck and a small mountain of burlap bags filled with potatoes. Nearby stood four American airmen whose planes had been shot down. Each of them was holding an empty bag.

Before Henri could ask what was going on, his contact pointed to the American and said, 'Get those guys into their sacks and let's get loaded up before anyone sees us.' The four Americans climbed onto the truck and, with help from Henri, crawled into their bags. Henri and his contact then lugged the sacks containing potatoes over to the truck and piled them on top of the airmen to until they were completely hidden from view.

Henri was instructed to drive them to Ambonnay and hide them for two days. Someone else from the Resistance would then arrive and help them escape to Spain.

Henri threw his bike into the truck and started the engine. It had stopped snowing and was becoming light. As the truck moved slowly down an icy hill, a German encampment came into view. This was the most dangerous part of the journey. If there was any place Henri would be stopped, this was where it would happen. Despite an overwhelming urge to speed up to get past the Germans, he knew he did not dare. He held his breath and continued on. Two minutes later, Henri breathed a sigh of relief. The German camp was behind him.

Henri drove straight to his grandfather's house on the outskirts of Ambonnay and explained the situation. 'It's just for a couple of days,' he said. His grandfather allowed two of the airmen to stay in his house.

Henri's next stop was a café run by a friend, who agreed to hide another of the Americans in a room just above the establishment.

By now, it was midmorning and German soldiers would be about, but Henri still had another airman to hide, a bombardier named Edmund Bairstow. Henri decided to take a chance. Turning his truck, he headed straight for home. His mother was there when he arrived. 'Are any of the Germans around?' he asked, quickly explaining that an American flier was hidden in his truck. When she assured him they were out, Henri rushed back to the truck, helped Bairstow out of the bag and ushered him into the house. He put Bairstow in his bedroom, warning him to be quiet because German soldiers were living in the next room. At first, Bairstow did not understand. 'There was no one in Ambonnay who spoke English and Bairstow didn't speak French,' recalled Henri, 'so I was a little worried but I figured we could manage for two days.'

Henri's worries, however, had only begun. Two days later, someone from the Resistance arrived at his house to say that the person who was supposed to spirit the Americans away had been captured and tortured by the Germans and sent to a concentration camp. Henri was told he would have to take care of the airmen until other arrangements could be made.

It was about the worst news Henri could imagine. To continue hiding an American in his bedroom with German soldiers quartered in the same house was unthinkable. He decided to contact the one other person in the Resistance he knew, a surgeon, who might be able to help him. But before he could get to the surgeon's house, Henri learned that the Gestapo had gotten there first, dragged the man from his house and shot him.

Henri was in despair, worrying that the Gestapo was closing in and could arrive at his door next. To make matters worse, the four Americans were going stir-crazy as the days wore on, frustrated by being confined to small spaces and not having anyone to talk to. Ed Bairstow was suffering the most. 'He was incredibly depressed and cried all the time,' Henri said. 'He feared that all the men on his plane had been killed and he was desperate for news.'

Henri felt he had no choice. With the help of a friend, he got the airmen civilian clothes and escorted them into the village so they could get together, warning them to be careful and not speak English. For the most part, they followed his instructions. Sometimes, with Henri's friend acting as a lookout, the Americans would linger over drinks and smoke cigarettes at the local café.

Sometimes, much to Henri's dismay, one of them would slip off to watch the village soccer games. On one occasion, they persuaded Henri to take their picture as they posed outside Henri's house, trying their best to look very French. It did not help Henri's nerves.

One night, he decided the safest thing was to bring the men over to his house to play cards. The Germans were scheduled to be out. All went well until Henri's sister Denise came running in. 'You've got to get them out of here,' she said frantically. 'The Germans are on their way back!' Henri motioned the Americans to follow him, his sister's panic leaving no doubt in their minds that something was wrong. Henri led the men outside, across the courtyard and down into his wine cellar. Then he scurried back to the house.

Almost at the same time, a group of German soldiers entered the courtyard and headed for the house. It was March, and Allied planes had just conducted their first daylight bombing of Berlin.

The Germans told Billiot that Hitler would be making a major speech shortly and that they intended to listen to it on Billiot's radio. Billiot's spirits sank. Who knew how long the Führer would talk? How long could he keep the airmen closed off in the darkness of his *cave*?

Amazingly, his sister Denise smiled serenely. 'I'll be right back,' she said.

The Germans, about a dozen of them, pulled their chairs around the console and began trying to tune in the broadcast. All they got was static and strange noises. Denise returned a few minutes later and gave Henri's hand a reassuring squeeze.

The Germans were puzzled. They could not get a thing from the radio. Henri was puzzled too, saying he had been listening to it only an hour or so earlier. One of the soldiers was a communications specialist and he began checking the radio. 'There's nothing wrong with it; it seems fine to me,' he said.

The Germans glanced at their watches. Hitler's speech was about to begin. After fiddling with the radio one last time, the Germans got up and announced they were going elsewhere to listen to the speech. As the soldiers went out the door, Henri heard one of them say, 'Who cares anyway? The Führer is crazy.'

'I can't figure it out,' Henri said to Denise. 'The radio was working perfectly.'

'Yes,' she said, 'but that was before I took a piece of lead out of the electric meter. You learn a few things in the Resistance.'

The next day, Henri went to the café to tell his friend that the strain was too much. His vineyard needed attention and something had to be done about the four Americans; they had been there more than a month. The friend replied that he had heard that a certain Monsieur Joly in Reims was working for the Resistance and could probably help.

Henri and his friend got on their bikes and headed toward Joly's home, about thirty kilometers away. When they arrived and explained their problem, Joly said he did not know what they were talking about. He refused to let them in and slammed the door in their faces.

As they turned to leave, another man emerged from Joly's house and, as he walked past, said under his breath, 'He'll see you tonight.'

The meeting was not satisfactory. Joly was noncommittal. Henri and his friend were dejected as they made the long, dangerous ride back to Ambonnay in the dark after curfew.

Less than a week later, however, a railroad worker knocked on Henri's door and said he was there to collect the Americans. They had been in Ambonnay forty-two days.

After their departure, the exhausted Billiot went to his bedroom to collapse. There, on his pillow, he found two hundred-franc notes. On one of them was a handwritten message: 'Dear Henri, To you I owe very much, more than words can express. May your future be as bright as those days I have spent with you.'

It was signed Edmund N. Bairstow.

SEVEN

The Fête

G aston Huet felt like vomiting. If there had been anything in his stomach he probably would have.

Staring out from the dish of soup in front of him was a giant bedbug. Huet was tempted to push the bowl away, then thought better of it. Instead, he dipped his spoon into the thin milky substance and flipped the bug onto the floor. Then he shut his eyes and drank the soup.

What he would have given for a juicy *poulet rôti* or *rillettes de porc* to eat, washed down by a bottle of his own sweet Vouvray! But after more than two years in a German prisoner of war camp, the fantasy was almost too much to bear.

Ever since June 17, 1940, when the gates of Oflag IV D in Silesia slammed shut behind him following his capture at Calais, life for the Vouvray winemaker had steadily deteriorated. He had weighed seventy-two kilos when he arrived; now he was down to forty-eight.

It was much the same for the more than 4,000 prisoners, packed into twenty cement-block buildings, two rows of ten each divided by a narrow strip of dirt the prisoners called Hitlerstrasse, or Hitler Street. The entire complex was surrounded by fortified guard towers and rows of barbed wire.

Running through the center of each of the buildings was a line of cement sinks. On each side was row after row of bunk beds, three high. The mattresses were stuffed with wood shavings, and aside from one blanket per bed, there were no other covers. The windows were bare, as was the cement floor. On the day before Huet arrived at the camp, the Germans had distributed one roll of toilet paper to each barracks. With 180 men in each, that came to one square per person.

Oflag IV D was what its name said it was, an *Offizier-Lager*, or camp for officers. Under the Geneva Convention, officers who were taken prisoner were to be housed and fed 'no worse' than the troops who captured them. They could practice any religion, were exempt from hard labor and could correspond with their families and friends. If they were caught trying to escape, they were to be subjected to nothing more than a month of solitary confinement.

Grim as officer camps were, they were far better than regular POW camps and nothing like concentration camps where Jews, Slavs, Gypsies – those the Nazis called *untermenshen*, or subhumans – were thrown. Once clear of interrogation, an officer POW had nothing to do but wait for the war to end. Mind-numbing boredom was the worst enemy, but hunger was a close second. Food was an incessant preoccupation.

Gaston Huet awoke one morning with breakfast on his mind. He could barely stomach the thought: 'panzermilch again,' a diluted soy milk he and the other prisoners were given every single morning for breakfast along with a bit of bread. Lunch would be no better: broth, perhaps with some boiled potato ground into it. Dinner would feature a dab of pâté, ground meat of an unknown origin held together with a great deal of lard.

The monotony of the day was interrupted when a German guard entered Huet's barracks just before noon and announced that mail had arrived for some of the prisoners. Although the rules of war stipulated that officers could correspond with their families, the rules were often conveniently overlooked. It had been weeks since any mail, always censored, had been allowed into Oflag IV D. This time it included several packages, all of which had been torn open and inspected by the German authorities.

Huet beamed when his name was called. There was a letter and a parcel from his wife. He put the letter in his pocket, holding the best for last, and opened the box. Inside were three eggs, packed in flour so they would not break, provisions the POWs cherished most since they could be used in so many ways to stretch their meager food supplies. Huet sifted through the flour with his fingers, not wanting to miss anything else that might have been packed, such as a bar of soap or a bouillon cube. The latter especially was something German censors kept a watchful eye out for after they discovered that secret messages had been scribbled to several prisoners on the inside of the wrappings of the tiny cubes.

Satisfied there was nothing more in the flour, Huet placed his box of food in a locked storage area and retreated to his bunk to read his letter. '*My dearest husband . . .*,' the letter began, and Gaston was transported to another world, a world of home, family and friends. He savored every word and lingered over the description of his growing daughter, trying to picture what she must look like. He had last seen her on her first birthday. He had missed her first steps, her first words. She would be nearly four now and he was about to miss yet another birthday.

News of the family vineyard added to his melancholy. Just before being recalled to active duty in 1938, Huet had taken full charge of running Le Haut Lieu when his father's health, already fragile as a result of World War I, deteriorated further. 'It's a bit of a struggle but the vines are okay,' Huet's wife wrote. In between phrases that had been blacked out by the censor, Huet learned there had been rain in Vouvray. The term *mauvaises herbes*, or weeds, also stood out. Even with the censored passage eliminating some of his wife's words, Huet could easily picture what the vineyard looked like. Because it was early summer, he knew the grapes would still be green and tiny, but if it did not rain too much, there was a chance the vintage would turn out to be a decent one. He longed to be home for the harvest but that, he knew, was impossible.

Tucking the letter back in his pocket, Huet went looking for his friend Daniel Senard. He found him stretched out on his bunk. Any news from home? Huet asked. Senard, the winemaker from Aloxe-Corton in Burgundy, shook his head. Unlike Huet, Senard had not received a letter. From earlier ones, however, he knew that German soldiers had occupied his home, pillaged his wine cellar and even burned some of the family's antique furniture to keep warm. Huet filled Senard in about the news he had received. Their conversation soon turned to the problems winegrowers throughout France were facing. Before long, other *vignerons* in the camp had joined them.

Of the million and a half French soldiers languishing in German POW camps, most came from rural areas, which meant that many, including hundreds in Oflag IV D, were directly or indirectly connected to the business of wine. To get through the long, boring days, those in the camp had formed groups to share news about their vineyards and compare notes about viticultural practices.

It was during one of the group meetings that Huet came up with an idea that startled everyone. 'Let's have a wine banquet,' he said. At first, no one said anything, and then there was a torrent of chatter. Finally, someone asked the obvious: how do we have a wine banquet without any wine? Huet confessed he did not have an immediate answer. 'But I have an idea. Let me think about it.'

Afterward, he explained what he had in mind to Senard and another winemaker friend, André Cazes, owner of Château Lynch-Bages in Bordeaux. 'I can sum it up in one word,' Gaston said. 'Blackmail.'

He had learned from a prison work crew that a nearby camp for criminals had wine and liquor circulating in it, which was against regulations. 'Let's threaten to blow the whistle,' Huet said. 'You know as well as I do that our camp commander is scared to death of the Gestapo. Maybe he'll let us bring in some wine for ourselves if we promise to keep quiet.' Senard and Cazes agreed it was worth a try.

A few days later, the three prisoners confronted the commander. He reacted nervously. 'Where did you get that information? For God's sake, don't tell anyone!' Huet replied that their silence could be had for a price, then he outlined what he and his friends had in mind.

The commander was reluctant at first, but the last thing he wanted to do was stir up trouble or call attention to himself.

'You can have the wine,' he said, 'but I am not going any further than that. You will have to use your *tickets colis* to get it.'

Those were the labels French prisoners of war were issued to obtain food and other provisions from home. They were like shipping permits, and each POW was given one label a month to send home. No package sent back could weigh more than five kilos, and it had to have the label attached. However, there was never any guarantee the Germans would deliver them, and when they did, the packages were always opened and inspected.

Huet and his friends were ecstatic, scooting from the commander's office like little boys who had been given a treat, congratulating each other and exclaiming, 'We did it, we're going to get our wine!' They rushed back to their barracks to report the good news and begin planning.

News of their victory spread through the camp faster than rumors of liberation. 'Is it true?' other POWs asked. Many were skeptical and thought it was a joke. But by the end of the day, the common refrain was 'Can we help?'

Huet named a committee composed of representatives from each of the country's wine regions. It was decided that 700 bottles of wine would be needed. That way, every prisoner would get one glass. Their goal was to have everything ready by the fall of 1942, timing their party so that it coincided with the grape harvest back home.

The work became all-consuming. After months of unrelenting boredom, now they had a party to plan. Huet and the other committee members worked every day, putting out word that each prisoner with a wine connection should beg three bottles of wine from home. After careful calculations, they were sure that three bottles per package would come in under the five-kilogram weight limit the Germans had imposed on packages.

When the first packages of wine began arriving late that summer, there was euphoria. 'This is really going to happen,' the POWs thought. That was when things started to go wrong.

The first headache came after too much champagne. Most champagne at that time was bottled in 80-centiliter bottles, five centiliters larger than the other wines, which meant that all the champagne packages being delivered to the POWs slightly exceeded the five-kilogram limit. The German commander had promised that none of the packages would be opened as long as they met specifications. Those from Champagne did not, and overzealous guards pounced on them.

It was left to Huet to break the news. 'We've lost most of our champagne,' he told the POWs. 'The Germans who seized the parcels probably drank everything inside.' Huet said that without the champagne they would not have enough wine in time for the party, so they would have to postpone it for a couple of months.

The announcement came as a crushing blow. There was momentary silence as the other POWs absorbed the impact of his words. All those labels wasted. Would they ever get enough wine? But it was much more than that.

'The party meant everything to us,' Huet recalled years later, 'and suddenly it seemed like it was all being taken away.'

That sense of loss was exacerbated by news from home: German forces that November crossed the Demarcation Line and placed the entire country under occupation. Mail from home, which was irregular at best, became even more erratic. As morale plummeted, anger began rising. Prisoners raised their arms and mockingly shouted 'Heil Hitler' at every guard who passed by. They also built a Tombe d'Adolph, Adolf's Tomb, and conducted a sham funeral service there. Fearing the problem could escalate, authorities threw hundreds of POWs into the *bloc des isolés*, or isolation block, accusing them of harboring 'anti-German' sentiments.

Huet was worried as well. Calling his wine *fête* committee together, he declared, 'For everyone's sake, we've got to go ahead with the party. Even if we don't have as much wine as we wanted, we've got to do it. Let's fix a date and stick to it.' The date they picked was January 24, 1943, the feast day of St Vincent, the patron saint of French winemakers.

It was an inspired choice, for the German winter had set in with a vengeance. Snow fell heavily and temperatures dropped below zero, but hardly anyone noticed. The POWs were obsessed with planning for the grand event, and everyone wanted to be involved. Artists volunteered to make posters and maps of different wine regions. A theater group offered to stage skits about wine and even make costumes. A priest who directed a camp chorale group said they would put down their hymnals and start practicing drinking songs.

One day while Huet was working on the program, he was approached by a representative of the carpenters' group. 'What about a winepress? We can build you a model of one,' he said. Huet thought it was a great idea but wondered if it might be too complicated. After all, where would they get the wood? The carpenter replied it was not a problem and that Huet would be doing them a big favor by letting them build a press. 'Them,' as Huet discovered, were five POWs who were intent on escaping. An underground tunnel was being dug and wooden bed slats were being used to prop it up. The winepress, the carpenter said, would help explain to any suspicious German why all the bed slats were disappearing. In addition, noise from construction of the press would help cover up sounds from the tunneling.

Huet was amused but not surprised. There had been numerous attempts at escape from Oflag IV D, several of them successful. As the prisoners' logbook noted, 'So many tunnels are being dug that it's like living on an anthill.' The most memorable attempt occurred when 150 officers tunneled from beneath the latrines to the woods beyond the camp, but not before getting the cooperation of the other POWs to refrain from using one part of the facilities until after they had made their break.

Escape was something Huet never considered. Like many POWs, he was afraid of what the Germans might do to his family. Those who tried to escape were usually unmarried men without families to worry about.

The carpenters' offer, however, intrigued him. He shrugged his shoulders. 'Why not? Go ahead and build the press,' he said.

By now, Huet's one-night wine tasting had evolved into a two-week extravaganza of exhibits and seminars celebrating the glories of the wines of France. A leaflet distributed by *vignerons* of the camp proclaimed,

> *We want to sing about the sun and the breezes blowing through the vineyards. We want to sing about what the eye cannot see from behind the barbed wire and walls of this camp, and about what one cannot imagine growing here on this hard, infertile ground of the Silesian plain. We want to sing about wine to stomachs washed out and swollen by three years of nothing but water. We want our celebration to be like the grape which has grown, ripened and been harvested in beauty and generosity.*

A few days before the grand fête, the more than 4,000 POWs of Oflag IV D had been asked to list, in order of preference, the wine they would most like to drink. Burgundy? Bordeaux? A sweet wine from the Loire? Choices ran the gamut, and pretty soon the POWs were exchanging stories about wines they had drunk, arguing at times about which vintages were better and which region of France produced the greatest wine. All had been asked to indicate three choices in case their first choice was unavailable.

Meanwhile, Huet and his organizing committee went to the locked storeroom and began counting the bottles of wine. When they had finished, they were crestfallen. There were only 600 bottles, 100 fewer than what they had hoped for. 'This means one bottle is going to have to serve seven men,' Huet told the others. 'It's going to be a very small glass of wine.'

By January 24, everything was ready to kick off the Quinzaine des Vins de France, the two-week wine celebration. As *vignerons* demonstrated how the newly constructed winepress worked, colorful posters depicting the glories of wine were hung on the walls of the barracks. A troupe of actors dressed in paper costumes went through a final rehearsal of the skit they had prepared. The camp choir warmed up with a few scales and measures from a drinking song they had learned, 'Farewell, baskets, the harvest is over . . .'

Beneath all this activity, five POWs were getting ready to say their farewells. A splurge of unusually warm weather in January had enabled them to finish their tunnel earlier than expected. As colleagues stood watch by the window, the five men shoved one of the beds aside and slipped through a hole in the floor. Each clutched a small disguise kit as they crawled through the tunnel toward the woods, about 125 yards away. There, hidden by the trees, they donned their disguises, homemade German uniforms which had been fashioned from the cardboard the wine had been packed in. Back in the barracks, other POWs checked one last time from the windows to make sure no Germans were around, then slid the bed back into place.

As evening fell, all attention shifted to the moment everyone had been anticipating. A jubilant Gaston Huet, overcome with relief and emotion, called members of his committee together to give them one last message. 'It's time,' he said simply.

The wine fête was held in the so-called Hall d'Information, the name given the barracks where plans for the soirée were first conceived. Because space was limited – the building could hold only 235 people at a time – it was decided that the celebration would be staged seventeen times over the course of several days in order to accommodate all of the POWs.

As that first evening got underway, the atmosphere was surreal. Many of the POWs could hardly believe it was happening. As each man took his place, he found a small piece of paper with a typewritten message attached to his chair:

This evening will give us time to recall and glory in one of France's purest treasures, our wine, and to alleviate the misery with which we have had to live for so long. A party to celebrate wine? No, it is not just that. It is also a celebration of us and how we have survived. With this little glass of wine that we are going to drink together tonight, we will savor not only a rare fruit but also the joy of a satisfied heart.

The 'rare fruit' would come later, however. First, one of the speakers said he would like to correct a few misunderstandings. 'Some of you labor under the assumption that there is no more beautiful sound in this world than the pop of a champagne cork,' he said. 'You are wrong. Champagne must be opened not with a pop or bang but with a whisper.' To open it otherwise, he warned, allows the carbon dioxide to escape prematurely and the result, 'though spectacular, is usually a mess.'

Unveiling a fake bottle of champagne that had been prepared for the demonstration, the speaker announced he would now show them how a bottle of champagne should be opened. As the bemused audience looked on, he meticulously peeled off the foil capsule, undid the wire holding the cork in place and gently set about easing the cork from the bottle. 'Remember,' he reminded his listeners, 'always with a whisper.'

Soon, however, it was the audience that was whispering, then chuckling out loud. The cork refused to budge. He tried again. Nothing happened. Realizing there was no alternative, he pinned the bottle between his knees, gripped its neck with his left hand and pulled with all his might. The pop sounded like a gunshot. Had there been anything in the bottle, towels would have had to be distributed to the audience. Sheepishly, the speaker said, 'Well, you get the idea.'

Laughter and applause increased when the theater group took over and began performing skits depicting life in the vineyards. The skits had them laughing so hard that German guards came to see what was going on. Fortunately, the guards did not speak enough French to understand the slang and country patois the *vignerons* were using, because the sketches were often rude and made fun of the Germans.

Most of the time, the guards just shook their heads and walked away.

The real star of the evening, the wine, came out at inter- mission, but not before a few introductory remarks and paeans to wine.

'It is French to smile and sing,' one speaker said.

Another told the audience, 'Many of you do not come from wine areas, so tonight we want to introduce you to all the beauty and purity of wine.' He then began to rhapsodize about France's different wine regions. 'We take pride in each of them,' he said. 'Tonight we travel with Rabelais to the banks of the Loire, we visit the *chais* of Bordeaux and Cognac, we will bask in the luminous waves of light that flood the hills of the Languedoc and Roussillon, and the blue sky of Provence, we will savor the pleasures of Burgundy, the Kingdom of Tastevins, we will walk through Champagne, the country of Dom Pérignon, and over the hills of Jurançon. We shall go as far even as Suresnes, which should not be forgotten in any wine tour.'

Gaston Huet, however, had not forgotten what everyone was waiting for and pushed to the front of the stage. 'Enough,' he said. 'To talk about wine, that is a wonderful thing, but drinking it, that is much better.'

With those words, which were nearly drowned out by cheers, tables were set up and bottles of wine were carried out, one bottle to be shared among seven men. The men had to bring their own glasses, most of which were small glasses that had contained mustard sent from home.

Huet urged the men to quickly find their respective groups, the ones to which they had been assigned according to the wines they had chosen. 'We have tried to do this correctly,' Huet said. 'The wines that should be chilled were left outside. Those that should be served at room temperature were brought inside a couple of hours ago.'

With so little wine, however, Huet encouraged the men not to hurry. 'Take your time to appreciate what is in front of you,' he said. 'Admire it before you bring it to your lips, this mustard glass now filled with nectar, and take the time to remember that tonight our goal is to do nothing but glorify one of our greatest treasures.'

For a moment, it was almost as if the POWs were in a cathedral. The silence was that deep, even reverent.

And then a spontaneous cheer went up. 'I don't know when I have ever felt so moved,' Huet said.

Once everyone had been served and gaiety was in full swing, the priest and his choir took over, leading the POWs in rousing drinking songs and a few melancholy airs of France.

Huet retreated to a corner of the room to savor his little mustard glass of wine. He sighed with satisfaction. It was a dry white wine from the Loire Valley, not one from his vineyard, but a taste of home nonetheless. He looked deep into its greenish-golden color, then paused to breathe in its aromas, its flowery bouquet with hints of lemon, pear, apple and honey.

As he brought the glass to his lips, the winemaker in Huet took over. 'Hmmm, a bit acidic,' he thought. 'Green on the middle palate and the finish is weak. I doubt the Chenin Blanc grapes fully ripened.'

Such analysis lasted only a few brief seconds, however, as the wine lover in Huet suddenly emerged and the flavors and aromas of the wine enveloped him.

Years later, Huet would recall that moment, and all the work that went into planning and organizing the affair. 'It saved our sanity,' he said. 'I don't know what we would have done without that party. It gave us something to hold on to. It gave us a reason to get up in the morning, to get through each day. Talking about wine and sharing it made all of us feel closer to home, and more alive.'

Huet did not remember precisely what wine he drank or the vintage. 'It was nothing special and there was only a thimbleful,' he said, 'but it was glorious, and the best wine I ever drank.'

'The best wine I ever drank? Hmm. Let me think about that.'

Roger Ribaud was stretched out on his bunk at Oflag XVII A,

a German POW camp near Edelbach, in lower Austria. It was Christmas Day 1940, and all he and his fellow POWs could think about was home and everything they were missing.

'We had a marvelous Burgundy last Christmas with the turkey,' he said to his friend, who was sitting on the end of the bunk. 'It was a '37 Echézeaux, light in color but very rich. But the best I have ever had? No, I don't think so. There was a . . .' And on the conversation went as the men thought about wines they had drunk and the occasions on which they had drunk them.

'That's the thing,' Ribaud said. 'It all depends on who and what you drink them with. Haven't you ever had a cheap little rosé with a special girl and thought, "This is great!"'

After his friend had left, Ribaud continued lying in his bunk, staring at the ceiling and thinking. It was his first Christmas away from home and the loneliness was almost unbearable.

Dreaming, however, was not enough to get him through that bleak winter day, so he reached into his bag, took out a pencil.

On this Noël of 1940, I have begun to write a little book in an effort to dispel some of the sadness that we are living with and share some of the hopes we still cling to in our captivity, of returning to our homes and loved ones and the values we hold most dear.

Ribaud began to make a list of French wines, every wine he could think of: some he had tasted, others he hoped to taste. He sorted them by region: Burgundy, Bordeaux, Champagne, Alsace, the Loire. He classified them according to their finesse, body and bouquet.

By then, his friend was back and peering over his shoulder. He was impressed but told Ribaud he had made a few mistakes. You're wrong about the Nuits-Saint-Georges, he said. It's much more full-bodied.

Their ardent discussion soon drew the attention of several other prisoners from Barracks IV, among them the Marquis Bertrand de Lur-Saluces, owner of the famed Château d'Yquem. All were fascinated with what Ribaud was writing.

As snow continued to fall and the wind of those cold winter days whistled through the cracks of their barracks wall, the men gathered more and more frequently around the rough wooden table where Ribaud was writing. With no books or any other reference material, the discussions sometimes became heated.

'I want this book to be for everyone,' Ribaud told the others, 'not just for rich people. I want to be able to show that with all the wonderful things our France produces, everyone can live well and have a decent wine cellar. This is the responsibility of the *maître de maison*.'

What began to take shape, as Ribaud continued writing, was a kind of gastronomic guidebook in which Ribaud, a lawyer by training, noted the food he had eaten with various wines and whether he thought the combinations worked.

In the same breath, however, he worried about what the Germans were doing, and feared that many of the greatest wines would be seized and 'prematurely sacrificed' – that is, consumed before they were ready to be drunk. He could easily imagine a group of young soldiers washing down a plate of sauerkraut and sausage with a rich velvety Margaux. The thought made him shudder.

> *I hope, dear reader, for your own satisfaction and that of your friends and family, that when this war finally ends, you will still find that the most venerable bottles you have hidden from the Germans are still safe, that they will have escaped the torment of these years and be ready to fête their resurrection.*

Now, more than ever, Ribaud was convinced that the book he was writing was important.

He called it *Le Maître de Maison de Sa Cave à Sa Table* (*The Head of the Household from His Cellar to His Table*). 'This is a memoir of great food and wine and how they can be brought into perfect harmony,' he wrote in the introduction.

Suddenly, the long cold lonely days seemed shorter. Ribaud saved every scrap of paper he could find, including the wrapping paper on packages from home, so that he would have something to write on. And every spare minute, that is what he did, work on his book. He asked other POWs about their favorite wine-and-food combinations, what grapes grew best in their region and how they prepared certain foods.

Over time, he compiled a huge core of information and knowledge, not only about the more famous wines but about small country ones that were barely known outside their villages. There was Crépy, a white semi-sparkling wine from the Haute-Savoie on the French side of Lake Geneva, Vic-sur-Seille, a *vin gris* from the Lorraine, and Irouléguy, a wine that can be either red, white or rosé and comes from the slopes of the Pyrenees. The Crépy, Ribaud said, is wonderful with cooked shellfish and very spicy dishes. The light, pleasant fruitiness of the Vic-sur-Seille, he said, makes it a wonderful match for a *tourte-chaude*, a crusty, creamy potpie filled with ham and cheese. Irouléguy, on the other hand, is more suited to anchovies and sardines, oily salty foods of the Basque country.

Ribaud stressed that one did not have to be an expert to know these things, that most of this could be learned by reading, tasting and talking to others. Nor was it necessary to have a wine cellar that was stocked with every wine in the world. Better, he said, to have a *cave* with wines you like and which fit your budget. To help in this process, Ribaud drew up a chart for matching wine and food.

'The choice of wine is specific to what you want it to do,' he explained. 'It can bring out the characteristics of each dish, or it can establish the importance you want to give each dish.'

For an hors d'oeuvre such as *aspics de foie gras*, Ribaud suggested a Brut champagne, a white Hermitage or a white wine from Corsica or Provence. Oysters, on the other hand, called for a white Graves from Bordeaux. However, if that was not in your *cave*, try a Vouvray, a Pouilly-Fuissé or a Cérons.

Ribaud cautioned that regional characteristics should be carefully considered. A foie gras from Périgord should be accompanied by a sweet white Sauternes because the goose, fed primarily on cornmeal noodles and mush, is larger and fattier. The smaller Strasbourg goose, fed on wheat noodles, produces a foie gras with less fat and therefore should be accompanied by a hearty red Pommard.

Ribaud realized that because of the food shortage in France, nothing was going to be wasted, and he had ideas for wines to go with every conceivable dish. For the hungry Bordelais who had been trapping pigeons in the city square, he recommended a Moulis, a Margaux or a wine from Château Beychevelle.

For those who bartered wine for something to eat, pork chops from a freshly slaughtered pig, for instance, Ribaud suggested a Santenay or some other light red from Burgundy.

For breaded pigs' ears, he proposed a woody, straw-flavored Arbois or an inky black wine from Cahors. For pigs' tails, it was a Joigny, a minor red wine from northern Burgundy, or Bouzy, a still red wine from Champagne. Pigs' feet, or pigs' trotters, required an unfinished champagne or a robust white from Algeria.

Brains, Ribaud said, require serious thought. Much depends on how they are prepared. Served in a browned butter sauce, he suggested a glorious Montrachet or white Mercurey, wines that would enhance but not overpower the delicate, if unusual, flavor of the *cervelle*. But if the brains were deep-fried, a more rustic wine such as a Viré or a white Mâcon would be more appropriate.

Ribaud's book covered everything from the first course to dessert. He described what to drink with grapefruit (a Condrieu), stuffed cabbage (Chassagne-Montrachet) and stuffed carp (Chablis or Cassis).

For frogs, Ribaud would have served a Saumur from the Loire Valley or a Sylvaner from Alsace. Snails would go well with a cold Chablis or a white Hermitage, even a white from Algeria.

What was essential to remember, he said, was that wine can bring a special quality to any meal, whether it is highlighted by a great rack of lamb (a Pauillac or Saint-Estèphe) or a *croque-monsieur*, a grilled ham and cheese sandwich (a Chinon or Auxey-Duresses).

'It is an art to choose the best moment to savor the great wines and select the dishes that will artistically blend the aromas and flavors of the wine and food,' he wrote.

The wines Ribaud chose during his prison days could only be savored in his imagination, but they nevertheless provided comfort. 'They were like a tree we could hang on to,' he said. 'A tree whose roots were deeply anchored in the soil of our country and whose branches spread throughout the world.'

After the war, his book was published to great acclaim and hailed as one of the first books that paid serious attention to regional wines and food.

Roger Ribaud sent a copy to each of his fellow prisoners of war. 'I hope this will help erase the pain of our imprisonment and yet be a souvenir of friendship and the years that we shared together.'

EIGHT

Saving the Treasure

CHAMPAGNE CACHE IN FOXHOLE

With the American Third Army, West of Bastogne, Belgium, Jan. 8 (AP) – Lieut. William T. McClelland of 318 Forest Avenue, Ben Avon, Pa., may dig plenty of foxholes in this combat area, but it is doubtful whether he will maintain the standard set by his first. While excavating for his first combat-zone home, he uncovered a cache of 400 bottle [sic] of champagne and other wines.

—*The New York Times*, Jan. 9, 1945

The treasure was everywhere: in wine cellars, warehouses, ports, as well as on trains and airplanes. Some of it was even buried in the ground.

But when Allied leaders, in 1943, began laying plans for Operation Overlord, the code name for the Allied invasion of northwestern Europe, treasure was the last thing on their minds. Their goal was to defeat Hitler and bring the Third Reich to its knees.

Nevertheless, saving the treasure, 'France's most precious jewel' as one French leader described it, became a prime objective.

It had rained heavily most of the night. Although fields were muddy and skies still threatened, Jean-Michel Chevreau was eager to start work. His vines had just begun to flower and he wanted to see how they had withstood the storm.

Pulling on a sweater, the Loire Valley winemaker glanced out the window and suddenly stopped. To his amazement, not a single German soldier was in sight. Troops who had been there the day before and had occupied his village for four years had completely vanished, almost as if they had never been there.

The reason quickly became clear. It was D-Day, June 6, 1944. The long-awaited invasion of Europe was underway. Hitler and his generals were desperately pulling troops from the Loire Valley and other parts of France and rushing them to Normandy.

For Georges Hugel, the landings did not come as a total surprise. On that late spring day, he was at home in Alsace recuperating from wounds received on the Russian front. He had set up three radios within arm's reach of his bed, one of them tuned to Radio Berlin, another to Radio Vichy and one to the BBC in London. Georges kept switching among them; he sensed something was going on.

For several days, Radio London had been increasing the number of cryptic messages it broadcast, such as 'The apple trees are blooming,' 'Jean, put on your hat,' and 'The speckled cat has meowed three times.' On June 5, 1944, there were eight hours of these 'action messages.'

The next day, the pain in Georges's feet woke him very early. He automatically reached across and turned on the radios, one after another, rotating the dials for the best reception. Something about the urgency in the BBC broadcast caught his ear, and Georges turned it up.

'This morning at six-thirty, the combined forces . . .'

Georges fell back in his bed. 'It's about time,' he thought.

It was the largest sea and air offensive ever mounted. Five Allied divisions, 7,000 ships and landing craft along with 24,000 American and British paratroopers were involved. The paratroopers arrived first, just after midnight, and took up positions on the flanks of the invasion beaches. Six hours later, the main assault force landed on beaches code-named Utah, Omaha, Gold, Juno and Sword. As ships and landing craft bombarded German positions, thousands of troops swept ashore.

All day long, Georges was glued to his radios, checking one and then another for the latest news. He listened as Charles de Gaulle addressed the people of France: 'The supreme battle has begun!

After so many battles, so much fury, so much sorrow, the time is here for the decisive confrontation that has been awaited for so long.'

No one followed the drama more closely than France's one and a half million prisoners of war who had been languishing in POW camps for more than four years. One of them, Gaston Huet, heard about D-Day over a radio he and other prisoners had made and managed to conceal from their guards. 'It was a moment of great joy for us,' Huet said. 'We thought we would soon be going home, maybe even in time for the harvest.'

Their exhilaration was shared by winegrowers throughout France. News of the landings sent many straight to their vineyards to assess the conditions and speculate: 'If it doesn't rain too much, if there's no mildew, if we get fertilizer, if, if, if . . .' And the biggest 'if' of all, if we win and the war is over by fall, maybe we can make some good wine.

Their hopes were premature, for the Germans did not go quietly. Instead, they dug in their heels and retaliated more ferociously than ever against all who opposed them.

That is what happened in Comblanchien, a tiny village of winegrowers and quarry workers in the heart of Burgundy's Côte d'Or. For a long time, the Germans had been convinced it was a Resistance stronghold. One train after another was blown up in the region, and there was so much sabotage that German units became skittish, refusing to allow trains to pass until the water tank of each station had been filled. The Maquis had often hidden in them to stage ambushes. Although many Maquisards drowned when the Nazis suddenly filled the tanks, the attacks and sabotage continued.

On August 21, about 9:30 P.M., eleven-year-old Jacky Cortot was finishing dinner when gunfire suddenly erupted. The electricity went out, then came back on. Jacky rushed to the window of the kitchen and, with his mother, peeked out through the closed shutters. They saw flames shooting up from a house and barn just down the street. A minute later, they heard the sound of wine bottles being broken and cries of 'Help, help!'

'The Germans are burning people alive in their homes,' Jacky's mother screamed. She ran to another window. Several other houses were in flames too. 'Run, hide in the vineyard,' she told Jacky. Pressing some money and important papers into his hand, she warned, 'Stay there and don't move until I come for you.'

Jacky slipped out of the house and into the nearby vines. He was not alone. A dozen other children, some with their mothers, were already there.

Crouching in the vines, the little group watched as one house after another was set on fire. Throughout the night, they heard the clock on the *mairie* sound the hour, 'each hour increasing our fear and anxiety,' Jacky wrote in a memoir. 'Would we still be alive at dawn?'

About five o'clock in the morning, Jacky saw his own house burned. Two hours after that, smoke began pouring out of the church. 'The steeple itself burned away, leaving only the four beams supporting the bell,' Jacky recalled. 'The bell was so hot, it turned red, until finally the whole structure fell. All that was left standing was the confessional.'

When it was finally over, eight people had been killed, fifty-two houses had been burned to the ground along with the church, and at least 175 villagers were left homeless. Among them was Comblanchien's deputy mayor, Ernest Chopin, and his family, who had hidden in their wine cellar when their house above was set on fire.

Chopin emerged the next morning and learned that twenty-three of his neighbors had been arrested and taken to Dijon. Fearing they would be executed, he rushed there and arrived just as the Germans were lining them up against a wall. Chopin begged the Germans to spare them. Eleven were eventually freed, the young and the elderly. The rest were deported to work camps in Germany.

*   *   *

Pierre Taittinger knew what the Germans were capable of. He remembered how frightened he was when his son François was thrown into jail for sending weinführer Otto Klaebisch adulterated champagne. He also recalled how worried he and other champagne producers had been when they were threatened with imprisonment for protesting the arrest of Robert-Jean de Vogüé.

But now, Pierre Taittinger was truly terrified. He was afraid his beloved city of Paris was about to be destroyed, and no one seemed more certain to do it than General Dietrich von Choltitz.

Von Choltitz was an old-school Prussian officer who had supervised the destruction of Rotterdam in 1940 and Sebastopol in 1942. He arrived in Paris in August 1944 with Hitler's orders ringing in his ears: 'Turn Paris into a front-line city; destroy it rather than surrender it to the enemy!'

Taittinger, the Vichy-appointed mayor of Paris, knew he had to do something – anything – to save it. Police, postal, telephone and railway workers had gone on strike. Barricades appeared in the streets as the Resistance intensified calls for insurrection. Realizing that they could be facing a full-scale uprising, the Germans decided to leave the city to combat troops and began pulling out all other personnel.

It was a surreal sight as Parisians sitting at sidewalk cafés watched what one resident, Jean Galtier-Boissière, called *la grande fuite des Fritz*, or the big flight of the Fritz. As he wrote in his journal on August 18, 'I saw dozens, hundreds of trucks, overcrowded cars and vehicles pulling cannons; there were ambulances full of wounded; they followed each other, crossed in front of each other and tried to pass each other. Monocled generals with blond elegantly dressed women on their arms poured out of sumptuous hotels near the Étoile and got into their sparkling open touring cars, looking for all the world as if they were off to a fashionable beach.'

But the most startling sight was the stream of loot flowing out with the departing occupiers. According to Larry Collins and

Dominique Lapierre in *Is Paris Burning?*, 'Paris was being emptied by the truckload. Bathtubs, bidets, rugs, furniture, radios, cases and cases of wine – all rode past the angry eyes of Paris that morning.'

A day later, sporadic street fighting broke out, orchestrated primarily by communists in the Resistance, whose slogan *Chacun Son Boche* ('To Each His Boche') soon became a battle cry.

Heeding the cry was Frédéric Joliot-Curie. In 1939, he had headed a team of physicists who were partially successful in producing the first atomic chain reaction. Now, however, Joliot-Curie was concerned with a different kind of reaction, one produced by mixing sulfuric acid and potassium in bottles. He was making Molotov cocktails for the Resistance. There was only one problem: not enough bottles. Joliot-Curie had found a few in the laboratory where his mother-in-law, Marie Curie, had discovered radium, but he needed more. With the help of friends, he found them in the cellar of the Préfecture de Police: dozens of cases of champagne, all of the bottles full and all bearing the label of Pierre Taittinger's champagne house.

With only momentary hesitation and slight regret, Joliot-Curie and his colleagues began uncorking the bottles and pouring their precious contents down the drain.

Taittinger, meanwhile, had finally gotten the appointment he had requested with von Choltitz. The Paris mayor walked into the Hôtel Meurice, down its marble-floored corridor and up the stairs to the sumptuous room that was the headquarters of the commander of Paris. The ivory-colored paint on the *boiserie* was nicked and the gilded trim had tarnished and flaked off in places, but with its massive crystal chandelier, it was still imposing. Von Choltitz, in his neatly pressed uniform, his medals gleaming, fit in perfectly.

The general got right to the point. Paris, he warned, would suffer the fate of Warsaw if there was an uprising by the Resistance. If any Germans were fired at, he would 'burn all the houses in that particular block and execute every inhabitant.'

Taittinger pleaded with von Choltitz to reconsider. 'Paris,' he said, 'is one of the few great cities of Europe that remain intact; you must help me to save it!'

Von Choltitz replied that he had his orders. In the same breath, however, he admitted that he had no wish to destroy Paris. Leading his guest to the balcony, he confessed that one of his great pleasures was looking outside at the city and watching people move about.

The reflective, almost philosophic comments surprised Taittinger, who tried to take advantage of what he sensed was a change in the general's mood. Turning to von Choltitz, he said, 'Generals rarely have the power to build, they more often have the power to destroy.' He urged von Choltitz to imagine what it would be like to return to Paris one day and stand on the same balcony. 'You look to the left, at the Perrault colonnade, with the great Palais du Louvre on the right, then the Palais de Gabriel and the Place de la Concorde,' Taittinger said. 'And among these splendid buildings, each one charged with history, you are able to say, "It was I, Dietrich von Choltitz, who, on a certain day, had the power to destroy this but I saved it for humanity." Is that not worth all a conqueror's glory?'

Taittinger's eloquence had a telling effect. 'You are a good advocate for Paris. You have done your job well,' von Choltitz said, but he did not tell the politician what he would do.

Taittinger returned to his office to wait. He knew that explosives had been planted throughout the city. In addition, 22,000 troops, mostly SS, 100 tiger tanks and 90 bombers were standing by, waiting for the signal to level the city. That signal, however, was never given.

For the first time in his life, von Choltitz disobeyed an order. On August 25, when General Leclerc's French 2nd Armored Division rolled into Paris, the German general surrendered the city intact.

The following day, Charles de Gaulle made a triumphal entry into Paris with a parade down the Champs-Elysées. Excited French soldiers, a bottle in one hand and a rifle in the other, scampered across the city's rooftops looking for German snipers. One of them,

Yves Fernique, was checking out the roof of the Hôtel Continental when the maître d' appeared with a silver tray, a crystal glass and a cold bottle of Sancerre.

But the Germans were not quite through with Paris. While they did not try to destroy the Eiffel Tower, the Arc de Triomphe or any of the city's other great landmarks, they did go after a different kind of monument: Paris's Halle aux Vins, the city's wholesale wine center.

Earlier, before von Choltitz surrendered, the Germans had tried unsuccessfully to commandeer the stocks which leading wine merchants stored there. Now, as celebrations were taking place in other parts of the city, German planes suddenly descended on the wine center and dropped several bombs. Champagne corks popped and thousands of valuable bottles of cognac and other spirits burst like bombs from the heat of the fire. As firemen poured streams of water on the wreckage, bottles continued to explode, sending showers of glass into the air. Soon, only the walls of the Halle aux Vins were left. Inside were piles of melted glass that had been stores of outstanding wine.

One wholesaler tried to make the best of it. Retrieving two large casks of Bordeaux from the inferno, he hooked up a rubber hose, and, as one witness recalled, 'began serving the wine in quaint, shallow silver cups to firemen and anyone else who seemed thirsty. It was being poured like water, and more was hitting the ground than the cups.'

About the only one who did not lift a glass that day was Charles de Gaulle. At the Hôtel de Ville, Paris's city hall, a Vichy-appointed official offered the general a flute of champagne; de Gaulle refused it, saying he did not drink with collaborators or those soft on Nazis.

The bombing of the Halle aux Vins sent shivers down the spines of wine merchants in Bordeaux. They could easily see their precious stocks suffering a similar fate.

Bordeaux was still occupied by 30,000 German troops, but

everyone, including the Germans, knew that it was just a matter of time before they had to pull out. As in Paris, the question was whether there would be anything left after they did so. Much of the city, especially its port, had been planted with 1,700-pound bombs, which were to be set off when troops abandoned the city.

With millions of bottles of wine stored in warehouses around the port and millions of others hidden away, destruction of the port would spell disaster for Bordeaux's wine trade. The worst seemed inevitable with the Allies on the march and activity by the Resistance increasing.

Last night, oil reservoirs were bombed. Machine-gun fire is constant, wrote May-Eliane Miaihle de Lencquesaing in her diary. *But I am repairing the flag! The Anglo-Americans are coming toward Bordeaux and we are waiting for them!*

Louis Eschenauer was waiting too – apprehensively. The 'king of Bordeaux' had made a great deal of money selling wine to his close friends from the Third Reich. He worried about what would happen to him now, so he made some final calls to his German friends. 'Don't blow up Bordeaux when you leave,' he begged.

One of the first he called was Captain Ernst Kühnemann, commander of the port. It would be the captain's job to carry out the destruction when such an order was issued. With wine merchants and others in Bordeaux pushing him to use his influence, Eschenauer invited his distant cousin to lunch. Kühnemann, a wine merchant himself, was not surprised. He loved good food and wine as much as Louis did and the two had dined together regularly, often at Louis's restaurant, Le Chapon Fin.

Eschenauer pleaded with his cousin to save the port, describing in detail the anguish and hardship its destruction would cause. Kühnemann listened sympathetically. He said he did not want to destroy the port, that such a move now would be nothing more than an absurd act of vengeance. 'But if Berlin orders me to do it, I will be in a very difficult position,' he said.

On August 19, an order marked 'top secret' and numbered 1–122–144 arrived at Kühnemann's headquarters. Destruction of the port was to start in five days at precisely 1700 hours. The atmosphere in Bordeaux suddenly changed.

> *The city has been closed off, surrounded by German troops. It is like a state of siege. There is no water, no gas, no electricity, absolutely no food to be seen, and no traffic either.* (Diary of May-Eliane Miaihle de Lencquesaing.)

While Kühnemann agonized about what to do, a subordinate who shared his commanding officer's feelings took matters into his own hands and blew up the blockhouse where the detonators were kept. The blast killed fifteen German soldiers and was heard miles away. German authorities mistakenly blamed the Resistance.

> *Aug. 24: Last night, a terrific explosion from the direction of Bordeaux. Unclear why. Although the Maquis has liberated Château Beychevelle and other parts of Bordeaux, we still hesitate to fly the flag because there is only one Resistance group near us. Nevertheless, at 5:30 this afternoon, we sang the Marseillaise with our staff. The Americans are only fifteen kilometers from Bordeaux!'* (Diary of May-Eliane Miaihle de Lencquesaing.)

In fact, the Americans were nowhere near Bordeaux, but the Germans did not know that and began making preparations to evacuate. Fearing the Resistance was far stronger than it was, the Germans decided to bluff, warning they still had enough explosives to destroy Bordeaux if their troops were fired on during withdrawal. The Resistance agreed to hold its fire.

On the evening of August 27, German troops began evacuating Bordeaux. The last one out was Ernst Kühnemann.

FAMOUS WINE COUNTRY FOUGHT OVER

Rome, Sept. 10 – The French and Americans have been fighting the Germans over perhaps the most famous vineyards in the world – the Burgundy district. How much damage has been done to this heritage has not yet been reliably assessed, but, according to many reports, the Germans have already gone a good distance toward the total ruination of the envied countryside.

—*The New York Times*, Sept. 11, 1944

There was just one problem with that report. It was wrong. The vineyards of Burgundy survived. The Germans and Allies may have fought *over* them but they did not fight *in* them.

It was called 'the Champagne Campaign,' a name conjured up almost at the very moment French and American troops landed on the Côte d'Azur in southern France. 'We had put down a tremendous barrage before dashing for the shore,' wrote British war correspondent Wynford Vaughan-Thomas. 'We were expecting to be mown down by machine guns but not a single bullet whistled past us: the Germans had tactfully pulled out a few hours before, and in their place an immaculately dressed Frenchman advanced out of the dust of war. He carried a tray with a magnum of champagne and ten glasses. "Welcome, gentlemen, welcome," he beamed; "but if I may venture a little criticism, you *are* four years late!"'

The goal of the Champagne Campaign, officially known as Operation Anvil, was to push north through the Rhône Valley and Burgundy and link up with forces which had landed in Normandy. Sometimes it was difficult to keep that goal in mind. There were too many distractions.

Among them was a sumptuous watering hole called the Hôtel Negresco, which the Americans had taken over for their head-quarters. The Negresco, located in Nice on the Riviera, was known for its fine cuisine, exquisite wines and one of the best nightclubs

in the world. One of those who 'checked in' as often as possible was
Sergeant Major Virgil West. 'We would go out on patrol during the
day,' he said, 'maybe getting into a little firefight, perhaps getting all
bloody and muddy in the process, then five hours later be sitting in
one of the biggest nightclubs in the world with a babe and a bottle
of champagne.'

But it was not all babes and bubbly. According to another soldier,
'The overwhelming thing was the strange character of the combat
there. It was hard, it was tough and we lost a lot of men. We didn't
destroy the beautiful Riviera, so we'd go back and have a bottle of
wine and a bath, then go back up into the mountains for another
battle.' Even when bullets were flying, however, soldiers described
how 'women kept trying to give us wine and flowers.'

Other gifts were sometimes offered as well. Just after arriving,
war correspondent Vaughan-Thomas was sitting at an outdoor café,
rhapsodizing about how the wine he was sipping reminded him of
a beautiful woman, when he was suddenly confronted by 'a large
imposing lady followed by five charming girls.' It turned out she was
the madame from the local *maison de tolérance*. Pointing to her girls,
she said, 'For you, the brave liberator.' When Vaughan-Thomas
drew back, she quickly added, 'Have no fear. My ladies have
been patriotic. Only the one with crossed eyes slept with the
Germans.'

While the Champagne Campaign never captured the public's
imagination as D-Day did, it did signal the first time, and probably
the only time, that gastronomic considerations had a direct bearing
on military planning. It was not by chance that French general
Lucien de Monsabert, who helped plan the campaign, made sure
that French troops advanced up the western side of the Rhône,
where the best vineyards were planted. The Americans went up
the other side, where the lesser growths were.

The French general later explained his strategy to Vaughan-
Thomas. 'Their job was vital,' said de Monsabert of his American
allies, 'but the vinously-minded historian will note that it did not

take them near a single vineyard of quality. Now follow the advance of the French army. Swiftly they possessed themselves of Tavel, and after making sure that all was well with one of the finest *vin rosés* in France, struck fiercely for Châteauneuf-du-Pape. The Côte Rôtie fell to a well-planned flanking attack.'

Vaughan-Thomas captured the spirit of the Champagne Campaign in a delightful reminiscence entitled *How I Liberated Burgundy*. At one point, he described meeting an American officer who was clearly disturbed about something.

'Thomas,' he said, 'you're going back to see the Frogs this afternoon, I hear. Well, there's a little problem that's got us kinda worried. I've got a feeling that the Frogs are doing a little bit of a go-slow on us. I've a hunch that our friends are staying a bit too long in this place Chalon something or other.'

'Chalon something or other' was actually Chalon-sur-Saône, the southern gateway to the famous slopes of the Côte d'Or, or the Golden Escarpment, where Burgundy's greatest vineyards lay. And the American officer was right; the French were doing a 'go-slow' in order to avoid turning the vineyards into a battlefield.

'I need hardly tell you,' a French intelligence officer told Vaughan-Thomas later that day, 'the terrible consequences of such a decision. It would mean war, mechanized war, among the *grands crus!* Would France forgive us if we allowed such a thing to happen? We must not forget 1870.' That was when one of the last battles of the Franco-Prussian War took place around Nuits-Saint-Georges as German troops swept through the vineyards of La Tâche, Romanée-Conti and Richebourg.

'This must never be allowed to happen again,' the officer said.

Moments later, a young officer burst in, hurriedly saluted and, with a smile illuminating his face, declared, 'Great news, *mon colonel*, we have found the weak point in the German defenses. Every one is on a vineyard of inferior quality.'

General de Monsabert was quickly informed and the attack began. Within twenty-four hours, the Germans were 'bundled out of Burgundy,' Vaughan-Thomas said. 'A blown bridge here, a demolished house there, what could these matter beside the great overriding fact of the undamaged vineyards stretching mile after mile before us.'

Ten years later, Vaughan-Thomas wrote, 'Time softens controversy and the history of distant wars grows mellow like '49 Burgundy.' The controversy he was alluding to involved a gift the French military gave to their American allies as their drive up the Rhône reached its end.

To show their appreciation, the French decided to present the Americans with an assortment of the finest wines Burgundy had to offer. Vaughan-Thomas volunteered to help collect wine for the occasion, a mission that led him to at least twenty wine cellars and enabled him to fill his jeep with some of the rarest treasures of Burgundy. These he then handed over to the Americans.

'All of them? Let me be honest,' Vaughan-Thomas wrote. 'Some of them, by an unaccountable chance of wartime transport, found their way to my cellar in the year after the war.' The rest, he dutifully surrendered to a young officer.

'These are the greatest wines of France,' he said. 'Guard them with care; rest them; then make certain they are at room temperature before they are served.'

'Don't worry,' the American replied. 'The Doc knows all about this Frog liquor, and while we are about it, we'll invite them over to drink it.'

The party took place in an eighteenth-century palace with the French guests advancing up a flight of stairs while the American command, as Vaughan-Thomas noted, 'awaited them in a salon worthy of a reception for Madame de Pompadour.' As trumpets sounded, a column of waiters marched in bearing the bottles on silver trays. Immediately, Vaughan-Thomas sensed something was wrong. 'My heart gave a warning thump – the bottles of Burgundy were bubbling gently. "We're in luck," my American colonel whispered to me, "the Doc's hotted up this stuff with medical alcohol!"'

As Vaughan-Thomas later described it, 'A look of incredulous horror flickered over the faces of the French. All eyes were turned on General de Monsabert. He had led them through the deserts of North Africa and over the snow-clad mountains of Italy. Faced with the greatest crisis so far in Franco-American relations, how would he behave? He fixed his staff with the stern glare of command. "Gentlemen, take up your glasses." Reluctantly the French reached out their hands. "To our comrades in arms, *les braves Américains*," he ordered in a ringing tone. He drained his glass with panache – every drop. Then, in a quieter voice that only the nearest Frenchmen and myself could hear, he murmured, "Liberation, liberation, what crimes have been committed in thy name!"'

Despite that hiccup, there is no denying that the Champagne Campaign was one of the most successful operations of the war. Meeting only token resistance, the French and American armies moved faster up the Rhône Valley than anyone dreamed was possible. Along the way, they were aided by an unusual kind of early-warning system: if towns and villages were decorated with flowers and flags, and people were standing along the roadside holding out bottles of wine, they knew the Germans had fled and the way ahead was clear.

'Of course, we drank some very good wine, but not as much as we would have liked because we were pretty busy and moving quite fast,' Jean Miaihle said. A few months earlier, Jean had been making copper sulfate under the noses of the Germans. When Bordeaux was liberated, he joined the French army as it fought and imbibed its way up the Rhône. Sometimes people would invite Jean and his buddies into their cellars and uncork a few bottles they had hidden away. 'One thing I remember was finding a lot of bad bottles with good labels,' Jean said. 'This was the wine people had been passing off to the Germans. They saved the good stuff for us.'

During the night of September 6, Robert Drouhin was awakened by something he had not heard for days: silence. He, his mother and sisters had been spending most of their time in their wine cellar because of heavy bombing and shelling near Chalon-sur-Saône. That night, however, the bombing suddenly stopped. They all sat up on their mattresses on the floor of the *cave* and listened. There was no doubt about it. The bombing had ceased. When they verified that it was safe, the family emerged from the cellar and went upstairs to bed.

Around six o'clock in the morning, they were awakened again, this time by a different sound. Robert jumped from his bed, went to the window and peeked out. There, he saw an American jeep make a U-turn in the square in front of the church, then leave. A short time later, another vehicle arrived and soldiers got out. They were wearing American uniforms. Robert watched as they undid a large roll of white fabric on the paving stones and made a cross with it. The cross was a sign to let Allied planes know Beaune had been liberated.

It was the beginning of what Robert would later call 'a day when everything was extraordinary.' Church bells began ringing as Beaune filled up with tanks and other military vehicles. People poured into the streets to celebrate what the local newspaper called 'this blessed and magnificent hour of liberation. French and Allied flags bloomed from the windows. Long-hidden in the attics, they now came out to float on the wind of liberation.'

Bottles and barrels of wine also came floating out as residents toasted and cheered their liberators. The cheers, said one person, could be heard forty kilometers away.

'Beaune was liberated with American equipment and American chewing gum,' recalled Robert Drouhin. 'It was a *scène classique*, like something out of the movies.'

Yet while celebrations were happening in one place, fighting was still going on in another. Mademoiselle Yvonne Tridon, secretary for the Syndicat des Négociants in Beaune, was dancing in the street with an American soldier when someone stopped and began berating her. 'Aren't you ashamed to be celebrating when people are still fighting?' the person asked. Tridon was taken by surprise. It had never occurred to her that the war was still going on.

Less than twenty kilometers to the north, German troops were trying to escape from the Château du Clos de Vougeot, a Burgundian landmark which they had seized at the beginning of the war to store their ammunition. They had loaded the ammunition on a train and were trying to get it back to Germany. A few hundred meters from the château, the Resistance opened fire on the train, setting off the ammunition it was carrying. The explosion blew the roof off the château, scattering its 200,000 ancient tiles over a three-acre area. The sound was heard all the way to Beaune.

But it was the sound of a quiet knock on the door that Robert Drouhin remembers most. He ran down the stairs to see who it was. Standing there was his father. Nine months after fleeing through his wine cellar to escape the Gestapo, Maurice Drouhin, who apparently had been hiding in the Hospices de Beaune, had come home.

'Hey, Al, get over here! We need you right away.'

Al Ricciuti, a boy from Baltimore and lifelong Orioles fan, was a translator in Patton's Third Army. He had been drafted and landed on Utah Beach just after D-Day. Now he was participating in the liberation of France. His unit was bivouacked outside the Champagne village of Avenay-Val-d'Or, a town his father had marched through in World War I.

Al was planning to do some sightseeing and take a few pictures for his father, when his buddies suddenly hollered at him. He rushed over to see what they wanted. 'These girls are trying to tell us something and we can't understand a thing they're saying.' There were three girls and they were all talking at once, and pointing back toward a house. Al, whose mother was French, listened and then explained, 'These girls are sisters. They say they've hidden two U.S. airmen from a B-17 in their house.'

Al and the others followed the girls to their house to get the

airmen who had been shot down. After the fliers had been taken
to the American camp, Al went back to talk to the girls and their
parents. They described how they had found the men and took
care of them during the last days of the German occupation.

The Revoltes, a family of small champagne growers, invited Al
to stay for dinner. Paulette, one of the daughters, took him on a
tour of their vineyards. 'We were lucky this time,' she told Al. 'No
real battles here, not like World War I, but we're still worried.'
Like many throughout Champagne, the Revoltes had heard that
the Germans had planted dynamite in some of the cellars of the
big champagne houses. Paulette wondered if it were true.

Al confessed he was not sure. He said the Germans had mined
some of the bridges but did not have time to detonate them because
Patton came in so fast. Patton, he said, laughing, would be very
upset to see any champagne ruined. 'He is a man with a terrific
palate,' Al said. 'He usually drinks the best whiskeys, but he loves
champagne too, and he knows his stuff.'

Champagne, however, was something Al knew nothing about.
He admitted he had never even tasted it. At dinner, the Revolte
family made sure he could never say that again as they brought
out the whole range of champagnes for him, from the sweetest
to the driest. It proved to be a revelation to the young man from
Baltimore, who had, until then, considered himself a beer man. 'I
tried some, and I thought, "Hey, this is for me."'

But there was little time to savor it. Patton was moving swiftly,
and the following morning the U.S. Third Army was on the march
again. Paulette came to see Al off. 'I'll write,' he promised as they
moved out.

When the Germans in Alsace realized how fast the Allies were
moving, they began raiding the cellars of winegrowers. People
including Georges Hugel watched in dismay as soldiers went from
one cellar to another, loading as much wine as they could carry onto
trucks and driving it to an airstrip outside Riquewihr. The cargo was

then transferred to airplanes, which began revving up their engines. The first plane lurched forward fifty meters, then came to a stop, as if someone had thrown out an anchor. None of the other planes, their engines groaning under the exertion, could take off either.

'Their planes were too light,' Georges said, 'and they didn't have enough fuel to take off fully loaded, so, fortunately, most of our wine remained in the country.'

Alsace was the last part of France to be liberated, and it happened just as the harvest was getting underway.

'It was a huge harvest but also a sad one,' said Georges's brother André. Their father was in hiding from the Gestapo after refusing to join the Nazi Party and their brother Johnny was still in the German army. Georges himself was still recuperating from the wounds he suffered in Russia and could only get around on crutches.

Bringing in the grapes was nearly impossible. Many vineyards had been sown with anti-tank mines in anticipation of an Allied attack. There were also unexploded bombs that had been dropped by the Allies, a few of which went off when vineyard workers stepped on them. As grape picking got underway, Allied planes began attacking departing German convoys. Georges and André were bringing in a load of grapes when a plane, its machine guns firing, passed just yards over their heads. Georges pushed André down and fell beside him. Grapes and chunks of earth flew everywhere as bullets from the plane riddled the vineyard. When the two brothers got up, the first thing they saw was a German truck a short distance away in flames. But as the smoke cleared, they suddenly realized that several of their workers had been killed.

When Georges and André returned home, their mother told them that a German officer had just been there. She said she had been reluctant to let him in, but he had insisted. 'I have a message for you,' he told her. 'Madame, you may tell your husband that it is safe to come home.' Fearing a trap, Madame Hugel replied that she did not understand what the officer was talking about and that, in any case, she had no idea where her husband was. The German smiled grimly. 'Madame, you understood me perfectly. There is no longer any risk of him being arrested. The air is pure now. Everything here has changed.'

As the rumble of Allied artillery became louder, the Hugels and others huddled for protection in their wine cellars. On the night of December 3, mortar and artillery shells began landing in Riquewihr.

Two days later, the streets of Riquewihr were full of Texans, some in tanks, some herding German prisoners and others conducting house-to-house searches.

'We were stunned by how laid-back the Americans were and the absence of noise,' André Hugel said. 'The sound of their rubber-soled boots was such a change from the hob-nailed boots the Germans wore.'

It was 7:30 in the morning when the Americans, part of the 36th Infantry Division, headquartered in San Antonio, arrived. Grandpa Emile Hugel had awakened an hour earlier. When he realized Riquewihr had been liberated, he decided to put on his best suit to greet the Americans. As he was pulling on his pants, however, a nervous young GI looking for Germans burst into the room. At first, the eighty-year-old Hugel, whose eyesight was weak, did not realize who it was, but his grandson André, who accompanied the soldier, quickly explained. The old man was so overjoyed that he rushed across the bedroom and threw his arms around the American. As he did so, his pants dropped to the floor. The soldier was so startled that he leveled his gun at Hugel. The misunderstanding was quickly cleared up and the now impeccably dressed Emile soon joined the jubilant throngs outside.

The celebration was even more special for the Hugel family because Jean Hugel had emerged from hiding. He had been ensconced in a hotel in nearby Colmar, pretending to be one of the staff, when a friendly telephone operator called him and said, 'Monsieur Hugel, you can quit hiding now. The Americans are here.'

Once he was back, he began doing a little horse trading, bartering wine for fuel, one jerry can of wine for two jerry cans of fuel. The Texans considered it a bargain. So did Jean, who now could drive his car and truck again.

A week after Riquewihr's liberation, the Germans launched a counterattack to retake the town. As they raced through the village, the Texans fired at them from the windows of homes and buildings. Soon the cobblestone streets were filled with dead and wounded. Casualties were carried to the courtyard of the Hugels' winery, which the Americans had converted to a first-aid station and morgue.

Vineyards suffered as well. American tanks ground through fences and vines, some setting off land mines and unexploded shells as they attempted to drive the Germans back. As battles raged, an American plane crashed in the Hugels' vineyard, killing all aboard.

Similar scenes were taking place in towns and villages throughout Alsace. In Ammerschwihr, heavy bombardment by Allied planes sent residents scurrying to their wine cellars for safety. Dozens found shelter in the cellar of the Kuehn wine firm, whose name, ironically, was the *Cave de l'Enfer*, the Cellar of Hell. They were not alone, because the *cave* had already been filled with statues of saints from one of Ammerschwihr's churches. The statues had been placed there for safety. (People still refer to it as the time when the saints went to hell.)

The real inferno was upstairs. Fires burned everywhere as American planes, having spotted two German tanks, repeatedly bombed the sixteenth-century town in the belief that the Germans still held it. The Americans did not realize that the tanks had been abandoned and that all of the Germans had left.

As terrified residents tried to put out the fires, the water suddenly stopped as wells ran dry. A bomb had hit the reservoir. In desperation, people began hauling bottles and barrels of wine from their cellars, hooking hoses to the casks and spraying the contents on the fires. Jean Adam was thirteen years old as he helped his mother and father try to save the family winery. 'The wine we were using was pretty generic, very low in alcohol because harvests had been so bad, so it didn't cause any explosions,' Jean said. 'But it might have been different if we had been using Gewürztraminer.'

With their wine, the Adams were able to save their stable and animals but very little else. It was the same throughout Ammerschiwihr. Eighty-five percent of the town and many of the surrounding vineyards were destroyed.

In Riquewihr, Georges Hugel looked at the destruction with sadness and pain. He had witnessed the brutality of war as a German soldier on the Russian front, and nothing, he felt, could ever be as bad as that. But seeing his own home threatened and his friends and neighbors under attack convinced him there was something he had to do. 'I'm going back to war,' he told his family. 'I'm joining the French army.'

It was the worst news his parents could have imagined. One son still fighting for the Germans, and now one with the Allies.

NINE

Eagle's Nest

W here are the French?
     That was the question nearly every American soldier was asking as Allied forces moved through Germany.

With the war in its final days, the Allies were moving swiftly toward Berlin. Everyone, the Americans, British, French, Canadians and Russians, had wanted to get there first.

Another race was underway as well, this one across southern Germany toward Berchtesgaden, Hitler's retreat in the Bavarian Alps. For the French, the route held deep historical significance. It was the same path Napoleon took when his armies scored a great victory over the Austrians in Ulm in 1805. For a brief time, from 1809 to 1810, the region, including Berchtesgaden, had been under French rule.

History, however, was only part of the reason Berchtesgaden was so important. Of far greater importance was the treasure everyone knew was there. It included gold, currency from a dozen countries, priceless jewelry, masterpieces of art, luxury cars and something the French could hardly wait to get their hands on: hundreds of thousands of bottles of the world's greatest wine, wine that had been stolen from their country.

Berchtesgaden may have been Hitler's hideaway and the place where Himmler, Göring, Goebbels and others of the Nazi leadership had flocked for vacations, but it was also a storehouse, a veritable maze of underground cellars and passages that had been carved out for salt mines in the twelfth century. Now it served as a vast warehouse for loot the Nazis had collected during the war.

The race to recover that treasure began on April 22, 1945, when General Philippe Leclerc got the green light to take his 2nd Armored

Division back to Germany. Earlier that month, he had been pulled back to France by Charles de Gaulle, who decided he did not want to have any part of the country in the hands of Germans when Germany finally surrendered.

There were still several pockets of resistance, the main one around Royan on the tip of the Médoc peninsula, where German troops had orders to hold out until the last bullet. Royan was a vital piece of real estate because it controlled traffic entering and leaving the port of Bordeaux. Without it, the Bordelais would have no way of shipping their wine to the rest of the world. Leclerc's orders were to clean it out.

He was furious. This was not where he wanted to be; the main action was in Germany. Leclerc, who had liberated Paris and Strasbourg, wanted to be there for the kill. He got de Gaulle to agree that as soon as his forces captured Royan, he would be sent right back to Germany.

Royan surrendered on April 18. Four days later, Leclerc and his men were on their way. Their dash across France was unprecedented. In a letter to his wife, Leclerc wrote, 'It will be terrible for my men if we miss this epic moment by only a few meters.' He was determined that would not happen. In just five days, Leclerc and his division had covered more than a thousand kilometers and crossed the Rhine into Germany.

To get into the action as quickly as possible, Leclerc agreed to break his division into separate units and attach them to American forces. His 5th Tactical Group was assigned to the American 21st Army Corps, whose destination was Berchtesgaden.

Side by side, like horses in a starting gate, they set off for the Bavarian town, each side determined to get there first.

Fearing the French might beat them, American commanders assigned the 5th Tactical Group a more distant objective, Salzburg, which was across the river from Berchtesgaden.

Not to be outmaneuvered, Leclerc ostensibly accepted the orders but broke his group into three subgroups. Two went to

Salzburg as the Americans instructed. The third kept moving toward Berchtesgaden. Its mission: get there before the Americans.

It did not take long for the Americans to realize that something was not quite right. The French unit that was supposed to be advancing on their right flank, the third subgroup, kept popping in and out of sight. Then it vanished altogether. When the Americans tried to make radio contact, there was only silence.

'After begging to hook up with us, they just disappeared,' grumbled one GI. 'One minute they were here, the next they were gone.'

By the time the Americans realized what had happened, the French were 200 kilometers down the road and closing in on their destination.

On May 4, with Berchtesgaden tantalizingly close – it was only fifty kilometers away – the Americans finally caught up. The French, they saw, had been held up at a ravine, pinned down by long-range fire from the SS. This was their big chance, the Americans decided. Turning their convoy around, they decided to take a more roundabout route to Berchtesgaden, the autobahn, gambling that the new fast highway Hitler had built to move his troops more quickly to the front would get them there first.

It was a bad decision. Late that afternoon, they ran into a bridge that had been blown out and were forced to spend the night there while engineers struggled to repair the structure.

The French, not wanting to take casualties at this late stage of the war, sat patiently at their position and waited out the SS. When the Germans ran out of ammunition and scattered, the French were on the move again.

Late that afternoon, a French tank column entered Berchtesgaden without firing a shot. It was led by a young man from Champagne. Bernard de Nonancourt could hardly believe he was there.

His first sight of Berchtesgaden on that fourth of May took his breath away. It was just as another visitor had described, 'a fairy-tale land with snowcapped mountains, dark green woods, tinkling icy

creeks and ginger-bread houses which were a delight for the eye.'
According to legend, somewhere in the crags of those mountains
were Barbarossa and his knights, lying in an enchanted sleep. One
day, it was said, Barbarossa would awake and usher in a golden age
of peace and prosperity for Germany. That time had not yet come.
As Barbarossa slept on, Adolf Hitler plunged the country into war
and ruin.

It was at Berchtesgaden that many of his plans for a Thousand-
Year Reich were first conceived. Over the years, the idyllic setting
was converted into a fortress. His rustic little chalet became a
monumental retreat bristling with antiaircraft guns and even a
smoke-generating machine that enveloped the area in a vast cloud
whenever there was danger of an air raid. Trees were chopped down
so that forest paths could be turned into paved roads. Tiny votive
chapels and villas were ripped out to make room for ugly concrete
buildings that housed troops, guests and a fleet of fancy cars.

But Hitler's most self-indulgent fantasy was an elevator that could
carry him to Eagle's Nest, his private mountaintop retreat several
thousand feet above Berchtesgaden. According to biographer Robert
Payne, 'It occurred to Hitler that the mountain could be tunneled
in such a way that he could be propelled up to the summit in an
elevator, thus permitting him to survey the surrounding landscape
like a god surveying all the kingdoms of the earth.'

It took workmen three years to cut the shaft out of solid rock.
The elevator they installed had a gold-plated door, carpeted floor
and cushioned seats. A bank of phones linked it with Berlin, Paris,
London and every other important city in the world. Although the
project cost 30 million marks, Hitler was pleased. It was a present
he had given himself for his fiftieth birthday.

Unfortunately, by the time Bernard de Nonancourt and his men
arrived, the elevator was out of order. The retreating Germans had
sabotaged it.

Perched on the rim of his tank, Bernard gazed toward the
mountain peak, mesmerized by the beauty. Eagles flew in slow

circles above the 8,000-foot summit, their wings glowing in the fading sunlight. It had been a long day, but it was not quite over.

'You, de Nonancourt, over here!' It was his commanding officer. Bernard slid down from his tank and hurried over to report. 'You're from Champagne, right? So you must know something about wine.' Bernard nodded and was about to answer when the officer continued, 'We have a special assignment for you. You're going mountain climbing tomorrow.' The officer explained that military intelligence believed that much of the wine the Nazis had stolen from France had been stashed in Eagle's Nest. 'I want you to take a team up and see what's there. Get some rest since you'll be starting early. It won't be an easy climb.'

It took a few moments for the officer's words to sink in. Then Bernard realized he was about to enter a place where few others had ever set foot. No one knew for certain what was there or what condition it was in. The retreating SS had already flooded the cellars of several villas with gasoline and set them on fire. What had they done to Eagle's Nest? he wondered.

Although Berchtesgaden had been the target of Allied bombing runs in recent days, Bernard and several other soldiers found a chalet that was still intact and began unloading their equipment. For the first time in weeks, they would be sleeping in beds.

But Bernard could not sleep. Instead, he pulled out a sheet of paper and began writing a letter to his mother. So much had happened that it had been difficult to stay in touch. Now he found there was so much he could not tell her. How could he explain the things he had to do as a commando in the Resistance? How could he ever describe the horrors he had seen at Dachau when his army unit helped liberate that camp? 'I know how you felt after we lost Maurice,' he wrote. 'Not a day goes by that I don't think about my brother and what his struggle has cost all of us, but I can now say for certain that fighting in this war was the right thing for me to do.'

Bernard woke his men before dawn. General Leclerc had arrived during the night and he had one more order for the men who would be scaling the mountain. He wanted the French flag raised over Eagle's Nest.

The first part of the journey was the easiest. Bernard and his team drove from Berchtesgaden to a teahouse further up the mountain, about twenty minutes away. There was a parking lot there and an entrance to the elevator Hilter had built. Bernard double-checked with engineers who had been sent up earlier to see if there was any way of repairing it. It is impossible, they told him.

Bernard and his team began their climb. It was warm and the going was slow in the early morning light. Often, the men had to stop while an advance group checked the slope for mines and booby traps.

Within a couple of hours, the men were finding it difficult to breathe. That was one of Hitler's complaints and why he himself rarely visited Eagle's Nest. The air, he said, was too thin.

A few hundred feet from the summit, the path became steeper. Bernard sent a squad of Alpine climbers ahead to drop ropes. Then, one by one, the men hauled themselves up the face of the cliff.

All were exhausted by the time they had reached the top. Even at an altitude of 8,000 feet, it was still warm. The view, however, was magnificent and the men paused to take in the sight while they tried to catch their breath.

From the outside, Eagle's Nest was dull, almost nondescript, not unlike a bunker. Bernard realized at once it would not be easy getting inside. The entrance, a steel door, was jammed. Tugging on it availed nothing, and sledgehammers had no effect either. Bernard stood aside as engineers set off a small charge of explosives. When the smoke and dust had cleared, the door stood slightly ajar. Everyone squeezed through; Bernard headed for the *cave*.

Once again, there was a door to open. Like the first, it refused to give, but finally Bernard forced his way through.

Inside it was dark. Bernard switched on his flashlight. It took him only a few seconds to realize what was there. He shouted for the others to come. 'You're not going to believe this!' he said. Wherever Bernard pointed his flashlight, there were bottles, some in wooden cases, others on iron racks.

The other men rushed in with their flashlights; the sight before them was overwhelming. It was an enormous room filled from floor to ceiling with wine. 'There was every great wine I had ever heard of, every legendary vintage,' Bernard later said. 'Everything that had been made by the Rothschilds was there, the Lafites, the Moutons. The Bordeaux were just extraordinary.'

Bernard made a quick calculation. There had to be at least a half million bottles, many of them magnums.

The Bordeaux, however, were only part of it. There were also outstanding Burgundies as well as rare ports and cognacs dating from the nineteenth century. Bottles from every major champagne house were there too: Krug, Bollinger, Moët, Piper-Heidsieck and Pommery, all of the grand marques. And then Bernard spotted Lanson, the house his uncle owned. 'I helped make that champagne,' Bernard thought to himself.

But that was not what surprised him most. 'What I really remember is the 1928 Salon, that unforgettable champagne. It was so good and there were only minute quantities of it.' Nearly five years earlier, de Nonancourt had watched Göring's men haul that very champagne away when he was working at Delamotte, a champagne house across the street from Salon.

Bernard touched some of the bottles as if to convince himself it was real. Then he started to laugh. Some of the champagne, he saw, was little more than plonk. There were huge numbers of bottles stamped 'Reserved for the Wehrmacht'; others were labeled only Category A, B or C to designate quality. They represented one-third of all the sales of champagne from 1937 through 1940, an amount the Wehrmacht had requisitioned to 'maintain the morale of its troops.' Those bottles, Bernard knew, were ones producers used to get rid of their worst champagne.

Now, Bernard had a problem to solve: how to get a half million bottles of wine down a mountain. He called to the engineers. 'Are you sure that elevator isn't working? Are you positive there's no way to fix it?' They shook their heads, explaining that the damage was so extensive that repairing it required more equipment than they were carrying.

Then Bernard remembered a certain group of men who knew how to handle things carefully, especially in the most difficult circumstances. He radioed for medics. 'And bring all the stretchers you can find,' he said.

What happened next constituted one of the most bizarre wartime evacuations ever mounted, an exercise that would involve more than two hundred soldiers and take several days to complete. Cases of wine were lugged out of Eagle's Nest and strapped onto the stretchers. With help from the Alpine team, the stretchers were carefully lowered a few hundred meters from the peak to where pairs of stretcher-bearers waited below. The stretchers were then carried slowly down the mountain to where tanks, trucks and other military vehicles were waiting. Bernard scrambled to get ahead, stopping at times to watch as the strange procession of stretchers, each one loaded with wine, wound its way down the slope.

Bernard reached his tank just before the first stretcher of wine arrived. 'Bring that one over here,' he ordered, motioning the stretcher-bearers to his tank. '*Faites le plein* [fill 'er up],' he said. The men lifted a case off the stretcher and handed it to Bernard on the turret. It was a case of 1928 Salon champagne.

As more stretchers arrived, the same astonishing scene repeated itself. Soldiers stripped their tanks and trucks of everything that was not essential, tossing out clothes, tools, even extra ammunition, to make room for the new cargo. Some of the men emptied their canteens and refilled them with such legendary greats as Latour '29, Mouton '34 and Lafite '37.

It was quite a party. As the French flag was raised over Eagle's Nest, Bernard opened his first bottle of Salon '28 and lifted it in a toast. The soldiers called it *le repos du guerrier*, or the warrior's break between battles.

One last skirmish lay ahead. Their American 'cousins' had just arrived in Berchtesgaden and they were less than pleased to see that the French had beaten them there. The Americans had always assumed they would get to Berchtesgaden first. To be outmaneuvered, outfoxed by a bunch of guys who were officially under their command galled them.

Bernard and his men were not terribly concerned. By then, most were well into their celebration and they were not about to let some sore losers spoil the party, especially since there was more than enough booze to go around. It did not take the Americans long to realize that. There were wine cellars everywhere. Nearly every villa had its own well-stocked *cave*. The new arrivals found one that belonged to Field Marshal Göring. It was bursting with more than 10,000 bottles. Soon, about the only sound that could be heard was the popping of corks.

One American, however, was in no mood to celebrate. General Wade Haislip, commander of the 21st Army Corps, had just arrived in Berchtesgaden and the first thing he saw was the French *Tricolore* flying above Eagle's Nest. He was angry and embarrassed.

'You were under our orders and you still are,' he barked at General Philippe Leclerc. 'Get that flag down and put the Stars and Stripes up!'

Leclerc did as he was ordered, then shrugged. What did it matter? He knew who had won the race.

Not long afterward, he ran into one of his group commanders, General Paul de Langlade.

'Well, it's done,' said Leclerc. 'It's been a long and hard road but it's ended well, wouldn't you say?'

De Langlade nodded and smiled. 'God loves the French.'

TEN

The Collaborator

I t was impossible to ignore Louis Eschenauer.
   'He was a big man with a big cigar and an even bigger personality,' Jean Mlathle said. 'Everyone knew Uncle Louis.'

Uncle Louis was Bordeaux's most prominent wine merchant, an indefatigable *négociant* who bought wine in bulk, bottled it and then sold it to customers throughout the world. He was fluent in English, French, German and Russian, and wrote his own business letters in those languages. He knew as much about the wine business as anyone in Bordeaux. A typical day would find him visiting several châteaux, tasting their wines and negotiating what he felt was a 'fair' price, as well as dealing with piles of correspondence and orders and overseeing bottling, packing and shipping. Uncle Louis was so successful and made so much money that he rarely had to borrow from a bank. He would buy up a grower's entire crop and pay cash on the barrel-head.

'Eschenauer was very talented, a real expert,' said Heinz Bömers, Jr, who, like his father the Bordeaux weinführer, knew and worked with Louis. 'He could detect the slightest nuances and flaws in wines. During the war, he and my father would go out and taste dozens of wines together. They trusted each other's judgment and were very good friends.'

It was that friendship and his close ties with the German leadership that enabled Eschenauer to greatly increase his fortune during the war by selling wine to the Third Reich.

It also got him into trouble. After the war, he was arrested and put on trial for economic collaboration.

Although the trial took place in 1945, many in France still feel it is too sensitive or embarrassing to talk about, that it represents a dark chapter of history they prefer to forget, a period when more than 160,000 people were brought to trial or investigated for collaborating with the enemy. Even President Charles de Gaulle worried about that period and, for the sake of national unity, preferred to portray France as 'a nation of resisters.'

The Eschenauer case, however, raises uncomfortable questions about that portrait, questions which are still being debated. Was he a collaborator? Did he use his connections with the Germans to enrich himself illegally? Or was he merely one of many people in France who simply did what they had to in order to survive?

Those who knew and admired Uncle Louis argue that it is inappropriate and distasteful to be digging up a man's past when he is no longer able to defend himself. Let him rest in peace, they say, and let the rest of us live in peace.

That attitude is shared by the French legal system. Documents relating to Eschenauer's trial, part of which was held behind closed doors, have been sealed by a law that protects a person's privacy by restricting access to personal papers until sixty years after the person's death.

Eschenauer died in 1958.

He was born in 1870. His family, which lived in Strasbourg, ran a successful wine business there until the Franco-Prussian War broke out. With Alsace about to be annexed by Germany, the family fled to Bordeaux, where they hoped it would be safer, and where Louis was born that same year.

It was a propitious move. Bordeaux's port and other commercial facilities provided the perfect setting for the family to resume business. Within a year, Maison Eschenauer had become one of the best-known names in the region.

On the personal front, however, it was a much different story. Louis's father was a womanizer, something Louis's mother made sure her son realized. One of Louis's earliest memories was seeing his mother in tears because his father was with another woman. Often, she would drag little Louis out of the house and down to the port as she searched the bars and dives for her husband. 'I want you to see what your father is doing; I want to show you the horror of debauchery,' Louis remembered his mother telling him. For a little boy, it was a traumatic experience, he later told friends, one that would stay with him and affect his relationships with women for as long as he lived. He would one day take a mistress but never marry her or legally acknowledge the child he fathered. He couldn't, he said, because his mother would not approve.

In 1900, when his father died, the twenty-nine-year-old Louis took over Maison Eschenauer and turned it into one of the leading *négociant* firms in Bordeaux by specializing in fine wines, the *grands crus*. He was shrewd and exacting, and ran his firm with flair and ingenuity. During Prohibition in the 1920s, he managed to get wine to his customers in the United States by bottling it in perfume bottles. The best wines, such as Château Ausone and Château Suduiraut, were shipped in genuine crystal. Dry white wines were labeled 'water from the Roman baths.'

In social circles, Uncle Louis, as he was popularly known, was considered a warm and generous host. Women adored him and friends practically begged for reservations at Le Chapon Fin, the restaurant Eschenauer owned. 'You couldn't get in unless you had a zest of British humor, a rosette of the Legion of Honor or a personal invitation from Uncle Louis,' one Bordelais recalled. The restaurant featured the greatest wines of France and a clientele to match. King Alfonso XIII of Spain and England's Prince of Wales were just two of his regular customers. Alfonso was particularly partial to the truffles served in silver cups alongside delicately prepared meat dishes. The Prince of Wales gravitated between *écrevisses à la nage* (fresh water crayfish floating in its sauce) and *lièvre à la royale* (hare cooked in the royal style). Because Eschenauer was called the 'king of Bordeaux,' visiting royalty felt right at home.

As the region's most prominent wine merchant, Eschenauer presided over a society which, in many ways, was secretive and closed. The Chartrons, whose name was derived from the Quai des

Chartrons, the strip along the port where they lived and worked, were *négociants* of English and German descent, Protestants whose ancestors had settled and begun trading in the port city two hundred years earlier. They had names like Lawton, Johnston, Kressman and Schÿler. They intermarried, played tennis and golf, spoke English and German as well as French, and they worked assiduously to maintain contact with their countries of origin, making annual pilgrimages to their ancestral homes to place flowers on family graves. Behind the closed and nondescript doors of the Quai des Chartrons, they lived in grand apartments of restrained elegance, surrounded by antique mahogany and family silver.

Although Eschenauer considered himself 'one of them,' that was not his style. He lived away from the Quai in a mansion decorated with modern paintings. Instead of golf and tennis, he preferred horse racing; he owned several prize-winning horses, which, he said, helped make up for a family life that he did not have.

Cars were another passion. He owned one of the first in Bordeaux and had several custom-built for him. The flashy cars attracted a great deal of attention, especially as he cruised down the coast to the resort of Biarritz, where he had installed his mistress.

'Louis had a real love of luxury,' said Florence Mothe, a Bordeaux winemaker and writer. 'With his sumptuous limousines and winters spent in Egypt, he seemed like a character out of F. Scott Fitzgerald.'

Eschenauer was equally flamboyant in his business life, flaunting his famous German clients and worldwide contacts. One of his closest associates was Joachim von Ribbentrop, the Third Reich's Foreign Minister, whom Eschenauer had hired before the war to sell some of his wines in Germany. When France declared war on Germany in 1939, Eschenauer, who did more than half his business with that country, found himself in an uncomfortable position: some of his best friends and customers were now 'the enemy.' With exports to Germany cut off, Eschenauer was suddenly stuck with a huge stock of wine he could no longer sell.

The crisis was short-lived. In June 1940, after German forces over-ran France, an old friend and client came knocking on Eschenauer's door. It was Heinz Bömers, head of Reidemeister & Ulrichs, Germany's largest wine company. Bömers told Louis he had just taken on a new job: buying wine for the Third Reich. 'It can be profitable for both of us because I am here not just for the Third Reich; I have permission to buy wine for my own company as well,' he said, 'so we can continue our regular business as usual, plus you can sell straight to the German government.' Bömers explained that before he accepted the job of weinführer, he had insisted on total independence with no restrictions on how much money he could exchange to buy for his personal business. He added that France, now an occupied country, would only be permitted to sell its wine to Germany; all of the other usual export markets such as Britain, Russia and the United States were being cut off.

Louis needed no convincing. He realized that the arrangement Bömers was proposing was not only practical but potentially lucrative – for both of them. A deal was quickly worked out as other wine merchants looked on with envy.

The new political and economic realities governing France seemed to agree with Eschenauer, despite the traumas of occupation. Like most other Chartrons, he was politically conservative and leery of anything that might impede business. What scared him most was the specter of communism, social upheaval and labor unrest.

It was almost with a sigh of relief that he greeted the return of Marshal Philippe Pétain in 1940 to head the country. Pétain's hatred of communism and decision to collaborate with Germany, Louis felt, offered the best assurance that France would avoid the kind of economic stagnation that had crippled the country in the years before the war.

Collaboration, at that time, had few sinister overtones. It signified the working relationships Pétain wished to establish with Berlin which would help France rebuild itself. In that spirit, Eschenauer joined Groupe Collaboration, an organization that supported Pétain's

program and took its name from the Marshal's speeches advocating
Franco-German collaboration. Its membership – as Louis would
come to regret – also contained hundreds of people whose political sympathies were distinctly fascist and pro-Nazi. Uncle Louis
donated 10,000 French francs to the Groupe.

By 1942, the meaning of collaboration had changed dramatically.
It meant hunting down and deporting immigrant Jews, arresting
communists and other perceived enemies of the state – doing
whatever Berlin wanted in hopes that France would be guaranteed
a favorable position in a new Europe dominated by Germany.

Did Eschenauer realize what was happening? If he did, would it
have made any difference?

'Business was his first priority,' explained Florence Mothe, who
knew Eschenauer and whose stepfather worked for Uncle Louis. 'But
he was not an anti-Semite. I never heard him say one word against
Jews.' Indeed, he was a friend of Baron Philippe de Rothschild,
who was later to defend him.

When the Germans tried to requisition the wine of Châteaux
Lafite-Rothschild and Mouton-Rothschild, Eschenauer urged Bömers
to step in and prevent it from happening. The weinführer agreed.
He had already assured the Bordelais he would do all in his
power to protect their best wines. The Rothschilds' wine remained
untouched. Baron Philippe, who knew and worked with both
Eschenauer and Bömers, later confirmed the story to Florence
Mothe and referred to Uncle Louis in his book as 'a great friend
of mine.'

And yet, with the Germans seizing other Jewish wine estates,
which they then sold to non-Jews, Eschenauer was quick to take
advantage. He formed a company, the Société des Grands Vins
Français, which allowed him to discreetly buy up such properties.

'He was an opportunist, absolutely,' Mothe said, 'but he was
not pro-Nazi; he was just pro-Louis. For Louis, business always
came first.'

But many in the Bordeaux business community considered

Eschenauer's behavior provocative. They resented the way he flaunted his German friendships. Frequently he invited Nazi officials such as Heinz Bömers to join him for an afternoon at the racetrack. Louis's distant cousin Ernst Kühnemann, the German officer who commanded the city's port and submarine base there, was an even more frequent guest. The two were very close because Kühnemann was also in the wine business and head of the Berlin wine company Julius Ewest. Often, they could be seen strolling arm in arm beside the track, a sight many French spectators found infuriating and disgusting.

'They may have been cousins,' recalled one Bordeaux wine merchant, 'but it created a scandal in Bordeaux to see this "emperor of the Chartrons" on intimate terms with the commander of the naval base.'

Off the track, the cousins could be seen at Uncle Louis's restaurant, where other German officials, many of them sent by Foreign Minister Ribbentrop, were being entertained as well. To accommodate its German clientele, Le Chapon Fin was granted a number of exemptions. The restaurant was allowed to serve wine around the clock; it was not restricted to certain hours as other restaurants were because of rationing; nor did it have to post four different fixed-price menus daily with meals for 18, 50, 70 and 100 francs. It could charge what it wished. Although meat and fish were almost impossible to come by elsewhere, one could still dine very well at Le Chapon Fin.

Such privileges left a bitter taste in the mouths of other Bordelais. While they struggled to survive, Uncle Louis continued living the high life.

By the summer of 1944, nearly everyone realized that Germany was about to collapse. Even Heinz Bömers, who was visiting his family in Bavaria, knew the end was in sight and had refused to return to Bordeaux.

After D-Day, as one town after another was liberated, swastikas began appearing over doors of suspected collaborators. The hand-writing was literally on the wall; only Louis Eschenauer did not seem to see it.

Despite warnings from Charles de Gaulle that those who collaborated with the enemy would be punished, Louis's glamorous lifestyle continued unchanged. There were trips to Biarritz in his custom-built cars (unlike others, he still seemed to be able to get fuel), afternoons at the racetrack with his German friends and lunch nearly every day with Captain Ernst Kühnemann.

It was probably during one of those lunches that Kühnemann informed Eschenauer that with the Allies sweeping into France, it would not be long before German forces occupying Bordeaux would be pulling out. That may have been when Uncle Louis first realized the tide truly had turned and that he could be in serious trouble.

He watched with growing anxiety as German troops, caught on the run, lashed out with atrocities and mass executions, and he saw how the Resistance struck back, chasing down suspected collaborators as well as Germans.

That August, Eschenauer learned that the Germans planned to blow up the port of Bordeaux just before they evacuated the city. When a local politician with connections to the Resistance pleaded with him to use his influence to try to save the facility, Louis jumped at the chance. It was a way to make sure he was on the winning side and it might even save his neck. Besides, it was definitely the best way to protect business. He needed that port to ship his wine.

Eschenauer immediately contacted Kühnemann to set up an emergency meeting with other German officers. There, he argued that destroying the port would be a big mistake, that it served no military purpose and that many innocent people could be hurt or killed. What neither Eschenauer nor the Resistance realized was that the Germans probably would not have been able to destroy the port anyway because most of their detonators had been sabotaged just a few days earlier by a German soldier who opposed the plan. But that was a secret the Germans were keeping to themselves. In a bluff, they promised not to blow up the port if their troops were allowed to leave Bordeaux peacefully without being fired at. The Resistance agreed.

There was one other demand by Kühnemann: no harm was to come to Uncle Louis; he was to be left alone after the troops departed.

At 6:30 P.M. on August 26, French flags went up around the port to signal that an agreement had been reached. Eschenauer and Kühnemann were together at Louis's home at that moment, saying their farewells over a bottle of wine.

By the following day, the Germans were gone. Eschenauer breathed a sigh of relief.

Four days later, he was arrested by the Resistance.

Eschenauer's arrest followed that of Marshal Philippe Pétain, who had resigned a week and a half earlier. Taken into 'protective custody' by the Germans, who may have been trying to keep Vichy alive, the eighty-eight-year-old Marshal was forcibly moved to Germany and shunted from one castle to another. It was particularly humiliating because he had vowed he would never leave French soil. Before his departure, Pétain was given one last chance to address the people of France.

'When this message reaches you, I shall no longer be free,' he said. 'I had only one goal, to protect you from the worst. Sometimes my words or acts must have surprised you. You may be sure that they were more painful for me than they were even for you. But I have never ceased to fight with all my might against all that threatened you. I have led you out of certain dangers; but there were some, alas, which I could not spare you.'

Although the new French government under Charles de Gaulle hoped Pétain would stay away from France, the old Marshal was determined to return. He said he wanted to defend his role as head of the Vichy government. In June of the following year, he did return. He was promptly arrested, charged with treason and put on trial.

Appearing before the High Court of Justice, Pétain, who had been ignored by de Gaulle when he offered to hand over his powers, put up a spirited defense, claiming that he had tried to act as a shield to protect the French people. 'Every day, a dagger at my throat, I struggled against the enemy's demands,' he said. 'History will tell all that I spared you, though my adversaries think only of reproaching me for the inevitable . . . While General de Gaulle carried on the struggle outside our frontiers, I prepared the way for liberation by preserving France, suffering but alive.'

Many agreed with him and still do. May-Eliane Miaihle de Lencquesaing is one of them. 'People say it was de Gaulle who liberated France, but de Gaulle was nothing without the Americans,' she said. 'It was Pétain who stayed, who gave himself to the country, and who kept us from suffering much worse. Some people say he was on the German side. No; he hated the Nazis.'

Nevertheless, Pétain was found guilty and sentenced to death. Several weeks later, de Gaulle commuted the sentence to life imprisonment. Others in the Vichy government, like Prime Minister Pierre Laval, were tried and executed.

The prospect of spending the rest of his life in prison, or worse, had left Louis Eschenauer severely shaken. After helping to save Bordeaux from the Germans, being arrested had come as a great shock. If the court had been willing to sentence Marshal Pétain to death, what would they do to him? he wondered.

As he languished in a prison cell awaiting trial, the seventy-five-year-old wine merchant learned of the summary judgments being handed down by various tribunals. Women who had consorted with Germans were given what Gertrude Stein called the '*coiffure* '44' – their heads were shaved. Businessmen, especially those in northwestern France, who had committed the very crime Eschenauer was charged with – economic collaboration – were marched before firing squads and executed.

It was a time of retribution, of settling old scores. At least 4,500 persons were summarily put to death by tribunals set up by the Resistance.

'No Resistance historian should try to minimize the incidents of injustice, malicious indictment and personal vendetta,' said historian H. R. Kedward. 'In the months following liberation, hardly a day passed without some new revelation of the horrors of torture, deportation and execution for which the Gestapo and Milice had been responsible. As the shallow graves of mutilated resistors were found in country areas surrounding most of the large towns, and the cellars of the Gestapo revealed their inhuman secrets, the popular demand for retributive justice against the collaborators grew more insistent.'

In Bordeaux, according to one winegrower who knew Louis Eschenauer, 'there was a "healthy" denouncing of others. No one could be sure where the finger would point next.'

As purges continued, about 160,000 people were formally charged with collaboration by the new French government. More than 7,000 were condemned to death, although the sentence was carried out in only 800 cases; another 38,000 were given prison terms.

Fearing the situation was slipping out of control, a spokesman for the Minister of Justice, in March 1945, went on the radio to remind the people of France that doing business with the enemy did not necessarily constitute a crime. 'Not all of it is of the same character,' he said. Some of it may be interpreted as 'normal' and 'legitimate.' The law against economic collaboration, the spokesman added, is 'aimed at punishing the guilty and not disturbing the innocent.'

In September, the regional director of Economic Supervision in Bordeaux went even further. In a letter to courts of law in his area, he encouraged them to 'conclude their cases and investigations as soon as possible.'

It was in that growing atmosphere of 'Let's put this behind us' that the trial of Louis Eschenauer began on November 9, 1945. It had been just over a year since his arrest. Eschenauer

appeared nervous and frail. A psychiatrist who examined him
testified that he was suffering from severe depression. The only
good news for Uncle Louis was that he would not be executed.
An investigating magistrate had determined that Eschenauer's
crime of 'trafficking with the enemy' had not affected the security
of the state and that, therefore, he should not be tried in a
military court or by any other body that could apply the death
penalty.

Eschenauer was charged with three counts of economic collaboration: first, that he 'voluntarily entered into correspondence and
relations with agents of the enemy'; second, that he 'illegally conducted commerce' which provided France's enemy with 'important
economic support'; and third, that he 'knowingly gave direct or
indirect assistance to Germany that could bring harm to the unity
of the nation.'

On the stand, Eschenauer denied the charges. 'I am not a
collaborator,' he said. 'I did business with the Germans because
I had to. I had to save my business. I also wanted to protect the
interests of other *négociants* and winegrowers.'

Eschenauer testified that his 'intimate relationship' with weinführer
Heinz Bömers enabled him to prevent the Germans from get-
ting their hands on Bordeaux's best wines, such as Châteaux
Lafite-Rothschild and Mouton-Rothschild. His friendship with Ernst
Kühnemann, he said, helped him persuade the Germans not to
destroy the port of Bordeaux and other parts of the city. 'I admit
that I was well acquainted with many of the Germans here, but
I also knew how to trick them and string them along,' he said.
'I despised the Nazis; I never helped them. It was the Allies I was
trying to help.'

He also reminded the court of his role on a committee to help
refugees in Bordeaux during the Phony War of 1939–40. His role,
however, did not go much further than accepting a check from
American banker Clarence Dillon and turning it over to certain
charities.

Eschenauer's testimony seemed to be the desperate words of a tired and frightened old man, a man who, in a moment of weakness, was prepared to say anything to save his neck, even if it meant turning against Heinz Bömers, whom Eschenauer, just before his trial, described as a 'close family friend.'

In court, Eschenauer branded Bömers a 'vulture,' a 'violent man' who was trying to take over his business and who nearly caused him to have a nervous breakdown. 'He thought that because I was an old bachelor, my business should go to him. He dreamed of becoming master of Maison Eschenauer after my death.'

Eschenauer complained that he had been under constant pressure from Bömers to supply him with more wine. 'He promised he would buy everything from me, but I said that was unfair and that he should buy from other *négociants* as well.'

Portraying himself as a hero who 'saved Bordeaux's wines,' Louis explained that he tried to act as a buffer between Bömers and the wine community. 'I prevented him from seizing the best wines,' he said. 'Instead, I gave him duds, junk.'

Junk? According to court records, some of the wines Eschenauer sold to Bömers in 1944 included: Château Margaux 1939 (2,400 bottles), Château Mouton-Rothschild 1939 (3,000 bottles), Château Ausone 1939 (3,600 bottles), Château Rausan-Ségla (4,500 bottles), Château La Lagune (6,000 bottles), Château Cos d'Estournel 1937 (2,400 bottles), Château Brane-Cantenac 1937 (2,000 bottles), Château Talbot 1939 (8,000 bottles).

Although neither 1939 nor 1937 was a great year (indeed 1939 was to prove itself awful), these wines can hardly be called 'duds.' They came from some of the greatest estates of Bordeaux. At the time Eschenauer sold them, they constituted a more than satisfactory drink.

Eschenauer's testimony was even less consistent and convincing when he was questioned about a company he set up, the Société des Grands Vins Français. Its purpose, he said, was to buy property for Bömers. In the spring of 1941, the company purchased Châteaux Lestage and Bel-Air, two Jewish-owned wine estates that had been seized and 'Aryanized' by the Vichy government.

When he was first asked why he bought the châteaux, Eschenauer testified that it was because he wanted to 'avoid pressure' from Bömers, who was trying to take over his business; if Bömers got those châteaux, maybe he would not try to take Maison Eschenauer too.

Under subsequent questioning, however, Eschenauer said the real reason he had bought the two properties was that he was 'trying to save them' for their rightful Jewish owners. 'I knew Germany would lose the war and that any promise I made to Bömers during the war would be null and void afterward.'

The court judges were skeptical. When they asked Eschenauer for documents to back up his testimony, Uncle Louis said there were none, that everything had been handled on a verbal basis. 'Bömers had complete confidence in me,' he said. Then he added, 'The truth is, I actually had very little involvement in the company; everything was handled by my bookkeeper.' The bookkeeper claimed this was false.

Florence Mothe said she was among those stunned by Eschenauer's testimony. 'Why would a man who had been denied nothing in life, from the smallest thing to the greatest luxury, behave in such a way? Turn on those who worked with him? That is what I cannot understand.'

From the moment the trial began, it had been watched with growing anxiety throughout Bordeaux. Other *négociants* who had sold wine to Germany knew it could easily have been any of them on the stand. Some, in fact, had already been fined and seen their goods confiscated. Others had actively competed for Bömers's attention and business by inviting him to parties and trying to demonstrate their interest in German music and literature. According to notes kept by Bömers's secretary, the weinführer found all of this 'ridiculous.' Now the Chartrons were worried, because soliciting business from the enemy was grounds for charging a firm or individual with economic collaboration.

Consequently, although many in the Bordeaux wine trade had resented and were jealous of Eschenauer's business connections during the war, most now rallied to his defense. Some wrote letters describing him as a 'patriot' and a 'man of integrity.' One supporter claimed Eschenauer helped the Resistance by loaning it trucks to haul food and weapons. Another said he had helped Jews escape from the Gestapo. Even Baron Philippe de Rothschild of Château Mouton-Rothschild wrote a letter in his behalf.

As his three-day trial neared its end, Eschenauer denied any wrongdoing and reiterated that he was not a collaborator. He had joined Groupe Collaboration, he said, 'just to please a friend,' adding that he never really had anything to do with the group itself. He admitted, however, that he had made a donation to the organization.

His most important service, he said, was helping save Bordeaux from destruction. 'Thanks to my good relations with Ernst Kühnemann and other German officers, I was able to persuade them, after many long and intense negotiations, not to carry out their plans for destroying the port and other parts of the city.'

Uncle Louis's trial ended on Armistice Day, the day marking victory over Germany in World War I. It was the first Armistice Day to be celebrated after the war. Once again it had been declared a national holiday and large celebrations were planned. No newspapers would be published. That was the best part as far as the court was concerned. Publicity would be minimal when the verdict was announced.

The panel of judges retired to consider its verdict at 1:15 in the morning. By 3 A.M., they were back in the courtroom.

The verdict: guilty on all charges.

The judges dismissed Eschenauer's claim that he tried to resist demands for wine by Heinz Bömers. 'He willingly agreed to furnish

Bömers with what he wanted and at no point did he ever refuse.' The
court also dismissed Eschenauer's testimony that his company, the
Société des Grands Vins Français, had purchased two 'Aryanized'
Jewish-owned châteaux in order to save them for their rightful
Jewish owners. 'The company,' the court said, 'was created for
only one purpose, to do business with the enemy.' (Bömers had
made no secret of the fact that he wanted to own a wine property
in Bordeaux again after losing Château Smith-Haut-Lafitte in World
War I. Several years after World War II, he bought Château du
Grand Mouëys, which his firm still owns.)

Uncle Louis was sentenced to two years in prison and fined more
than 62 million francs for illegal profiteering. He admitted doing
957 million francs' worth of business during the war, but it was the
way he did that business that disturbed the authorities most. His
courting of German officials at his restaurant and at the racetrack
and his flaunting of those relationships made him a natural target.
As one Bordelais who knew him said, 'Louis just went too far.'

His property was confiscated and he was forbidden from doing
business in Bordeaux. He also lost all rights as a French citizen.

As Uncle Louis was led away, he broke down in tears. 'After 1918,
they gave me a medal for selling wines to the Germans, now they
fling me in prison for doing the same thing,' he sobbed. 'If Mama
were to see me now!'

De Gaulle intended that the purge process would be swift, that
after the more notorious collaborators had been punished, the
process of healing, restoring order and unifying the country could
begin. He was especially eager to see this happen in Bordeaux,
a region whose political support he considered important and
whose economic resources – its wine and its port – were vital
for the recovery of the nation. To that end, his government, in
1951, passed an amnesty law which allowed many businessmen
who had been found guilty of excess profiteering to return to
their offices.

Louis Eschenauer was amnestied in 1952. He spent the remainder of his days in his château at Camponac in Pessac, just outside Bordeaux.

Before Uncle Louis died, Heinz Bömers, Jr., son of Bordeaux's weinführer, came to Bordeaux to learn more about the wine business. Uncle Louis was there to welcome him, and take him to the races.

'There is something I wish to tell you,' he said, taking Heinz by the arm. 'I want you to know that I have always been a friend of your father. I was his friend before the war and I was his friend during the war. And I am still his friend today.'

ELEVEN

I Came Home Not Young Anymore

It was late morning when a bent, elderly-looking man, a handmade knapsack on his back, came trudging through the mud and slush of a warm February.

Gaston Huet was on his way home.

After five years as a prisoner of war, Huet and the men of Oflag IV D finally had been released. It happened without warning. They had been awakened early in the morning by sounds they had never heard before and a sight they could never have imagined. Charging straight for the camp were sword-wielding Cossacks on horseback, yelling at the top of their lungs. Huet and the other POWs watched in astonishment as the riders galloped through the gates and overran the guardhouses, sending the frightened Germans fleeing. Was it freedom, Huet wondered, or more captivity with different masters?

Through the confusion, one of the Cossack leaders finally made himself understood. 'Go,' he told the Frenchmen. 'Take just what you can carry.'

For Huet, it would not be much. There were letters from home, letters that helped sustain him through some of the worst moments of his captivity. There was also the piece of the French flag he had torn off in Calais just before he was taken prisoner in 1940. He had looked at it so many times, wondering if there would ever be a France again. The last thing Huet put in his bag was a copy of the program from the wine celebration he had organized, an affair that had done as much as anything to make his life as a POW bearable.

Huet took one last look around the camp. He stared at the barracks where he had lived, then at the guardhouses; the machine guns were still in place. So was the barbed wire which ringed the camp. Huet also looked at the Tombe d'Adolph, the mock grave of Hitler which the prisoners had built. Life in Oflag IV D had been a nightmare, the paralyzing cold of winter, the awful heat of summer and especially the lack of food. He shivered when he recalled the bitter January days when prisoners tried to catch rats for dinner. Yet some incredible friendships had been forged during those years.

He thought about those friendships as he proceeded down Hitlerstrasse, the name given to the dirt path which cut through the middle of the camp and led to the front gate.

Huet passed through the gate and started walking west, toward France and home.

He was not alone. The roads were full of frail sick men, all looking far older than their years. At times, the men tried to help and encourage each other as the mud sucked at their worn-out shoes and boots. They were so weak after their years of captivity that each step was painful. All that kept them going were thoughts of home. What would they say to their families? Would their friends recognize them? What had happened in the five years they had been gone?

For more than a hundred kilometers, Huet kept going, stumbling over roads that had been torn up by tanks and pockmarked by repeated bombing. The war was not quite over, Germany had not yet surrendered. At times, Huet and the other POWs had to throw themselves onto the wet and cold ground for protection as fighter planes and bombers flew overhead.

As they approached the Franco-German border, they met Allied troops coming toward them. The troops rushed to help them. 'This way, this way,' the troops said, escorting the POWs to trains bound for France.

It was late February when Huet finally arrived back in Vouvray. He returned to a welcome that needed no words. 'We just fell into each other's arms, my wife and I,' he remembered. 'We were laughing and crying at the same time. So many emotions.'

And then he saw his daughter. The baby he had last seen on her first birthday was now a little girl, nearly seven years old, and shy behind her mother's skirts. She peeked out at the man she knew only from his letters and her mother's stories and asked if he wanted to play. The question made him weep. 'She was so beautiful, I could hardly believe it,' Huet said.

It would be some time before he was ready to play, however. Huet had lost more than one-third of his body weight. Before being captured, he weighed nearly 160 pounds. When he was freed, he weighed less than 100.

Before he fell asleep that first night at home, he had one last question. 'And the vines? How are the vines?'

A few days later, Huet discovered the answer for himself and nearly wept again. Five years of war and neglect had taken their toll. No pruning had been done and the vines were gangly, their branches hanging down every which way. Gone were the tidy rows that once had been so carefully staked and tied neatly to the lines of wire. And weeds were everywhere, even though it was only March. Plowing had been impossible because the Germans had requisitioned the horses. Huet could clearly see what the lack of fertilizer and copper sulfate had meant as he looked at the number of sick and aged vines that needed replacing.

It was a plight facing nearly every winegrower, and the problems extended to their cellars as well. Wines that had lain in wooden casks for five years desperately needed bottling, but that was impossible because there was a bottle shortage. For many wines, it was already too late. They had dried out, lost their fruit and were undrinkable. The casks in which they had been aging were ruined as well. Some had become moldy from overuse, while others were damaged when overzealous Vichy inspectors poured oil into them to prevent *vignerons* from withholding their industrial alcohol quota.

Just when it seemed as if the picture could not be worse, Mother Nature conspired against winegrowers. On May 1, the early warm spring vanished when France was gripped by a deep freeze. Temperatures dropped below zero. Vines with young shoots already sprouting were frozen solid. One old winemaker in Bordeaux said he

had never seen such a hard frost so late in the spring. Many growers
lost their entire crop.

It was not much different in other wine regions. In Burgundy,
however, the worst was yet to come. Maurice Drouhin had been
heartened when, after the frost, temperatures soared again and his
vines showed new signs of life and began to flower.

Now, as he stared at the sky with his son Robert, dark clouds
advanced ominously from the northeast. It was 5 P.M., June 21. On
what should have been the longest day of the year, the whole of
Burgundy was suddenly plunged into darkness, almost as if night
had fallen. The wind rose and the house began to shake. Then
it began to hail. Balls of ice shredded vineyards throughout the
Côte de Beaune. Ten of the main villages, from Puligny to Corton,
were ravaged. Maurice could only shake his head. Like everyone
else, he wondered if there would be enough grapes to make any
wine at all.

The following morning, he and Robert went out to survey the
damage. Leaves of his vines looked like they had been sliced with a
knife. Flowers looked as if they had been trampled into the ground
by a stampede. Maurice stopped to talk to other *vignerons*, but there
was little to say. It was the same everywhere. Everyone realized they
would be lucky if they could salvage even 5 percent of their crop.

Maurice decided it was time to do something he had been putting
off until the German surrender had been signed and he was positive
the war was over. 'Grab a broom,' he told Robert. 'We're going to
get rid of a few cobwebs.'

Together, they went down to the *cave* and began brushing away
the webs and grime that had accumulated on the wall Maurice had
built five years earlier. 'Those little spiders of yours did a good job,'
he said to Robert. Then they began knocking down the wall. The
wines that had been hidden behind appeared to be in perfect shape,
including a complete stock from the Domaine de la Romanée-Conti
from 1929 to 1938.

Maurice took one of the bottles up for dinner that night and told

Pauline it was a celebration. With these wines, he said, we'll be able to pay our bills and get business going again.

It was a strategy many others were adopting as they recovered wines they had hidden from the Germans. Gaston Huet retrieved his wines from a cave along the Loire River. The weeds and brush he had planted now completely concealed the opening, but he had no trouble finding it.

His brother-in-law André Foreau, another Vouvray winemaker, dug up his garden to unearth the bottles he had buried. So did a neighbor, Prince Philippe Poniatowski. But Poniatowski was worried about what the time underground may have done to his wine, so he called in some wine experts to join him in a tasting. The verdict was unanimous: all the wines were in outstanding condition, even the 1875.

In Champagne, Marie-Louise de Nonancourt took her son Bernard with her when she broke down her wall at Laurent-Perrier. There was one casualty. Her statue of the Virgin Mary, which she had cemented into the wall to guard the hidden stock, shattered as sledgehammers hit the bricks. Marie-Louise, however, saw it as a sign of good luck, saying the Virgin had done her job and now it was up to the de Nonancourts.

In June 1945, the Marquis d'Angerville of Volnay in Burgundy was surprised to receive a letter from one J. R. Swan of New York City. The letter read, 'I am writing you to ask if you are still in possession of 10 cases of Volnay Champans '34 and 10 cases of Meursault Santenots '34 purchased from you for me and left in your care. It would be a great deal to expect that they had not been taken by the Germans but there is always the chance that I have been fortunate.'

The wine Swan had ordered represented just a few of the many bottles that had spent the war hidden and untouched behind a wall in d'Angerville's cellar. In a letter to Swan, the marquis informed him that the wine was still there and would be shipped to him immediately.

But it was a task the marquis approached with regret. His 1934
Volnay Champans was one of the best wines he had ever made and
he hated parting with it. 1934 had been an outstanding vintage,
certainly the best of the decade, and it had produced wines that
were rich, velvety and harmonious. His '34 Volnay Champans was
no exception. It was the wine he and his family drank to celebrate
the end of the war, and if there had been any way he could have
held on to some of it, he would have done so.

D'Angerville realized, however, there was no alternative. Unless
he let it go, there would be no way to start business again. So he
packed it up.

30,000,000 BOTTLES OF CHAMPAGNE
THAT GERMANS MISSED ARE AWAITING EXPORT

PARIS, Sept. 13 (UP – More than 30,000,000 bottles of champagne
are in French cellars waiting to be exported to the United States,
because the Germans were afraid to go into the underground caverns
to remove them.

Léon Douarche, former director of the International Wine Office,
said today that the Germans carried away only a small percentage of
this year's production of wine and champagne, which he estimated
at 3,700,000,000 liters, compared to the yearly average figure of
5,500,000,000.

—*The New York Times*, Sept. 14,1944

In July 1944, Otto Klaebisch, the weinführer of Champagne,
placed a large order for champagne for the German military with
the CIVC. Three weeks later he abruptly canceled it and fled back
to Germany.

With Patton's Third Army rapidly advancing toward Champagne,
the Germans had to leave quickly, so quickly, in fact, that they did
not even have time to set off all the explosives they had planted

under bridges. Nor did they destroy Champagne's vast cellars as Himmler had threatened to do.

Nevertheless, the German occupation had left companies and personal lives in tatters. There were millions of francs' worth of unpaid bills for champagne the Nazis had shipped to Germany. Champagne houses, notably Moët & Chandon, were in disarray after their executives had been imprisoned and the houses themselves had been placed under direct German control.

The Champenois were relieved when they heard that Robert-Jean de Vogüé, who had headed both Moët and the CIVC, was still alive after a year and a half in a slave-labor camp. They were horrified, however, when they saw his condition.

De Vogüé was not supposed to have survived. The Nazis had put the letters NN against his name – *Nacht und Nebel* (Night and Fog) – which meant work him to death and dump him into an unmarked grave. Just after he arrived at the camp, a sadistic guard told him, 'You know what they say about Ziegenhain, don't you? Those who come to Ziegenhain come here to die.'

De Vogüé almost did.

One morning he awoke to discover that an infection in the little finger of his right hand had become much worse. As he examined it more closely, he realized that gangrene had set in. When he asked for a doctor, the authorities ignored him. De Vogüé knew he would die unless he did what was necessary himself. He found a piece of glass and sharpened it as best he could. Then he began to cut. With no anesthetic, the pain was unbearable but de Vogüé continued to cut until he had removed his entire finger. Using the rags of his concentration camp clothes, he finally stopped the bleeding. The crude operation saved his life, but it was almost for naught.

When his camp was liberated, de Vogüé began walking. He had gone only a few kilometers before he collapsed. As he lay unconscious along the road, a British officer passed by and stopped. He was a man whom de Vogüé had once worked with in Champagne. The Englishman jumped out of his jeep and picked up de Vogüé; then he notified de Vogüé's family that he was bringing him home.

For de Vogüé's five children, it was an exciting moment. They had no idea of their father's condition and had decorated the living room with signs of 'Welcome Home, Papa.'

When de Vogüé arrived, all the joy vanished. No one recognized the frail, sticklike figure who could no longer stand on his own. He bore no resemblance to the elegant, dynamic man who had run the Moët & Chandon champagne house and who had faced down Otto Klaebisch.

Now he hung between the shoulders of the British officer and his brother-in-law. His greeting was so faint the children were not even sure he had spoken. Their mother began to cry as she ushered the men into the bedroom to help put her husband to bed. For days, there was doubt he would recover.

De Vogüé's assistant, Claude Fourmon, who was arrested with him in Klaebisch's office, arrived back in Champagne in even worse shape. Fourmon had been sent to Bergen-Belsen where each day was a test of survival. He would fix a date to live and then, when that date passed, he would pick another one. 'If I can just make it until January 13,' he would tell himself, 'then I can make it.' When January 13 arrived, he picked another date.

Those dates stretched on through the winter of 1943–44. The cold was unbearable. 'I sang,' Fourmon said. 'I sang against the cold. I sang hymns, children's songs, anything. Songs seemed to be the only thing that helped.'

When he finally returned home, Fourmon, like de Vogüé, was barely alive. He had been tortured and was no longer the ebullient young man whom the Gestapo had arrested in Reims two years earlier. 'I came back not young anymore,' Fourmon said.

He was thirty years old.

May-Eliane Miaihle de Lencquesaing was crying. She and her family had just returned to Château Pichon-Longueville, Comtesse de

Lalande. The Germans had left it only the day before, and the Miaihles, for the first time in four years, were getting a look inside.

'The Germans were brutes,' she said. 'They had dried their uniforms in front of the fires and sparks had flown everywhere. The beautiful *boiseries* were ruined and every pane of glass was broken. Even the marble fireplaces and doors were in pieces. Windows had been left open and rain poured in, ruining the parquet floors. Straw pallets on the floors where the soldiers slept were like mud.

'And the smell! It took us years to get the smell of the grease they used on their jackboots out of the château.'

It was same throughout Bordeaux as winemakers and winegrowers tried to erase the scars left by the occupation: swastikas carved into stonework, graffiti scribbled on walls, bullet holes.

Château Mouton-Rothschild had been occupied and damaged but not confiscated by the Third Reich. Like Château Lafite-Rothschild, the Vichy government had sequestrated Mouton to keep the Germans from declaring it a Jewish asset and making it German property.

When Baron Philippe de Rothschild came back to Mouton, however, he was already bearing a burden of sorrow. He had fled France to join de Gaulle's Free French Forces in 1942, leaving behind a wife and tiny daughter. For most of the war, the two managed to survive, living first in the South of France and then in Paris. The baron's wife, the Comtesse Elizabeth de Chambure, was not Jewish, so she was confident the Germans would leave them alone.

But she was wrong. Just before Paris was liberated, the Gestapo arrived at her apartment. In front of the terrified eyes of her daughter Philippine, the comtesse was dragged out of her home and put on one of the last trains bound for the German death camps. She was killed in the gas chambers of Ravensbrück only a few days before the concentration camp was liberated.

Upon seeing his beloved Mouton, the baron became even more

saddened. Although his wines were untouched, the château and grounds had been severely damaged by the Nazis, who had transformed it into a communications command center. There were even bullet holes in the walls of some of the rooms where the Germans had used paintings for target practice.

Baron Philippe was determined to eradicate all signs of the Nazi presence. He discovered that some of the soldiers who had occupied his property were being held as prisoners in a nearby camp. 'Who better to redo the château where there was devastation, everything to be cleaned, repaired, repainted,' he later recalled in a memoir. When Baron Philippe asked authorities for permission to put the Germans to work, officials agreed.

For days, the POWs labored to repair the damage they had done, ripping down miles of communications cables they had strung around the château and demolishing antiaircraft gun emplacements on the grounds. They also filled in the bullet holes.

But their work was far from finished. For years Baron Philippe had dreamed of creating a park around Mouton, along with a road that would link it directly with Mouton d'Armailhac, a neighboring wine estate he had acquired. The baron equipped the Germans with rakes, shovels and other tools and told them to get to work. Under a blazing sun, the prisoners began planting trees, flowers and shrubs, clearing land for a park and digging out a path for the road.

The project took months to complete but when it was finished, the baron pronounced himself well satisfied.

'I can never look at the road,' he said, 'without thinking of it as the "Route of Revenge."'

French winegrowers were overwhelmed by the amount of work that lay before them and the amount of money it would cost. Money for repairs, money for new high-axle tractors and other equipment, money for fertilizer and copper sulfate, money for replacing vines. Where were they going to get it?

Fortunately, winegrowers had an understanding ear in the man in charge of the country's economic recovery program. He was Jean Monnet, who was soon to espouse the idea of a European Economic Community. Monnet had grown up among the vines of Cognac, where his family made the French brandy. He understood their problems and was acutely aware that one and a half million French families depended on wine for their livelihood.

But the new government, pressured by all sectors of the economy for assistance, could only go so far. Its main goal where wine was concerned was making sure there was an adequate supply. Thanks to Monnet's urging, the government finally agreed to provide money for replacing old and sick vines.

The new program was especially welcome in Alsace, where most vineyards had been planted with high-yielding low-quality hybrids following the 1870–71 Franco-Prussian War.

After World War I, the French government had ordered growers to rip out their hybrid vines and replace them with the traditional grape varieties of Alsace. Growers dragged their feet, complaining it was too expensive. The government did not force the issue.

When Alsace was annexed by Germany in 1940, new pressure was exerted, this time by Berlin. Get rid of the hybrids or else, the authorities warned. Still nothing happened.

One day in 1942, Alsatians awoke to the sound of sawing. Looking out their windows, they saw that their vineyards were full of Hitler Youth from Baden, Germany. The Third Reich had sent truckloads of the young people into Alsace armed with detailed maps of the vineyards and secateurs and saws. In one fell swoop, the hybrids, which had comprised 75 percent of the vineyards, were gone from Alsace.

In the opinion of most Alsatians, it was the one good thing the Germans did for Alsace. Now there was no choice but to replant.

Work, however, began slowly. Most of the vineyards were littered with unexploded mines and artillery shells. There was also a labor shortage; nearly all of Alsace's young men had been drafted into the German army. Most were sent to the Russian front and a huge percentage had been killed. Those who survived were only now making their way home.

The waiting had been particularly difficult for the Hugels. Their eldest son, Georges, was now fighting in the French army; their second son, Johnny, still was in the German one.

Johnny returned home first. He had been in a German unit fighting near Lake Constance on the Austrian border when he spotted a column of French tanks approaching. Ducking into a nearby farmhouse, Johnny quickly shed his German uniform and traded it to a farmer for some old clothes. 'Look after yourself,' the farmer called as Johnny rushed out to greet the troops. He was back in Riquewihr a few days later.

One day after that, Georges returned as well.

That was when they discovered they had been in the same battle. Georges had been fighting at Lake Constance too.

With the Hugels reunited and Alsace now completely liberated, the real celebrating could finally begin. 'We went from cellar to cellar. We were plastered for three days,' Johnny said. 'Every day someone else, one of our friends, was coming home. Every day someone else came back.'

But many did not. At least 40,000 young Alsatian men were killed fighting in the German army, most of them in Russia. Before liberation, death notices were required to state that the victim *Gefallen für Führer, Volk und Vaterland* (died for the Führer, people and Fatherland). Now, grieving families could say without fear that their sons had died on the Eastern front.

As Alsatians reclaimed their French identity, it was also safe to speak French. Instead of having to greet friends on the street saying, '*Heil Hitler*,' people now could say '*Bon jour*.' Men could also sport berets. Names of streets, businesses, towns and villages were restored as well.

Richenweïer became Riquewihr. Hügel and Söhne was once again Hugel et Fils.

*   *   *

Another name was about to be replaced too.

Ever since Burgundian winemakers had given one of their best parcels of vines to the now discredited Marshal Pétain, they had been feeling increasingly uncomfortable.

Each day when they went to work, the imposing stone gate of the Clos du Maréchal seemed to mock them. There must be something we can do about this, they thought. They called on a friend who was an attorney for advice. The Marshal's property has all been confiscated by the government, they pointed out. Isn't there some way we can get the vineyard back?

The attorney agreed to take their case to court and ask that the gift of the Clos du Maréchal be declared null and void. Much to their relief, the court ruled in their favor, and the parcel of vines passed back into the hands of the Hospices de Beaune.

A day after the decision, winegrowers armed with sledgehammers and picks converged on the vineyard and began knocking down the stone gate they had once so proudly erected.

Mademoiselle Yvonne Tridon, who had presented Pétain with a gift of wine on behalf of the Beaune Syndicat des Négociants, admitted that it was all a little strange. 'We French are sometimes very hard to understand,' she said. 'One day we are singing "Maréchal, nous voilà," and the next day we don't ever want to hear about him again.'

Within an hour, the stone gate lay in ruins. But not quite all of it. During the bashing and smashing, Maurice Drouhin and his son Robert spirited away one of the posts.

Destruction of the Clos du Maréchal gate, however, did not end the controversy. There were still the wines made by the Hospices de Beaune on the Marshal's behalf. The wines had the right to be bottled and labeled with Pétain's name and a picture of the Hospices. It was an acute embarrassment to those who once had hailed Pétain as a savior.

Winegrowers, therefore, were alarmed when they heard that the government, which had confiscated Pétain's property, had decided to put the wines up for auction. Before the auction could begin, however, the auction site was taken over by several groups protesting the sale. Among them were war veterans, Resistance veterans, the Federation of Deported Laborers and the Federation of Political Deportees. All complained vehemently that the sale was unpatriotic.

The auctioneer, Georges Rappeneau, a newcomer to the profession who had only conducted one other auction in his life, did not know what to do. He called the protesters into his office and tried to reason with them. They refused to listen and demanded that the sale be called off.

Then Rappeneau remembered where he was and how things were done in the heart of Burgundy. 'Just a minute,' he told the protesters, 'I'll be right back.' Rappeneau went outside and asked one of his assistants to find glasses and a corkscrew. Once the glasses were handed out, he began filling them. He was pouring Clos du Maréchal. 'Gentlemen,' he said, 'let's drink to a successful conclusion.' It was not long before the problem was worked out and the sale went ahead.

And who bought the wine? The veterans themselves!

They bottled the wine with Clos du Maréchal labels and resold it at a profit, the money going to support their organizations. One person suggested the Hospices could do even better by bottling the wine from Pétain's former vineyard with the old Clos du Maréchal labels but with 'ex' printed in front. 'A good way to garner a little publicity and raise some extra money,' he suggested. The Hospices passed on that idea.

Although Maurice Drouhin was glad that Pétain's vineyard had been returned to the Hospices de Beaune, he was pleased that he and Robert had managed to salvage the gatepost from the ex-Clos du Maréchal. 'It's a piece of our history,' he told Robert. 'We ought to learn from it, not destroy it blindly as though we can change everything that has happened.'

It was in that spirit of facing up to history that Maurice responded quickly to a letter he received from Dr. Erich Eckardt shortly after the war. Dr. Eckardt was the German judge who presided at Maurice's trial in 1942 and ordered that he be released from prison. Now, Eckardt was pleading for help, saying that the Allied authorities in Germany had refused to let him practice his profession. 'Is there anything you can do, anything you can say that will help me?' he asked Maurice. Maurice remembered how Eckardt had been willing to listen to his defense at the trial. He had no hesitation about responding with a notarized statement saying Eckardt was a 'decent man who had judged me fairly and impartially.' Soon afterward, the Allies reinstated Eckardt as a judge.

Robert-Jean de Vogüé received a letter too. He was being summoned to court as a 'hostile witness' against Otto Klaebisch. The former weinführer of Champagne had been brought before a postwar tribunal investigating economic crimes. The court was stunned when de Vogüé, instead of condemning Klaebisch, spoke in his behalf. He conceded that he and the weinführer had had many sharp disagreements but emphasized that Klaebisch had always been very correct. 'He was in a difficult situation,' de Vogüé told the court. 'I don't believe for a minute that he himself would have ever ordered my arrest or those of my colleagues. It was the Gestapo.'

Klaebisch was exonerated.

Baron Philippe de Rothschild felt his heart sink a little when he saw the German postmark on the letter he had just received. He opened it up. 'Dear Baron Philippe,' the letter said, 'I have always loved the wines of Mouton, and I wonder if there is any chance you would let me represent them for you in Germany.'

The letter was signed Heinz Bömers, the former weinführer of Bordeaux.

Although the war years had brought the baron sadness and pain, his response was immediate. 'Yes, why not,' he replied. 'It is a new Europe we are building.'

*　　*　　*

'The wind of the apocalypse that blew from the east for sixty months, driving away laughter and happiness from the kingdom of vines, and leaving only the silence of death, has finally ended.' With those words, Grand Master Georges Faiveley declared open the thirty-second meeting of the Confrérie des Chevaliers du Tastevin. They called it the Chapitre de Résurrection. The Burgundy wine fraternity had been 'put to sleep' during the war.

But on November 16, 1946, it was resurrected with all the pomp and ceremony the wine community could generate. Government officials, foreign dignitaries, military leaders and Burgundy's greatest winemakers gathered for a feast of wine and food and to hear author Georges Duhamel, a member of the Académie Française, extol the virtues and values of wine.

Like everyone, Duhamel had gorged himself on a seven-course meal and had been plied with half a dozen wines, including a 1938 Beaune Clos des Mouches from Maurice Drouhin, a 1940 Clos Blanc de Vougeot, a 1942 Nuits Clos de Thorey, and a 1929 Nuits Château-Gris. Under such circumstances, it was not surprising that Duhamel positively overflowed in his praise.

'Wine was one of the first signs of civilization to appear in the life of human beings,' he said. 'It is in the Bible, it is in Homer, it shines through all the pages of history, participating in the destiny of ingenious men. It gives spirit to those who know how to taste it, but it punishes those who drink it without restraint.'

William Bullitt, who had been the U.S. ambassador to France at the beginning of the war, also had a message for the Confrérie. 'Like everyone else, when I became ambassador, I was told to keep my eyes and ears open and my mouth shut,' he said. 'Now, here I am doing just the opposite, opening my mouth to sing your songs and closing my eyes to savor your wine.'

It was an evening of shared pleasures and reminiscences. Time had already begun to soften some of the memories of the war. As the wine continued to flow, people began telling stories. One guest

recalled the experiences of a friend, a man from Chantilly who had
served in the French army.

His friend, he told the others at his table, was a great wine lover
who had been away from home for four long discouraging years.
When the war ended, he could not wait to get back to his cellar,
where he had locked up several hundred bottles of wine. With great
anticipation and some trepidation, he inserted the key that he had
carried with him for four years into the lock. It turned. The door
was still locked! Excitedly, he opened it and pushed into the dark
room. Pulling a flashlight from his pocket, he shined it around.

Everywhere there was a sparkle of glass from the bottles. Everything was just as he left it. Gingerly, he eased one of the bottles
out of the rack. It was still corked. So was the next bottle and
the next.

Carrying them from the *cave* out into the light, he saw that the
bottles were all in perfect shape.

Except for one small thing – they were all empty.

German soldiers had indeed broken into the cellar, prying open
the door without breaking the lock. They must have been ecstatic
when they discovered what was there. After consuming as much
wine as they could, the Germans pushed the corks back into the
bottles and put the bottles back on the racks. Before leaving, one
of the soldiers took time to write a thank-you note. 'Dear Sir, Our
compliments. Your taste in wine is impeccable!'

When the laughter at the table had died down, the Grand Master
of the Confrérie called on Duhamel to bring the evening to a close.
The old academician and wine lover returned to the podium with
pleasure.

'This celebration has given us optimism and confidence,' he said.
'It proves that our beloved France, so tested and so unhappy, still
has resources on which she can count. In coming here tonight, we
have proven that our France, this kingdom of wine, will live on.'

EPILOGUE

Intense heat, freezing temperatures, hail, then more heat. 1945 seemed like certain disaster.

But the peasants who worked the vines believed there was a special relationship between war and grapes. They had always said that the Good Lord sends a poor wine crop when war starts and a fine, festive one to mark its end.

And they were right.

1939, the year World War II began, was a horrendous vintage, whereas 1945, *l'année de la victoire* (the year of the victory), was one of the best ever recorded.

Wine critics ran out of superlatives: 'I give it six stars out of five!' one said. 'These wines will not be ready to drink for fifty years,' another predicted. Old-timers compared them to 1870, 1893 and other legendary vintages of the past.

Although the 1945 crop was minuscule, only half of what had been harvested in 1939, the wines were incredibly rich and concentrated, 'a recompense,' as one observer put it, 'for the years of misery, war and deprivation.'

Mother Nature did most of the work. Because winemakers lacked sugar, sulfur and other chemicals, the wines had to be made in an extremely natural way. To make up for sugar, winemakers increased the time that the must, or fermenting juice, remained in contact with the grape skins. Those skins had been packed with extra natural sugar by the hot weather. Because of a bottle shortage, wines remained longer in the cask, developing even greater character and complexity.

In a sense, 1945 was the last great vintage of the nineteenth century. For winemakers and winegrowers, the end of the war marked the beginning of the twentieth century as high-axle tractors

replaced horses, and bottling machines replaced women who
traditionally did that job, leaving no doubt that a new era in
winemaking had begun.

Vineyard life changed too. Time was no longer told by the church
bells; vines no longer set the rhythm and pace of life. 'Workers used
to be part of the family; now they are employees,' Robert Drouhin
said. 'Instead of a festival and big feast after the harvest, we pay
them, give them a glass of wine and say goodbye.

'The increase in economic well-being has led to a change in
mentality. More and more people are thinking about the profitability
of wine rather than the quality. I think there used to be a lot
more pride.'

Robert fondly recalls the walks he and his father took through
the vineyards and everything Maurice tried to impart to him. 'He
always said that when you are hiring someone, look at the quality
of the person. It is very easy to find a good technician, it's much
harder and more important to have a good person.'

In 1957, when Maurice suffered a stroke, Robert, who was
twenty-four, was forced to drop out of oenology school to take
over the operation. It was a rough beginning. 'I certainly made
enough mistakes,' he said.

Mademoiselle Tridon, who by then was working as Maurice's
secretary, remembers Robert coming into the office for the first
time after his father's stroke. 'He was a very sad young man, but he
listened very carefully to everything I had to say about the business,
and he listened to others as well. That was something Maurice had
always been very good at.'

Maurice died in 1962. A few years later, while going through his
father's papers, Robert discovered a letter Maurice had written to
his wife from prison in 1941:

*In my meditations, I find that nothing in life counts more than the
happiness we can give others, the good that we can do. This is what
we must teach our children, to think of others more than they think*

*of themselves, for it is in this way they will find the most noble
satisfaction of all.*

World War II was the defining moment in the lives of those who
would run France's vineyards. It shaped not only who they were
but all they would become.

Like Robert Drouhin, May-Eliane Miaihle de Lencquesaing credits
her father with instilling in her the principles of hard work and
commitment to quality in the 1970s.

'I owe everything to my father. He believed that discipline was
the key to education, and the most important principle was to train
children, especially the girls, to know how to handle all the tasks
they would face in life.'

Today, Madame de Lencquesaing runs Château Pichon-Longueville,
Comtesse de Lalande, a property that was severely damaged during
the occupation and was hovering near financial ruin until she
took it over. Under her direction, this second-growth estate, as
defined by the 1855 Classification, has produced brilliant wines
that rival and sometimes surpass those of first-growth properties
such as Château Lafite-Rothschild, Château Mouton-Rothschild
and neighboring Château Latour. The wines possess great finesse,
richness and depth of flavor, qualities enhanced by significant
investments Madame de Lencquesaing has made at Pichon since
the early 1980s.

'Those years during the war gave me all the basics,' she said.
'We had the feeling as children that we were heroes, that even
while bombs were falling we were helping in the liberation of our
country.'

Bernard de Nonancourt was eighteen when he went off to war,
inspired by Charles de Gaulle. Over the next four years, however,
his youthful enthusiasm would be tempered by the grim realities
he faced in the Resistance.

When the war ended, Bernard was faced with a completely
different challenge, reviving a moribund champagne house his

mother had purchased. In 1945, Laurent-Perrier was ranked at the bottom of the heap, 98th of the 100 major champagne houses.

Today, under Bernard's guidance, it is one of the top 10 with a staff of 360 people and an annual production of nearly 11 million bottles. Bernard attributes his success directly to what he learned in the Resistance, 'the knowledge of organization and how to make a team work together.'

There was something else he learned as well. 'Keep a love of risks,' he says. 'Don't be too self-satisfied.'

Some years ago, when Bernard was trying to come up with a name for a luxury line of champagne he was planning to produce, he sent a list of possible names to President de Gaulle. The response came back immediately: 'Grand Siècle, of course, de Nonancourt!'

Years later, after Grand Siècle had become the flagship of Laurent-Perrier, Bernard said, 'I can still hear his voice whenever I read that message.'

Douglas MacArthur inspired him too. There is a plaque with a quote from the American general on his desk. 'I look at it every day,' Bernard said. 'It says, "Be young." I am seventy-eight now, but when I look back, I find that I miss those times. Although the war was awful for the world, it was the most beautiful moment of my life. I felt so full of patriotism.'

After five years as a prisoner of war, Gaston Huet quickly became one of France's greatest winemakers. He also became mayor of Vouvray, a post he held for forty-six years.

At age ninety, he is still active. He spends a great deal of time visiting oenological schools and speaking to aspiring winemakers. His advice: 'Forget everything you've learned in school. Get rid of bad habits. Come back to traditions.'

Until recently, the one other thing he treasured was the annual reunion with those who had been imprisoned with him at Oflag IV D. After the war, the men got together every year to share memories and remind each other that yes, they really had survived. Each year, however, fewer and fewer attended. The men had grown older; one by one, they began passing away.

In 1997, for the first time, there was no reunion. 'There were not enough of us left,' Huet said.

Huet's belief in tradition is something Jean Hugel fiercely embraced. Over and over again, he told his three sons that 'a well-treated wine is an untreated wine,' and that the winemaker should allow Nature to follow its own course as much as possible.

Never were the wines he made better displayed than in June 1989. That is when the Hugels finally had their party – fifty years after they had planned it. The first one, scheduled to celebrate their 300th anniversary as wine producers in 1939, had to be canceled when war was declared. Now they were celebrating their 350th anniversary.

It was a glamorous event that included a tasting of some of the greatest wines from the Hugels' cellar. They included the 1945 Gewürztraminer Sélection des Grains Nobles, a wine of extraordinary sweetness, complexity and concentration. 'It's a wine that tastes like it will live forever,' Johnny Hugel said.

The tasting followed a plan laid down by Papa Jean Hugel in 1967. 'These wines,' he wrote, 'should only be tasted under the following circumstances: on their own, outside the context of a meal, with your best wine-loving friends, in a respectful atmosphere and without the slightest reference to their price. In such a way, you will do homage to the skill and honesty of the winegrower, and equally to Nature, without whom the production of such jewels would be impossible.'

Sadly, Jean Hugel, who died in 1980, was not there for the celebration.

A few years after the war, young Armand Monmousseaux came running home from school waving his history lesson in front of him.

'Papa, Papa,' he hollered, 'was this really you?' Armand's class had been studying the French Resistance when the boy came across a passage describing how a certain Jean Monmousseaux used his wine barrels to help the Resistance by smuggling arms and people across the Demarcation Line.

His father looked at the article. It was about a winegrower from the Touraine who joined Combat, one of the earliest Resistance organizations, and risked his life by hiding weapons, documents and Resistance leaders in his wooden casks, and then transporting them on horse-drawn wagons past German checkpoints. When Jean finished reading, he looked at his son and rather sheepishly admitted that the story was indeed about him.

Jean's wife, who was English and had tried to live 'very quietly during the war,' overheard what had just been said and was furious. 'All that time and you never told *me*?' she exclaimed. 'How could you? Did you think you couldn't trust me?'

'No, no,' Jean replied. 'I just didn't want you to worry or put anyone else in danger.'

Al Ricciuti was feeling restless; he had a stack of work waiting for him, but instead of attending to it, he started a letter. It was one of dozens he had written to Paulette Revolte in the years since the war had ended. 'I am thinking of coming back to France,' he wrote. 'I would like to retrace my wartime steps. May I stop by to see you and your family?'

Paulette's response was enthusiastic. 'We would love to see you again; please plan to stay with us. We have lots of new champagne for you to taste.'

Al packed his bags. Within two days he was back on Utah Beach, eighteen years after landing there with Patton's Third Army. Memories came flooding back, some of them grim and others that made him laugh out loud. How could he ever forget the first time he met General Patton? 'There were about a hundred of us, all naked and lined up, waiting to get into a portable shower, when someone yelled, "Ten-hut!" We snapped to attention still clutching our bars of soap when Patton marched up. He stopped right in front of the guy next to me and barked, "Soldier, when did you last take a shower?" The guy replied, "About a month ago, sir." "Good," said Patton. "Keep taking 'em regularly like that."'

Following Al's second 'landing' in Normandy, he was off to northern France and into the Ardennes Forest in Belgium. Finally, he arrived in Champagne.

'That's when it struck me, when I came back and saw her. It was love at second sight,' he said.

Al and Paulette were married on January 21, 1963, in Avenay-Val-d'Or. After a short honeymoon, they returned to Baltimore, where Al worked for the National Guard Armory and Paulette worked at not being homesick.

Seven months later they received a letter from Paulette's brother saying he could no longer run the family's champagne business. If Paulette did not want it, he was going to sell it.

Once again, Al packed his bags and, this time with Paulette, headed back to France. Al was planning on a U.S. civil service job there while Paulette ran the family business, but it did not turn out that way. France suddenly closed down all the American military installations in the country.

Paulette could not have been happier. 'I need the help,' she told him. 'You can work here with me.' He agreed to give it a try.

Al started by following her around. 'I made notes about everything and kept a diary every day,' he said. And he tasted as much as possible. 'I didn't really know anything about champagne but what appealed to me was seeing the end product. It wasn't like other jobs where you work and work and never see what you've done.'

That is how Al Ricciuti became the first American to make champagne. However, it did not happen overnight. Some of the locals looked down their noses at him and wondered what an American could possibly know about making champagne. 'They didn't really show it outwardly but I knew how they felt,' Al said. 'There were some sarcastic remarks.'

Over the years, jealousy and sarcasm gave way to admiration. 'He was a good student,' Paulette said. 'People were impressed with how hard he worked and how anxious he was to learn.' A spokesman for Mumm's, which buys 25 percent of Al's grapes, said Al was as much a part of the community as any French person. 'The Champagne community is tightly knit,' said George Vesselle. 'Penetrating the circle is difficult, especially for a foreigner, but Al succeeded.'

Al, however, is modest about his achievement. 'I like to drink champagne but I do not have what you would call a good palate. My wife is the one with the palate.'

That brought a laugh from Paulette, who said, 'I don't have to taste champagne. It's in my blood.'

Many of Al's best customers are former army buddies. Usually, they sit in the kitchen, swapping war stories under the watchful eyes of President Truman and General Eisenhower, whose portraits adorn certificates commending Paulette and her family for saving the lives of U.S. airmen.

In 1959, the head barman of the Hôtel Meurice in Paris noticed a short rotund man 'with impossibly correct posture' wandering around the bar. He seemed to be in a daze, almost as if he were in another world.

'May I help you?' the barman asked.

'Yes,' the man replied. 'I once lived here for a short while and was wondering if I could see my old room again.'

The barman, Pierre Lévéjac, recognized the man and asked him to wait while he phoned the hotel manager. 'Sir, you're not going to believe this but Dietrich von Choltitz is here and he would like to see his room.'

The manager rushed to the bar, where von Choltitz, elegantly dressed in a dark blue suit, introduced himself and repeated his request. 'I would be delighted to show you your old room,' the manager said. 'If you will follow me.'

The two went to the fourth floor, where the former German commander of Paris once lived. Von Choltitz spent several minutes looking around the room, mostly in silence, before opening a door and stepping out onto the balcony overlooking the Tuileries. 'Ah yes, this is what I remember,' he said.

Within a quarter of an hour, the manager had escorted von Choltitz back to the bar and suggested they open up a bottle of champagne. 'We must mark this occasion of your return, *mon général.*' But von Choltitz declined. 'I have done what I wanted to do and must now be on my way,' he said.

Von Choltitz had another engagement, this one with Pierre Taittinger, the wartime mayor of Paris. Taittinger had organized a luncheon in von Choltitz's honor, but the old general, who disobeyed Hitler by surrendering Paris intact, refused to be treated like a conquering hero. 'Von Choltitz was not an easy man,' said Taittinger's son Claude, who attended the luncheon. 'He was a Prussian and perhaps he felt uncomfortable about having once disobeyed his commander-in-chief. Later, however, while we were having coffee on the terrace, he told me something I shall never forget. He said, "I understood what your father was telling me. I made my decision not to destroy Paris after talking to your father."'

Three years later, in 1962, Parisians were surprised to discover German flags flying alongside French ones on the Champs-Elysées. For the first time since the war, a French President was welcoming a German head of state.

That evening, Robert-Jean de Vogüé sat down to watch the news on television with his son Ghislain. When the cameras switched to President Charles de Gaulle as he was about to shake hands with Chancellor Konrad Adenauer, Ghislain jumped up and said, 'Here, let me turn this off. I'm sure you don't want to watch this.'

His father stretched out his arm to stop him. 'No, stay where you are, leave it on,' he said. 'This is what I have worked all my life to see.'

GLOSSARY

APPELLATION D'ORIGINE CONTRÔLÉE (AOC) controlled place of origin. For French wine, it guarantees that the wine not only comes from the place listed (such as Burgundy or Bordeaux) but also meets the standards of quality for that area.

ARRONDISSEMENT district or borough of a city.

BLACK ROT a fungal disease that attacks grapevines, leaving black spots on the green parts of the plant and shriveling the fruit. Most virulent in warm weather and high humidity. Treatment is with copper sulfate.

BOCHES derogatory name given the Germans.

BORDELAIS a resident of Bordeaux.

CAVE a cellar, generally a wine cellar.

CHAMPENOIS a resident of Champagne.

CHÂTEAU (PL.: CHÂTEAUX) literally, castle, but generally used to signify an entire wine estate–house (irrespective of whether it is a castle), vineyards, *caves* and other buildings. Most Bordeaux wine comes from châteaux.

CHEMINOTS railway workers, derived from the French for railroad, *chemin de fer,* literally iron road.

CHEVALIERS literally, knights; now frequently used for members of a wine society, in French a *confrérie*, or brotherhood.

COMITÉ INTERPROFESSIONNEL DU VIN DE CHAMPAGNE (CIVC) the semi-governmental interprofessional body which regulates the Champagne industry.

COMITÉ NATIONAL DES APPELLATIONS D'ORIGINE the governing body for the guarantees on place of origin and quality in French wine.

COPPER SULFATE a copper salt, sometimes called blue stone, used to treat vines against fungus.

CÔTE D'OR literally, the Golden Slope or Escarpment; the area of Burgundy between Dijon and Santenay where some of the greatest Burgundies are made. Both red and white wines are made here.

CUVÉE contents of a wine vat or a special lot of wine.

DORYPHORES potato bugs, or Colorado potato beetles, probably brought to Europe in shipments from America in the 1930s. Came to be a derogatory term for German soldiers.

DOSAGE the sugar syrup made from champagne wine and sugar that is added to champagne before its final corking. The amount added depends on the sweetness of the champagne. The drier the champagne, the smaller the dosage used.

EAU-DE-SANTENAY a laxative; purgative water.

EAU-DE-VIE literally, water of life, but the generic name for distilled spirits, including brandy.

FEUILLES MORTES literally, dead leaves; used to describe the traditional color of bottles for Burgundy wine, a brownish-green color.

FROGS a derogatory name for the French.

GOLDEN ESCARPMENT see Côte d'Or.

GRANDS CRUS the great vineyards.

GRAND SIÈCLE literally 'great century'; the name of Bernard de Nonancourt's luxury champagne.

HOSPICES DE BEAUNE the charity hospital in Beaune in Burgundy, founded in 1443. The hospital is funded by the sale of wine from its vineyards, which have been donated to the Hospices by area vineyard owners through the centuries. The annual auction of its wines in November is considered an indicator of prices for the vintage.

INSTITUT NATIONAL DES APPELLATIONS D'ORIGINE (INAO) the administrative organization for guaranteeing place of origin and quality in French wine. The organization is based in Paris, but has technical experts in each of France's wine regions.

MADERIZED oxidized; a condition of older wines reflecting the gradual seepage of oxygen into the bottle as the space between the cork and wine increases.

MAIRIE French term for town or village hall.

MAISON DE TOLÉRANCE a licensed brothel.

MAISON DU VIN a wine business, usually that of a wine wholesaler, who buys wine from growers and bottles it under the house's own label or who buys grapes from growers and then makes and bottles the wine. A *maison du vin* may also own some vineyards and make wine from those grapes under its own label.

MAQUIS literally, the Corsican bush. During World War II, a general term for the French Resistance, the underground.

'MARÉCHAL, NOUS VOILÀ' song composed in honor of Marshal Philippe Pétain, France's head of state during the Vichy years. Especially popular among children in the early years of World War II, when it was regularly sung in schools and even at religious gatherings of young people. Title means 'Marshal, Here We Are.'

MILDEW downy or false mildew that is the most ruinous of the fungal diseases that attack the vines. It originated in America and is spread by the wind, so it is difficult to contain once it attacks a vineyard. High humidity and heat are the key factors in its development. Most American vines are resistant to it, so do not have to be treated with the copper sulfate so necessary to the French vineyards.

MONUMENT AUX MORTS a monument to the war dead of a community. In France every village, no matter how small, has one, usually bearing names of more victims of World War I than of World War II. Soldiers who died in battle are those who are *mort pour la France*, died for France.

MUST grape juice before it ferments completely and becomes wine.

NACHT UND NEBEL German for Night and Fog, but also the term the Third Reich used to designate prisoners it did not want to survive, that it wanted worked to death. They were to disappear within the system, buried in mass and/or unmarked graves, with no information given to families.

NARQUER DES ALLEMANDS   to taunt or make fun of the Germans.

NÉGOCIANTS   wholesale wine merchants who buy wine and/or grapes in quantity from growers and resell the wine. If they buy grapes, they will make the wine and sell it under the house's name. Prior to World War II, they also bottled most of the wine they bought, frequently selling it with the name of the maker on the bottles. This was particularly so in Bordeaux where most of the châteaux did not begin bottling on the property until after World War II.

OFLAG IV D   the German prisoner-of-war camp for French officers in Silesia in Germany where Gaston Huet and more than 4,000 others were held for the five years of World War II.

OIDIUM   powdery or true mildew, another fungal disease of the vines which came to Europe from America. Finely ground sulfur is used to combat it.

PANZERMILCH   the derogatory term for the soy beverage prisoners of war got in camps instead of coffee or tea. Literally, panzer milk, the panzers being the German tanks that so effectively routed the French in 1940.

PHONY WAR   the period between when war was declared (September 3, 1939) and when fighting actually began (May 10, 1940). Known in French as *le drôle de guerre*.

PHYLLOXERA   a burrowing plant louse that destroyed the vineyards of France at the end of the nineteenth century. Another import from America, but the cure also came from America when native

American vine rootstock was found to be resistant to the louse. All French vines had to be ripped up and burned, with new vines grafted onto the American rootstock.

PIQUETTE   wine made by adding water to the already pressed skins and husks of grapes. It is very low in alcohol and is usually given to vineyard workers as a daily ration. Also used as a derogatory name for any bad wine.

RUE   street

ST. VINCENT   the patron saint of French winemakers. His feast day is celebrated near January 24. He was chosen as the winemakers' patron saint because the first syllable of his name is the French word for wine, *vin*. For winegrowers, there is one other point in his favor: January is about the only month when there is almost no work to be done in the vineyards; hence they can take the time to celebrate. This they usually do with a procession to the church, then a mass where the local priest blesses the wine and the statue of the saint is passed to the winegrower who will look after it for the coming year.

SERVICE DU TRAVAIL OBLIGATOIRE (STO)   the forced labor program set up by Vichy in 1942 to meet German demands for labor. It did more to recruit members for the Resistance than anything else. Those called up for STO generally preferred to go into hiding with the Maquis than to go to Germany to work for the Third Reich.

TERROIR   all the natural conditions influencing the vine and the grape (climate, soil, landscape).

TOUR D'ARGENT, LA   one of Paris's best-known and oldest restaurants, especially famous for its duck. A favorite with German officers based in Paris during World War II. Owned then, as now, by the Terrail family.

TRÈS ANCIENNE literally, very old. Old-fashioned.

TRICOLORE literally, three-colored. The French flag with its wide stripes of blue, white and red.

VIGNERONS winegrowers.

VIN CHAUD DU SOLDAT literally, hot wine for soldiers, usually served at special canteens during the winter months. Considered a preventative against disease during cold weather. Kits for making hot wine were also sent to soldiers at the front lines.

VIN ORDINAIRE literally, ordinary wine. Common wine with nothing special about it, drunk with routine meals at home.

VINIFICATION winemaking.

WEINFÜHRERS a German-sounding word made up by the French to designate the men sent by the Nazis to buy French wine and oversee its distribution.

NOTES

Most of the information in our book came from personal interviews with those who actively participated in the events of the time and whose families were directly involved. Material from published sources that could not be included in the main text is cited in the following notes. Publication information about those sources is contained in the Bibliography.

Introduction

PAGE

2   *Berchtesgaden . . . the 'Valhalla for the Nazi gods'*: Stephen E.
       Ambrose, *Band of Brothers; E Company, 506th Regiment, 101st
       Airborne, from Normandy to Hitler's Eagle's Nest*, p. 271.

2   *'Behind those pleasant white walls'*: Robert Payne, *The Life and
       Death of Adolf Hitler*, pp. 351–54.

6   The use of wine in war by Cyrus the Great, Julius Caesar
       and other wartime figures is described by Herbert M. Baus,
       How to Wine Your Way to Good Health, p. 182.

6   *'A ration of wine is not expensive'*: *Bulletin International du
       Vin*, October/November 1939, p. 109.

6   *wine's apogee as a military tactic*: Baus, *How to Wine Your
       Way*, p. 183.

7   *Wine as 'a good counselor'*: André L. Simon, *A Wine
       Primer*, p. 11.

10   The study of wine's importance to the French character is
        from the article 'La Vigne et le Vin,' vol. 2 of tome 3 of
        Nora Pierre (ed.), *Les Lieux de Mémoire*, which were part of a
        French government survey, pp. 796–97.

11   *Mirepoix . . . gave a speech . . . in which he described how wine
        'contributed to the French race by giving them wit'*: quoted
        by Robert O. Paxton, *French Peasant Against Fascism: Henry
        Dorgères's Greenshirts and the Crisis of French Agriculture*,
        1929–1939, p. 22.

                    ONE *To Love the Vines*

15   Information about the International Conference of the Vine
        and Wine comes from Charles K. Warner, *The Winegrowers
        of France and the Government Since* 1875, p. 157, and from
        the *Bulletin International du Vin*, August 1939.

16   *'Our opponents are little worms'*: Paul Johnson, *Modern Times:
        The World from the Twenties to the Eighties*, p. 360.

20   *Phylloxera, a tiny insect:* discussed at length in Alexis
        Lichine's *New Encyclopedia of Wines and Spirits*, p. 31.

21   Bizarre remedies and a 300,000-franc reward described by
        Warner, *Winegrowers of France*, p. 4.

21   Vineyard conditions are discussed extensively by Warner,
        Winegrowers of France, p. vii-x, 70–79. Also by François
        Bonal in *Le Livre d'Or du Champagne*, pp. 4–5,
        174.

23   The birth of AOC is described by Remington Norman, *The Great Domaines of Burgundy*, p. 244.

23   blending *'is to some extent like kissing'*: André L. Simon, *A Wine Primer*, p. 71.

27   *the peasants' legend about war and wine*: Janet Flanner, 'Letter from France,' *The New Yorker*, September 15, 1945, p. 72.

27   *'This is a queer war so far'*: article by Janet Flanner in *The New Yorker War Pieces, London* 1939 *to Hiroshima* 1945, p. 6.

33   The planting of roses and gardens on the Maginot Line comes from Jean-Pierre Azema, *From Munich to the Liberation*, 1938–1944, p. 27.

33   *'Since you don't have anything to do'*: quoted by Herbert R. Lottman, *The Fall of Paris: June* 1940, p. 6.

34   *'Confidence is a duty!'*: and France's reaction to an imminent German invasion is reported in an article by A. J. Liebling in *The New Yorker War Pieces*, p. 40.

34   *'Wine is the good companion of soldiers'*: Édouard Barthe is quoted by Jean-Louis Crémieux-Brilhac in *Les Français de l'An 40, tome II*, p. 463.

35   *'Any Frenchman over thirty remembered the blind wastage'*: Robert O. Paxton, *Vichy France: Old Guard and New Order*, 1940–44, pp. 11–12.

35   The shipment of wine to the front being a state secret

is cited in a French Ministry of War report of January
26, 1938.

36   'Gentlemen, you are about to witness': *The Oxford Companion
to World War II*, p. 408.

36   'like a lot of small corks, to plug holes in the line': from Alistair
Horne's essay on the Fall of France, ibid., p. 411.

36   'We can beat the Boches': article by Liebling in *The New
Yorker War Pieces*, p. 39.

TWO *Nomads*

41   *biggest migration of people seen in Europe since the Dark Ages:*
The Oxford Companion to World War II, p. 392.

41   'They don't know, nobody knows, where they are going':
from the *Cahiers* of Paul Valéry, quoted by Robert
O. Paxton in *Vichy France: Old Guard and New Order,
1940–1944*, p. 13.

42   'Nearly every Frenchman had been nurtured on stories of
German atrocities', ibid., p. 15.

42   'It was a retreat without glory': René Engle, *Vosne-Romanée, un
Mémoire*, p. 24.

43   'The Germans swept in like angels of death': Florence Mothe,
Toutes Hontes Bues, p. 147.

44   *losses – 90,000 dead, 200,000 wounded*: cited in *Oxford
Companion to World War II*, p. 408.

44   *'le don de ma personne'*: Pétain quoted by Paxton, *Vichy France*, p.37.

44   *'the leader who saved us from the abyss'*: ibid., p.14.

44   *'Of all the shipments to the armies'*: from an essay written by Pétain for Gaston Derys's *Mon Docteur le Vin*, 1935.

45   *'No one admitted responsibility'*: H. R. Kedward, *Resistance in Vichy France: A Study of Ideas and Motivation in the Southern Zone*, 1940–1942, p. 11.

45   Marc Bloch's disillusionment with the French high command is described by Paul Johnson, *Modern Times: The World from the Twenties to the Eighties*, p. 364.

46   *'No one who lived through the French debacle'*: Paxton, *Vichy France*, p. 3.

49   *'it allowed the Germans to appear organized and generous'*: H. R. Kedward, *Occupied France: Collaboration and Resistance*, 1940–1944, p. 3–5.

49   *'Don't worry about the heating'*: Paxton, *Vichy France*, p. 19.

49   Hitler's lust for booty: ibid., p.xii.

49   *'The real profiteers of this war'*: Gordon Wright, *The Ordeal of Total War*, 1939–1945, p.117.

52   Château Haut-Brion's conversion into a hospital for French soldiers and later into a rest home for the Germans was

described to us during an interview with Jean-Bernard Delmas, manager of the estate. Delmas's father was in charge of Haut-Brion's winemaking during the war.

52   The use of bells at Cos d'Estournel for target practice: from an interview with Bruno Prats, former owner of the château.

53   The German takeover of Château du Clos de Vougeot was related to us by Jacques Chevignard, executive secretary of the *Confrérie des Chevaliers du Tastevin*, Burgundy's wine fraternity.

53   The German rampage at Sézanne-en-Champagne was described by Maître Antoine Petit in the catalogue for the auction of some of the Hôtel de France wines, November 29, 1998. He elaborated on the destruction during an interview with us following the sale.

53   *At least* 250 *trainloads of goods destined for Germany had been looted:* Wright, *Ordeal of Total War*, p. 119.

54   *'In the old days, the rule was plunder':* ibid., p. 117. Also quoted by Jacques Delarue, *Trafic et Crimes sous l'Occupation*, p. 80.

54   Göring's retort that the French franc be used for toilet paper: Delarue, ibid., p. 80.

54   The story of Félix Kir was discovered in a series of articles he wrote for the Dijon newspaper *Le Bien Publique*. The series, *Dijon sous l'Occupation*, was published in January and February 1965.

54   Vichy's rush to hammer out an armistice agreement is noted
      by Paxton, *Vichy France*, pp. 7–11.

55   The power struggle within the German command over how
      France should be treated is discussed by, among others,
      Wright, *Ordeal of Total War*, pp. 116–20.

55   The adoration of Pétain is cited by numerous sources, among
      them an essay by Kedward in *Oxford Companion to World
      War II*, p. 392.

55   Vichy philosophy and policy is extensively discussed by
      Paxton and Kedward throughout their books.

56   Story of the sleeping Pétain is related by Johnson, *Modern
      Times*, p. 365.

57   German soldiers behaving like tourists in Paris and their
      fascination with its restaurants is recounted in Alistair Horne's
      essay on the Fall of France, *Oxford Companion to World War
      II*, and in Bertram M. Gordon's article 'Ist Gott Französisch?
      German Tourism and Occupied France, 1940–1944,' published
      in *Modern and Contemporary France* in 1996.

                     THREE   *The Weinführers*

63   German leadership's ties to French wine trade came from
      interviews and other sources, including Florence Mothe,
      Toutes Hontes Bues, pp. 148–58.

63   The comments of Albert Speer about Göring's love of Lafite
      are found in his book *Inside the Third Reich*.

64   '*Spare me your little champagne peddler*': Mothe, *Toutes Hontes Bues*, pp. 157–58.

64   '*His asceticism was a fiction*': Robert Payne, *The Life and Death of Adolf Hitler*, p. 346.

64   '*To animate these rather barren evenings*': Speer, *Inside the Third Reich*, p. 91.

65   '*transform yourselves into a pack of hunting dogs*': Jacques Delarue, *Trafic et Crimes sous l'Occupation*, p. 80.

69   '*Will this integral part of French civilization be confiscated*': Mothe, *Toutes Hontes Bues*, pp. 153–54.

70   '*It was embarrassing how they bowed and scraped to him*': ibid., pp. 160–61.

75   Segnitz's reaction upon learning some Burgundy winemakers were trying to cheat him was told to us by his son.

80   The letters of Maurice Drouhin from prison were shared with us by his son Robert.

84   '*Thanks to you, I am now the owner*': Bulletin of the Centre Beaunois d'Études Historiques, No. 37, November 1990, p. 90.

85   The description of grim-faced soldiers preparing to move out to the Russian front came from an interview we had with the Marquis d'Angerville.

86   Segnitz's 'thank-you' letter came from the Drouhin archives.

86   The loss of two million bottles of champagne is cited by
François Bonal, *Le Livre d'Or du Champagne*, p. 192.

88   Much of the information about Robert de Vogüé's meeting
with Klaebisch comes from interviews with his son Ghislain
and with Claude Fourmon.

90   *'Work Sundays!'*: Cynthia Parzych and John Turner, *Pol
Roger*, p. 14.

93   *'How dare you send us fizzy'*: Claude Taittinger, *Champagne by
Taittinger*, p. 87.

93   Guy Taittinger's charming of Klaebisch was described to us
by Claude Taittinger in an interview and also in his book,
ibid., pp. 87–88.

94   Use of information about champagne shipments by the
Resistance and British intelligence: Parzych and Turner, *Pol
Roger*, p. 36.

98   *'Owing to the Germans' mania'*: *Janet Flanner's World:
Uncollected Writings, 1932–1975*. p. 51.

FOUR   *Hiding, Fibbing and Fobbing Off*

103   The story of Henri Gaillard is gleaned from two logbooks
that were discovered in a closet of Gaillard's former station
in the 1990s.

105   *'hiding, fibbing and fobbing off'*: Janet Flanner, 'Letter from

France,' *The New Yorker*, September 15, 1945, p. 72.

105   *the management . . . 'would be terribly, terribly sorry'*:
      Patrick Forbes, *Champagne: The Wine, the Land and the
      People*, p. 215.

106   *'It was almost a patriotic act'*: recalled by Claude Taittinger
      in an interview with us and in his book, *Champagne by
      Taittinger*, pp. 36–37.

107   The story of how one winegrower hid his wines in a pond
      was related by André L. Simon to Wynford Vaughan-Thomas
      in *How I Liberated Burgundy*, p. 155.

107   Mayor Vavasseur's encounter with the Germans was
      described to us in an interview with Gaston Huet.

108   *the Germans 'had the feeling that they were constantly being
      tricked'*: A. J. Liebling, *The New Yorker War Pieces*, p. 349.

109   Madame Gombaud's use of rat droppings is told by
      Nicholas Faith, *Victorian Vineyard: Château Loudenne and the
      Gilbeys*, p. 146.

109   *'We knew certain things were going on'*: from an interview
      with Professor Helmut Arntz, a former German soldier
      in Paris.

110   The story of Ronald Barton was told to us by his nephew,
      Anthony Barton, who now owns and manages Châteaux
      Langoa- and Léoville-Barton.

111   The heroics of Gaby Faux were described to us by Baron
      Eric de Rothschild and cited by Cyril Ray, *Lafite*, pp. 61–64.

114   '*minor gestures of defiance*': H. R. Kedward, *Occupied France: Collaboration and Resistance*, 1940–1944, p. 8.

114   '*I couldn't bring myself to touch*': from an interview with Suzanne Dumbrill in Champagne.

115   The clash between French students and German police is described by David Schoenbrun, *Soldiers of the Night: The Story of the French Resistance*, pp. 88–96.

115   '*If we had been "occupied," to use the polite term*': Jean Paulhan, *Summer of '44*, p. 91.

116   Jean Monmousseaux's exploits were noted by Schoenbrun, *Soldiers of the Night*, p. 134, and described to us in greater detail in an interview with Monmousseaux's son, Armand.

117   '*They pillaged it neatly*': from an essay by Robert Aron, 'Bordeaux Sauvé par Son Vin.'

119   *conditions of life . . . had 'declined from austerity to severe want*': Robert O. Paxton, *Vichy France: Old Guard and New Order*, 1940–1944, p. 237.

FIVE   *The Growling Stomach*

124   '*The French are so stuffed*': Jacques Delarue, *Trafic et Crimes sous l'Occupation*, p. 79.

125   The decision to limit the calorific intake of the French, reported by Michel Cépède, *Agriculture et Alimentation en France durant le Deuxième Guerre Mondiale*, p. 151.

125 'The old and the ill need wine': from Report to the Fifth
Congrès National du Vin de France, p. 12.

125 'We said, "Don't you want to get well"': ibid., p. 67.

126 France as the worst-nourished of Western occupied
countries, and the real voice being 'the growling stomach':
Robert O. Paxton, *Vichy France: Old Guard and New Order*,
1940–1944, p. 238.

128 'Ja, we're the doryphores . . .': Irving Drutman, ed., *Janet
Flanner's World: Uncollected Writings*, 1932–1975, p. 52.

128 The disappearance of pigeons from a park in Bordeaux was
reported by the newspaper *Sud-Ouest*, September 1997,
as part of a collection of articles entitled 'Procés Papon:
l'Histoire d'une Époque,' looking back at wartime Bordeaux.

128 'We were so hungry that we ate the goldfish': Varian Fry,
Surrender on Demand, p. 182.

129 'What helped a lot was wine': ibid., p. 121.

129 Laws restricting the amount of wine which producers were
allowed to make: Charles K. Warner, *The Winegrowers of
France and the Government Since 1875*, pp. 160–61.

130 The table of statistics concerning wine production,
ibid., p. 158.

135 'God made man': from a book of poems and essays
compiled and edited by Joni G. McNutt, *In Praise of
Wine*, p. 218.

135   Information about Vichy's antialcoholism policies can be
        found in Paxton, *Vichy France*, pp. 146–48.

136   Vichy's decision to allow growers to water wine in order
        to stretch the dwindling supply is described by Warner,
        Winegrowers of France, p. 161.

136   Black market problems are cited in René Terrisse, *Bordeaux
        1940–1944*, p. 160.

137   The story of Claude Brosse is found in *Alexis Lichine's New
        Encyclopaedia of Wines and Spirits*, p. 317.

138   '*No one could ever have imagined*': Lucie Aubrac, *Outwitting
        the Gestapo*, p. 52.

138   '*When they finished, they poured a glass of heating oil*':
        ibid, p. 51.

139   '*Sex and food are the only things that matter*': Paul
        Johnson, *Modern Times: The World from the Twenties to the
        Eighties*, p. 365.

139   '*le con qui se dort*': attributed to Georges Mandel, Minister of
        Colonies, by several sources.

139   Pétain's stomping through the Midi to criticize
        winegrowers is described by Warner, *Winegrowers of
        France, p.* 162.

139   Laval's plan to send French workers to Germany is explained
        by H. R. Kedward. *Occupied France: Collaboration and
        Resistance 1940–1944*, p. 61–62.

146   'war of annihilation': Johnson, *Modern Times*, p. 380.

SIX *Wolves at the Door*

153   The legend of the wolves is recounted by Robert J. Casey,
           The Lost Kingdom of Burgundy, p. 21–23.

157   Vichy's persecution of Jews is depicted by H. R. Kedward,
           Occupied France: Collaboration and Resistance, 1940–1944, p.
           28.

157   'They must all go': ibid., p. 63.

160   The flight of young men from STO is explained by Robert
           O. Paxton, *Vichy France: Old Guard and New Order,
           1940–1944*, p. 292, and Kedward, *Occupied France*, p. 62.

161   'With every week that passed': Kedward, *Occupied France*, p. 9.

162   The Piper-Heidsieck story was recounted by Patrick
           Forbes, *Champagne: The Wine, the Land and the People*,
           p. 215, and expanded upon in an interview with Claude
           Taittinger.

SEVEN *The Fête*

176   It was through a series of interviews with Gaston Huet that
           we pieced together the story of the wine banquet. Huet
           also loaned us a logbook he and other POWs kept, which
           helped us to better understand how much the fête meant to
           those being held prisoner.

184   Roger Ribaud's story is derived entirely from the book he
wrote in prison, *Le Maître de Maison de Sa Cave à Sa Table*,
which was published after the war.

EIGHT *Saving the Treasure*

193   *'France's most precious jewel'*: this term used by Defense
Minister Daladier was reported by the *Bulletin International
du Vin*, July/August 1938.

196   *'The Germans are burning people alive'*: part of a story told
to us by Jacky Cortot, who recalled during an interview how
German soldiers retaliated against the Resistance by torching
his village of Comblanchien.

197   *'Turn Paris into a front-line city'*: Larry Collins and
Dominique Lapierre, *Is Paris Burning?*, p. 38.

198   The role of Frédéric Joliot-Curie, ibid., p. 117.

198   The use of Taittinger champagne bottles for making Molotov
cocktails was confirmed by Dominique Lapierre.

198   In an interview with us, Claude Taittinger described how
his father pleaded with General Dietrich von Choltitz not to
destroy Paris.

198   *he would 'burn all the houses'*: David Schoenbrun,
Soldiers of the Night: The Story of the French Resistance,
p. 439.

199   *'Paris is one of the few great cities'*: ibid.

200   The bombing of the Halle aux Vins: *New York Times*, August
         27, 1944.

201   Louis Eschenauer's efforts to persuade Ernst Kühnemann
         not to carry out orders to destroy the port are described by
         several sources, among them Pierre Bécamps, *La Libération
         de Bordeaux*, pp. 57–75.

202   'top secret' order 1-122-144 is mentioned by Florence
         Mothe, *Toutes Hontes Bues*, p. 164.

203   *'We had put down a tremendous barrage'*: Wynford Vaughan-
         Thomas, *How I Liberated Burgundy*, p. 3.

204   *'We would go out on patrol'*: Robert H. Aldeman and Col.
         George Walton, *The Champagne Campaign*, pp. 111–16.

207   the unusual early-warning system in which the French held
         out bottles of wine is described by Stephen E. Ambrose,
         *The Victors: Eisenhower and His Boys, the Men of World
         War II*, p. 229.

209   The damage sustained by Château du Clos de Vougeot was
         described to us in an interview with Jacques Chevignard.

209   Al Ricciuti told us about his wartime adventures during an
         interview at his home in Champagne.

210   Ricciuti's claims that the Germans did not have time to set
         off explosives was confirmed by Patrick Forbes, *Champagne:
         The Wine, the Land and the People*, p. 216, who said he had
         been told that Himmler had also planted dynamite in the
         cellars of Epernay. The explosives were to be detonated if the

Germans were forced to evacuate the city. Himmler's motive
was to give Sekt producers in Germany a headstart after
the war.

211 The liberation of Alsace was described at length during
interviews with Georges, Johnny and André Hugel.

NINE   *Eagle's Nest*

218 *'It will be terrible for my men'*: from a letter quoted by André
Martel in *Leclerc: Le Soldat et le Politique.*

219 *'One minute they were here'*: Stephen Ambrose, *Band of
Brothers: E Company, 506th Regiment, 101st Airborne, from
Normandy to Hitler's Eagle's Nest*, p. 272.

219 The decision by the Americans to take the autobahn,
ibid., p. 273.

219 *'It was ... a fairy-tale land with snowcapped mountains'*:
ibid., p. 273.

220 The legend of Barbarossa is told by Robert Payne, *The Life
and Death of Adolf Hitler*, p. 354.

220 Hitler's efforts to turn Berchtesgaden into a fortress, ibid.,
pp. 351–54.

220 *'It occurred to Hitler'*, ibid., pp. 352–53.

220 Bernard de Nonancourt's exploits were described
to us during a lengthy interview at his home in
Champagne.

222   Hitler's reluctance to visit Eagle's Nest, Payne, *Life and Death
         of Adolf Hitler*, p. 353.

225   General Haislip's anger at having been beaten by the French
         is reported by Martel in his biography of Leclerc.

225   *'It's been a long and hard road'*: ibid.

TEN   *The Collaborator*

229   Much of the information about Louis Eschenauer's personal
         life came from an interview with Bordeaux journalist and
         winegrower Florence Mothe, whose stepfather worked for
         Uncle Louis. She expanded on that information in interviews
         with us and with Dr J. Kim Munholland of the University
         of Minnesota. She also described it in her book, *Toutes
         Hontes Bues*.

231   *'You couldn't get in unless'*: quote from Mothe.

236   Much of the information about the German departure from
         Bordeaux was discovered in the archives of *Sud-Ouest*.

237   *'I had only one goal'*: Robert O. Paxton, *Vichy France: Old
         Guard and New Order*, 1940–1944, p. 368.

238   'coiffure '44': from Gertrude Stein, who was quoted in
         Corinne Verdet's *Summer of '44*, p. 70, as saying, 'Today
         the village is tops-turvy, because they are going to shave the
         heads of the girls who compromised themselves with the
         Germans. It's what they call Coiffure 44 and it is terrible
         because they are shaved in public.'

239   *'No Resistance historian should try'*: H. R. Kedward, *Occupied France: Collaboration and Resistance, 1940–1944, p. 77.*

239   Statistics concerning those charged with collaboration, ibid., p. 77.

239   *'Not all of it is the same character'*: from government documents obtained by Dr J. Kim Munholland.

240   The charges against Eschenauer and his contention that 'I am not a collaborator' are contained in the November 10 and 12 editions of *Sud-Ouest*, 1945.

240   Details of Eschenauer's closed trial were discovered in government documents obtained by Florence Mothe, copies of which were shared with Dr J. Kim Munholland.

ELEVEN *I Came Home Not Young Anymore*

249   Huet's liberation from a POW camp was described to us by Huet during an interview.

251   Mother Nature's conspiracy against winegrowers is depicted in a wartime diary kept by the Lawton brothers of Bordeaux.

255   Robert-Jean de Vogüé's survival and return home were described to us by his son, Ghislain.

256   Claude Fourmon was still visibly shaken and could barely speak as he struggled to tell us how he survived.

257   Baron Philippe de Rothschild's return to Mouton and his

wife's arrest by the Gestapo were recounted to us by their daughter, Philippine.

258   '*I can never look at the road*': Baron Philippe de Rothschild, *Vivre la Vigne: Du Ghetto de Francfort à Mouton Rothschild*, 1744–1981, p. 70.

259   Jean Monnet and France's economic recovery program: Paul Johnson, *Modern Times: The World from the Twenties to the Eighties*, pp. 590–91.

259   The eradication of hybrids by Hitler Youth brigades was described by Georges Hugel in an interview.

261   Court action declaring that the gift of the Clos du Maréchal be null and void is cited in the *Bulletin of the Centre Beaunois d'Études Historiques*, No. 37, November 1990.

261   In an interview with Robert Drouhin, we learned how the gate of the Clos was torn down.

262   The auction of Pétain's wines conducted by Georges Rappeneau is cited by the Beaune Historical Society.

264   Most of the information about the Chapitre de Résurrection came from the archives of the Confrérie des Chevaliers du Tastevin.

BIBLIOGRAPHY

Aldeman, Robert H., and Col. George Walton. *The Champagne Campaign*. Boston: Little, Brown and Company, 1969.

Ambrose, Stephen E. *Band of Brothers: E Company, 506th Regiment, 101st Airborne, from Normandy to Hitler's Eagle's Nest*. New York: Simon & Schuster, Touchstone Books, 1992.

——. *The Victors, Eisenhower and His Boys, the Men of World War II*. New York: Simon & Schuster. 1998.

Aron, Robert. 'Bordeaux Sauvé par Son Vin,' *Nouveaux Grands Dossiers d'Histoire Contemporaine*. Paris: P. Perrin, 1972.

Association de Médecins Amis du Vin de France. *Report to the Fifth Congrès National du Vin de France*. Montpellier, France, 1951.

Aubrac, Lucie. *Outwitting the Gestapo*. University of Nebraska, Bison Books. Paris: Éditions du Seuil, 1984.

Azema, Jean-Pierre. *From Munich to the Liberation, 1938–1944*. Paris: Éditions du Seuil, 1979.

Baudot, Marcel, et al., eds. *The Historical Encyclopedia of World War II*. New York: Facts on File. Paris: Édition Casterman, 1977.

Baus, Herbert M. *How to Wine Your Way to Good Health*. New York: Mason & Lipscomb, 1973.

Bécamps, Pierre. *La Liberation de Bordeaux*. Paris: Hachette, 1974.

Le Bien Publique. Dijon, France.

Bonal, François. *Le Livre d'Or du Champagne*. Lausanne: Éditions du Grand-Pont, 1984.

Briggs, Asa. *Haut-Brion*. London: Faber & Faber, 1994.

Broadbent, Michael. *The Great Vintage Wine Book*. London: Mitchell Beazley, 1980.

Bulletin of the Centre Beaunois des Études Historiques, Beaune, France.

Bulletin International du Vin (a journal of the International Wine Association), Paris.

Casey, Robert J. *The Lost Kingdom of Burgundy*. London: Leonard Parsons, 1924.

Cépède, Michel. *Agriculture et Alimentation en France durant le Deuxième Guerre Mondiale*. Paris: Génin, 1961.

Coates, Clive. *Grands Vins: The Finest Châteaux of Bordeaux and Their Wines*. Berkeley: University of California Press. London: Weidenfeld & Nicolson, 1995.

Collins, Larry, and Dominique Lapierre. *Is Paris Burning?* London: Pan Books, 1974.

Comité du Livre-Souvenir. *Oflag IV D: Annales et Repertoire*. Arras: L'Amicale de l'Oflag IV D, 1946.

Cook, Don. *Charles de Gaulle: A Biography*. London: Secker & Warburg, 1984.

Dear, I. C. B., gen. ed. *The Oxford Companion to World War II*. Oxford, Eng.: Oxford University Press, 1995.

Delarue, Jacques. *Trafic et Crimes sous l'Occupation*. Paris: Fayard, 1993.

Derys, Gaston. *Mon Docteur le Vin*. Paris: Draeger Frères, 1936.

Diamond, Hanna. *Women and the Second World War in France, 1939–1948: Choices and Constraints*. Harlow: Pearson Education. Longman, 1999.

Drutman, Irving, ed. *Janet Flanner's World: Uncollected Writings 1932–1975*. New York: Harcourt Brace Jovanovich, 1979.

Duijker, Hubrecht. *The Wines of the Loire, Alsace and Champagne*. London: Mitchell Beazley, 1983.

Eyres, Harry. *Wine Dynasties of Europe: Personal Portraits of Ten Leading Houses*. London: Lennard Publishing, 1990.

Faith, Nicholas. *The Winemasters*. London: Hamish Hamilton, 1978.

———. *Victorian Vineyard: Château Loudenne and the Gilbeys*. London: Constable & Company, 1983.

Flanner, Janet. *The New Yorker*, 'Letter from France,' Sept. 15, 1945. New York.

Forbes, Patrick. *Champagne: The Wine, the Land and the People*.

London: Victor Gollancz, 1985.

Fry, Varian. *Surrender on Demand*. Reprint of 1945 edition. Boulder, Colo.: Johnson Books, 1997.

Gordon, Bertram M. 'Ist Gott Franzosisch? Germans, Tourism and Occupied France, 1940–1944,' *Modern and Contemporary France*. Boston: Addison Wesley Longman, 1996.

Hanson, Anthony. *Burgundy*. London: Faber & Faber, 1982.

Hastings, Max. *Overlord: D-Day and the Battle for Normandy 1944*. London: Michael Joseph, 1984.

Hutter, Clemens M. *Hitlers Obersalzberg*. Berchtesgaden: Berchtesgadener Anzeiger, 1998.

Johnson, Hugh. *The World Atlas of Wine*. London: Mitchell Beazley, 1971.

———. *Wine*. London: Mitchell Beazley, 1974.

———. *The Story of Wine*. London: Mitchell Beazley, 1984.

Johnson, Hugh, and James Halliday. *The Vintner's Art: How Great Wines Are Made*. New York: Simon & Schuster, 1992.

Johnson, Paul. *Modern Times: The World from the Twenties to the Eighties*. New York: Harper & Row, Harper Colophon, 1985.

Kaufman, William I. *Champagne*. New York: Park Lane, 1973.

Kedward, H. R., *Occupied France: Collaboration and Resistance*, 1940–1944. Oxford: Blackwell Publishers, Historical Association Studies, 1985.

Lawton, Hugues, and Jean Miaihle. *Conversations et Souvenirs Autour le Vin de Bordeaux*. Bordeaux, France: Éditions Confluences, 1999.

Lichine, Alexis. *Alexis Lichine's Guide to the Wines and Vineyards of France*. New York: Alfred A. Knopf, 1986.

———. *Alexis Lichine's New Encyclopaedia of Wines and Spirits*. 7th ed. London: Cassell Publishers, 1987.

Lottmann, Herbert R. *The Fall of Paris, June 1940*. New York: HarperCollins Publishers, 1992.

Loubère, Leo A. *The Wine Revolution in France: The Twentieth Century*. Princeton, N.J.: Princeton University Press, 1990.

Loubère, Leo A., ed. *The Vine Remembers, French Vignerons Recall the Past*. Albany: State University of New York Press, 1985.

Lynch, Kermit. *Adventures on the Wine Route: A Wine Buyer's Tour of France*. New York: Farrar, Straus & Giroux, 1988.

Martel, André. *Leclerc: Le soldat et le politique*. Paris: Albin Michel, 1998.

Matthews, Patrick, ed. *Christie's Wine Companion*. London: Webb & Bower, 1987.

McNulty, Henry. *Champagne*. London: Collins, 1987.

McNutt, Joni G., ed. *In Praise of Wine*. Santa Barbara, Calif.: Capra Press, 1993.

Mothe, Florence. *Toutes Hontes Bues*. Paris: Albin Michel, 1992.

The New Yorker War Pieces, London 1939 to Hiroshima 1945. New York: Schocken, 1947.

Norman, Remington. *The Great Domaines of Burgundy*. London: Kyle Cathi, 1992.

Parker, Robert. *The Wines of the Rhone Valley and Provence*. New York: Simon & Schuster, 1987.

Parzych, Cynthia, and John Turner. *Pol Roger*. London: Cynthia Parzych Publishing, 1999.

Paxton, Robert O. *Vichy France: Old Guard and New Order*, 1940–1944. New York: Columbia University Press, Morningside Edition, 1982.

—— *French Peasant Against Fascism: Henry Dorgère's Greenshirts and the Crisis of French Agriculture*, 1929–1939. New York and Oxford: Oxford University Press, 1997.

Payne, Robert. *The Life and Death of Adolf Hitler*. New York: Praeger, 1973.

Pierre, Nora, ed. *Les Lieux de Mémoire*. A French government survey. Paris, 1990.

Price, Pamela Van Dyke, and Christopher Fielden. *Alsace Wines*. London: Sotheby's Publications, 1984.

Pryce-Jones, David. *Paris and the Third Reich: A History of the German Occupation*, 1940–1944. London: Collins, 1981.

Ray, Cyril. *Lafite*. London: Christie's Wine Publications, 1968.

Ribaud, Roger. *Le Maître de Maison de sa Cave à sa Table.* Paris: Éditions Jacques Vautrain, 1945.

Robards, Sherman M. *Terry Robards' New Book of Wine*. New York: G. P. Putnam's Sons, 1984.

Robinson, Jancis. *The Great Wine Book*. London: Sidgwick & Jackson, 1982.

Rothschild, Baron Phillppe de. *Vivre la Vigne: Du Ghetto de Francfort à Mouton Rothschild*, 1744–1981. Paris: Presses de la Cité, 1981.

Schoenbrun, David. *Soldiers of the Night: The Story of the French Resistance*. New York: New American Library, 1980.

Simon, André L. *A Wine Primer*. London: Michael Joseph, 1946.

Speer, Albert. *Inside the Third Reich*. New York: Macmillan, 1970.

Stevenson, Tom. *Champagne*. London: Sotheby's Publications, 1986.

Sud-Ouest. Bordeaux, France.

Sutcliffe, Serena. *The Wines of France: The Indispensable Companion*. London: Futura Publications, 1985.

Sutcliffe, Serena, ed. *Great Vineyards and Winemakers*. London: QED Publishing, 1981.

Taittinger, Claude. *Champagne by Taittinger*. Paris: Éditions Stock, 1996.

Taylor, A.J.P. *The Second World War: An Illustrated History*, London: Penguin Books, 1976.

Terrise, René. *Bordeaux 1940–1944*. Paris: P. Perrin, 1993.

Vaughan-Thomas, Wynford. *How I Liberated Burgundy*. London: Michael Joseph, 1985.

Verdet, Corinne, ed. *Summer of '44*. Paris: Éditions Arthaud, 1984.

Vigreux, Marcel, and Jacky Cortot. *Comblanchien, Village-martyr: 21–22 août 1944*. Nuits-Saint-Georges: Imprimerie SBI, 1995.

Warner, Charles K. *The Winegrowers of France and the Government Since 1985*. New York: Columbia University Press, 1960.

Wildman, Frederick S., Jr. *A Wine Tour of France*. New York: Vintage Books, 1976.

Wright, Gordon. *The Ordeal of Total War*, 1939–1945. New York: Harper & Row Publishers, Harper Torch, 1968.
Young, Brigadier Peter, ed. *The World Almanac of World War II*. London: Bison Books, 1981.

ACKNOWLEDGMENTS

This book would never have been written, and certainly never finished, if it had not been for some very special people

Among them, Gerry Holmes of ABC News and Jennifer Ludden of National Public Radio, who kept insisting we had to do it and who put us in touch with the people who helped make it happen.

One of those was their friend Stefan Fatsis, a correspondent for *The Wall Street Journal* and the author of two books. 'The best thing you can do,' Stefan told us, 'is get in touch with my agent, Robert Shepard.' He was right. Robert has been far more than an agent. He is a friend, an advisor and a good shoulder to cry on when words and ideas are not lining up in the right order. He is, in fact, a very good shepherd.

Plus, he steered us to Charles Conrad, vice president and executive editor of Broadway Books. Charlie is a man who exercised the patience of Job and had the courage to let us 'do our thing,' even when we were not exactly sure what that thing was. His assistant, Becky Cole, ran interference for us over and over again. Broadway copy chief, Harold Grabau, saved us from ourselves more times than we can count. We thank them all.

None of them, however, would have had anything to work on if it had not been for John Lally, who kept us on line and in line as we struggled with new computers. Without John, we would still be using the quills that fall off the ducks in our pond.

Others we would like to thank include James Lawther, Master of Wine, for his advice and ideas; Larry Collins and Dominique Lapierre, whose help is as graceful as their writing; Marie Carnot and Yves Fernique, who plied us with good wine and stories about the war when our energies were flagging; Christel Kucharz and her family, as well as Renate Gozlan, who translated some nearly illegible letters from Old German to very clear English.

Then there is Leslie MacBee, a U.S. Foreign Service Officer who decided to buy an old station master's house in Burgundy as a vacation retreat. When he cleaned the closets, Henri Gaillard's logbooks tumbled out and with them, a rare glimpse of what working for the Nazis was like. Thanks, Les.

Our friend Doug Tunnell, who gave up the life of a foreign correspondent for CBS News to make wine at Brick House Vineyard in Oregon, did not leave behind his nose for news. When he heard Philippe Drouhin talk about his grandfather, Maurice, Doug called us and introduced us to the Drouhins. Doug has continued to be a wonderful supporter, and has he ever poured some great wine for us! (Does this entitle us to another glass or so, Doug?)

Debby Leff took part of her vacation to read the manuscript with a kind but critical eye, and gave us a boost when we needed it most.

Others who helped facilitate our work were Pascale Doussot at Maison Joseph Drouhin, Nicole Snozzi-Arroyo at Domaine Laurent-Perrier, Christine Riassa and Sophie Ferrer at Château Pichon-Longueville, Comtesse de Lalande, and Marie-José Baudoin at Maison Louis Latour. They took innumerable phone calls from us, responded to hundreds of our requests and remained good-humored and helpful throughout.

All of the wine people we have talked to, written to and called have been marvelous. They shared their time, their memories and their lives with us. Among them, the late Peter A. Sichel of Château Palmer, and his cousin Peter M. S. Sichel of Château Fourcas-Hosten, Jacques Chevignard of the Confrérie des Chevaliers du Tastevin, Louis Latour of Maison Louis Latour, wine writer and consultant Steven Spurrier of *Decanter* magazine, wine writer and consultant David Cobbold, champagne maker André Secondé, Champagne historian Colonel François Bonal, Henri Brunier of Domaine Vieux Télégraph, Professor Claude

Chapuis of the University of Dijon, Richard Dumbrill, the British Consul in Champagne, Burgundy winemaker Philippe Engel, writer Nicholas Faith, the late André Gagey of Maison Louis Jadot, Anthony Barton of Châteaux Léoville- and Langoa-Barton, Hervé Berland of Château Mouton-Rothschild, Bernard Pauzié of the World War II museum in Vraux, Christian Pol-Roger of Champagne Pol Roger, and German wine importers Heinz Bömers Jr. and Hermann Segnitz.

Several friends have observed that the people we focused on as principal characters are established stars of the French wine community. They are correct, but that was not how we planned it.

Our goal was to find people with stories to tell, people who were willing to share some of their most personal, and sometimes painful, memories. Today, it is true that Huet, Drouhin, de Lencquesaing, Miaihle, de Nonancourt and Hugel are famous names. But when World War II began, they were not. They were small businesses, typical of so many in France's wine community who were just trying to survive. How these people managed to do that is what caught our attention. We are grateful to all of them.

To May-Eliane Miaihle de Lencquesaing, who invited us to Château Pichon-Longueville, Comtesse de Lalande. There on the terrace, she read to us from a diary she kept as a young girl during the war, passages that helped us understand what life was like under the occupation.

To her cousin, Jean Miaihle of Château Coufran, who vividly illustrated to us the danger of defiance as he described how he built a secret laboratory for making copper sulfate.

To Robert and Françoise Drouhin of Maison Joseph Drouhin, who opened their hearts as well as their home to us. They went far beyond what we asked them to do by introducing us to others who lived through the war, and by searching out letters and historical documents that greatly enhanced our story.

To Bernard de Nonancourt of Domaine Laurent-Perrier, who reminded us that enthusiasm and patriotism are not only for the young. His spirit is as effervescent as the wonderful champagne he makes.

To Gaston Huet, who started us on this long journey several years ago. He has the rare gift of making time stand still and yet come alive. You have only to taste one of his wines to know that.

To the Hugels of Riquewihr: to André, whose keen sense of history helped us appreciate the unique circumstances of Alsace; to his brother Johnny, whose unflagging enthusiasm always made us feel welcome; and to their brother Georges, whose harrowing account of serving in Hitler's army made us shudder. His courage left us in awe.

It is impossible to exaggerate Georges's generosity and his willingness to put up with our constant questions and phone calls, even in the face of a serious illness. On one memorable occasion, he asked emergency medical personnel, who had just arrived in an ambulance to take him to a hospital, to wait so he could talk to us. We were incredibly embarrassed and apologized for bothering him with what was 'a stupid question.' Georges quickly replied, 'No, no, go ahead. There's no such thing as a stupid question. Better to ask it while I am still alive.' That was in the summer of 2000.

Georges died two months later.

There are two people we do not know how to begin to thank, dear friends who were with us from the very start, long before we were sure we had a book to write.

In fact, this book might never have been written had it not been for Kim and Anne Munholland. It was a collaborative effort in the best sense of the word. Kim, a professor of modern European history at the University of Minnesota and an expert on France during World War II, was unstinting in sharing his knowledge and expertise with us.

Essential to that process was the generous financial and institutional support extended by the University of Minnesota Graduate School. Thanks to a series of grants, Kim was able to travel to the

Library of Congress in Washington, D.C., as well as to archives and libraries in France. His research carried him to Paris, Bordeaux, Burgundy and Champagne. He spent long and often frustrating hours digging through records, files and books, poring through hundreds of reels of microfilm for information that was so vital to our book. Without his dogged persistence, we might never have known about Roger Ribaud, whose prison memoir was all but lost in the mountain of paper at France's Bibliothèque Nationale. Nor would we have discovered the details of Louis Eschenauer's arrest and trial, an event many in France still refuse to discuss. Given its sensitive nature, it is not surprising that many of the documents relating to Uncle Louis were 'misplaced,' put in files that had little or nothing to do with Eschenauer or his trial. But Kim managed to find them, along with many other things – documents, photos, old newspaper clippings – all of which helped shed light on a period of French history that only now is beginning to be openly discussed in France.

His work, however, went far beyond that. He also held our collective hand, answering questions over and over again until we gained a proper perspective and began to understand the myriad of dramas that were being played out under the Nazi occupation.

Anne, who is Kim's editor, was equally patient. She applied her careful eye to our manuscript repeatedly, asking questions, making suggestions and drawing up a list for the Glossary. Most of all, perhaps, she kept us honest. Any errors that may exist are ours, and ours alone.

Together, Anne and Kim helped assure that *Wine and War* would become a reality. They traveled vineyards with us, conducted interviews and provided encouragement to us every step of the way. When things were going well, they were our biggest cheerleaders. When we felt discouraged, they would not let us quit.

But they were much more than collaborators or consultants. They were friends, and we could not have done this without them.

INDEX

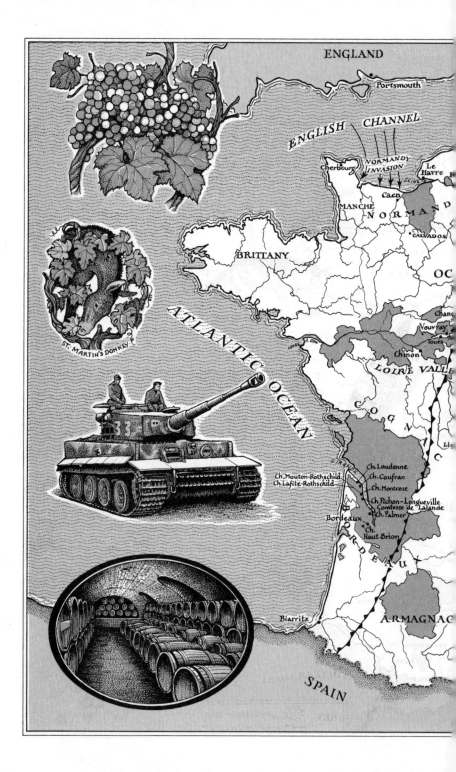

ENGLAND

• Portsmouth

ENGLISH CHANNEL

Cherbourg

NORMANDY
INVASION

SEINE

Le Havre

Caen

MANCHE

NORMANDY

• CALVADOS

BRITTANY

OC

LOIRE

Chang

Vouvray

Tours

Chinon

LOIRE VALLEY

ATLANTIC OCEAN

ST. MARTIN'S DONKEY

COGNAC

Li

GIRONDE

Ch. Loudenne
Ch. Coufran
Ch. Montrose

Ch. Mouton-Rothschild
Ch. Lafite-Rothschild

Ch. Pichon-Longueville
Comtesse de Lalande
Ch. Palmer

Bordeaux

Ch. Haut-Brion

BORDEAUX

Biarritz

A-RMAGNAC

SPAIN